WITHDRAWN

THE
STRUCTURE
OF POWER
IN AMERICA

THE STRUCTURE OF POWER IN AMERICA

THE CORPORATE ELITE AS A RULING CLASS

EDITED BY
MICHAEL SCHWARTZ

HOLMES & MEIER
New York   London

Copyright © 1987 by Holmes & Meier Publishers, Inc.
All rights reserved

Holmes & Meier Publishers, Inc.
30 Irving Place
New York, NY 10003

Great Britain:
1–3 Winton Close
Letchworth, Hertfordshire SG61 1BA
England

Book design by Elsa Danenberg

Library of Congress Cataloging-in-Publication Data

The Structure of power in America.

Bibliography: p.
Includes index.
1. Business and politics—United States.
2. Capitalism—United States.   3. Corporations—
United States.   4. Directors of corporations—
United States.   5. Elite (Social sciences)—United
States.   I. Schwartz, Michael, 1942–
JK467.S77   1988   322'.3'0973   87-14849
ISBN 0-8419-0764-1 (alk. paper)
ISBN 0-8419-0765-X (pbk.)

This book has been printed on acid-free paper.
MANUFACTURED IN THE UNITED STATES OF AMERICA

Dedicated to
Robert Gogel
1944–1981
Colleague and Friend

CONTENTS

PREFACE

For much of the decade of the 1970s, political sociology focused on the distinction between instrumentalism and structuralism as a device for understanding the origins of public policy. Though both of these perspectives derived in good part from Marxist origins, they have been taken over by non-Marxists and even anti-Marxists as part of the ongoing migration of political sociology away from electoral studies and into more detailed analyses of the policy formation process.

Instrumentalism traces its recent history to C. Wright Mills, whose path-breaking book *The Power Elite* argued that government policy was an extension of the interests and understandings of major government leaders. These leaders, in Mills' view, were disconnected from either constraint by or sympathy with the general population. A continuity of policy therefore developed inside government which reflected the independent interests of a governmental elite that sought to perpetuate its own privileges while maintaining popular quiescence. Later analyses by those who have been associated with the instrumentalist tradition, notably Ralph Milliband and G. William Domhoff, have sought to focus and modify this analysis by widening the lens of attention to include the elaborate process that precedes the official promulgation of public policy, and by exploring the relationships between government and other institutions, notably the largest corporations. Among the most significant contributions of this perspective have been to identify the processes by which leaders move between positions in business and government and to demonstrate that these ties determine the pro-business profile of much government action.

Structuralism, which traces its recent incarnation to Nicos Poulantzas' review of Ralph Milliband's *The State in Capitalist Society,* focuses attention on the internal structure of the government itself. For this perspective, the current shape of government is a result of a long process of institution building in which interests are congealed into organizational processes. The outcome is a set of interrelated agencies, connected together in such a way that only a limited range of policies is possible. This systemic limitation even constrains the actions of those who in theory run the government agencies. Only certain interests may be pursued through the state; if government leaders attempted to pursue opposing policies they would be unable to do so because of the very structure of the state.

Most structural arguments are aimed at demonstrating that government will inevitably pursue probusiness interests. If capitalists do not recognize their own interests, or even (ignorantly) oppose the policies necessary to promote capitalism, the state may have to oppose capitalists for the benefit of capitalism. This argument rests on a detailed analysis of structural processes within the government; the exclusion of certain policies is a consequence of a lack of openness of this structure to certain forms of influence. Ultimately, even a president cannot press beyond the constraints of government structure and must succumb to the internal dynamics which push government to maintain stability, provide a favorable investment climate for privately held businesses, and suppress any public discontent with the outcomes of these policies.

The contrasting logics that inform instrumentalism and structuralism are discussed in more detail in Chapter 6. In this introduction, we offer this brief outline in order to contrast both perspectives with the perspective presented here.

In the 1980s there has been a drift away from the instrumentalist-structuralist debate, partly because it remains unresolved and partly because it has ceased to offer guidance for empirical research. But there is a broader difficulty with working within the framework of this debate, since the two positions operate with an agreed-upon assumption that has been undermined by recent research. This assumption is expressed in both perspectives' exclusive focus on government as a source of social policy. Instrumentalists and structuralists assume that the government is the only source of policy in society. Instrumentalists express this postulate by focusing their attention on who obtains the reins of power in government and by assuming that those who do will have a relatively unlimited capacity to pursue whatever ends they choose. Structuralists express this postulate by focusing exclusively on the internal constraints of *government* and assuming that these constraints will determine policy without regard to the desires or needs of outside parties. Most explicitly, structuralists assume that the government can inevitably impose a set of policies on the capitalist class even when that class is (ignorantly) opposed to these policies.

Instrumentalists and structuralists disagree about the determinants of government policy, whether it results from the interests of its leaders or from the internal dynamics of the state. But both analyses agree that by understanding the policy thrust of government, it is possible to understand the policy thrust of society as a whole. They leave aside the set of interrelationships between government and business, except insofar as these relationships influence the recruitment of government leadership or the dynamics of change within government.

It is our contention that this narrow focus on government as a source of policy is incorrect. A large proportion of social policy does not derive from government at all. Indeed, much of what we might call "social policy" exists so independently of government that it does not appear as a policy. Perhaps the most significant case in point is the industrial decline experienced by the American Northeast starting in the late 1960s and continuing through the 1980s. This phenomenon has had a peculiar relationship to the policy formation process. Every presidential aspirant during this period blamed the industrial decline on the presidential incumbent and, to a lesser extent, policies enacted by Congress. Each incumbent president, on the other hand, declared the decline to be a process external to government and, to some degree, untouchable by government policies—at least those available within the framework of modern American politics. Only one of these diametrically opposed stances can be accurate.

The latter position is the correct one: the role of the U.S. government was peripheral to industrial decline; most of the process took place within the realm of private investment decision making. Only by looking at the structure of business, especially the interrelationships among large corporations, can we hope to understand the "policy" of deindustrialization in a more sensible and down-to-earth way. Government should be seen as an adjunct; the basic structural phenomenon is located largely in the realm of business. Despite the major contributions of instrumentalism and structuralism, neither perspective directs our attention to these issues. Both have fallen prey to the myth of government power.

An understanding of policy formation in the broader sense we advocate begins with an analysis of the structure of business, much as other literature has focused on the structure of the state. For that reason, we have included in this volume an entire section devoted to understanding the structure of interaction among corporations. This structure of interaction makes it difficult and potentially costly for corporations to be political or economic mavericks, while it simultaneously encourages coordinated activity by large corporations acting in groups under the guidance of central capitalists who share a common class interest.

The structure of business interactions helps explain: (a) coordinated activity by large numbers of corporations in pursuing a common economic interest; (b) coordinated activity by corporations vis-à-vis government; and (c) the coordinated activity of large numbers of corporations that produces patterns of social behavior that can be called social policy, though not bearing the imprimatur of government action.

The first form of unity—simple economic coordination—has become a major focus for the new field of economic sociology. In Part I, and especially Chapter 2, we offer many examples of this form, which we see as the building block of the broader forms that we discuss in later chapters.

The second form of coordination—in which business develops a united position outside government and then brings that position to the state—has gained recognition as an arena of analysis because researchers have followed the chain of logic from government decision making back into the business sector. Domhoff and others have looked at policy formation bodies and other groupings within business which allow for the articulation of a set of business policies bearing on government action. Our analysis pushes this logic a step further. We argue that the unity within business is what gives a foundation to the united voice of business. Government action is constrained precisely because business is able to coordinate its activities. This is a fundamental reason why government leadership must treat the wishes of the business community with respect and even deference. It is not just the united force but the capacity for united action which leads to this deference and to the intimate interconnection between business wishes and government action. In Part II of this volume we suggest ways in which this interface is produced so that government is responsive in a detailed but not mechanical way to business interest.

Finally, the least studied and least understood aspect of business unity is that which leads directly to a social policy. This aspect is addressed in Part III. Here we see the ways in which the inner circle of the business class may lead various institutions to coordinate their activities, thus creating social policy, with or without direct government involvement. For example, when the auto industry purchased street railways and transformed them into bus companies, it fully constrained government transportation policy. The government was left without much choice—public transportation had to be motorized. Similarly, the experience in Saint Louis, where banks redlined inner city housing while exporting capital to large corporations, constitutes a social policy of urban decline, a policy that not only did not involve the government at any level, but was not even acknowledged as a policy.

What is a ruling class? It is a group of people with a common structural economic position who make the key decisions that determine the character of ordinary life in a society. Once we set aside the commonly held notion of government dominance in decision making we recognize that many of the policies that most condition and constrain our lives are made in the "private sector," not in the government. We speak of the business elite as a ruling class not simply because it dominates many positions in government, but, more importantly, because it controls the places where many key public policies are decided: the boardrooms and executive suites of the major financial industrial corporations of America.

ACKNOWLEDGMENTS

The research on which this book is based has been undertaken over the course of more than a decade and in a great many locales. In the process, we have individually and collectively accumulated an enormous, unrepayable intellectual debt. The list that follows is necessarily an incomplete one. However, we cannot fail to give thanks to the following people and institutions: William Chambliss, Donna Di Donato, G. William Domhoff, Richard Eckstein, Mary Beth Gallagher, Bob Higgins, The John Simon Guggenheim Foundation, Maggie McLoughlin, Harvey Molotch, The National Science Foundation, Mary Romero, Edward Royce, and Michael Zweig.

THE
STRUCTURE
OF POWER
IN AMERICA

PART I

Business Unity and Intercorporate Coordination

Introduction

Ninety-eight percent of all companies in the United States account for only about 25 percent of the business in this country; the remaining 2 percent account for nearly 75 percent. The top 500 industrial corporations, which represent only one-tenth of one percent of this elite 2 percent, control over two-thirds of the business resources, employ two-thirds of the industrial workers, account for 60 percent of the sales, and collect 70 percent of the profits.[1]

A decisive trend of the last eighty years has been for fewer and fewer companies to orchestrate ever greater fractions of total economic activity, even as the economy itself has vastly expanded. The 200 largest manufacturing firms, for instance, have increased their share of total manufacturing assets by approximately one-half percent per year since the turn of the century. The rate of concentration has varied from year to year, but the overall trend has remained steady, so that by 1980, the top 200 firms controlled nearly two-thirds of all manufacturing assets; similar rates of concentration characterize other business sectors (Marris, 1979). The great bulk of the private economy is therefore now in the hands of fewer than a thousand companies. In one whimsical extrapolation, the managing editor of *Fortune* is foreseen to have quietly decided in 1998 to still apply the famous

"Fortune 500" appellation to a list for which only 479 companies could then be found (Tobias, 1976).

Accompanying concentration, particularly in recent years, is product diversification, paced by the so-called conglomerates but pursued to varying degrees by most large firms. Not only are large enterprises in control of an expanding, dominant share of all economic activity, but most are also increasingly familiar with a range of disparate market conditions, labor forces, and political climates.

At the same time, networks of economic relations among the firms are becoming more inclusive. Among the most significant trends is the rise of intercorporate ownership (see Chapter 2). The share of company stock held by financial institutions, for instance, was under 7 percent in 1900, but it had climbed to 17 percent by 1945 and reached 33 percent in 1974 (U.S. Senate Committee on Government Operations, 1974, pp. 143–161; Kotz, 1978, p. 65). The top stockholders of most large companies are now other corporations (Corporate Data Exchange, 1977, 1978, 1980). Typical of the present-day ownership is that of Mobile Oil Corporation, the fourth largest American manufacturing firm. In the mid-1970s, 9 of the 10 top shareholders, possessing in aggregate about 20 percent of the shares, were other corporations. The only noncorporate owner among the top 10 was the Rockefeller family interests (Corporate Data Exchange, 1977, pp. 224–225).

This centralization of the economic sector provides the foundation upon which corporate domination of American life is constructed. It is not just that the American economy is highly concentrated. It is also capable of systematic coordination—at least at certain crucial moments. Though this coordination would not be possible without a high degree of concentration, it depends upon a great many other factors as well. It is these factors which provide the subject matter for Part I of this volume.

The crucial issue in the construction of business unity has to do with the dynamics of intercorporate competition and power. For most of the post–World War II period, the analysis of American business has been dominated by managerialism, a theory which posits that American corporate policy is determined by professional managers, for whom high profits are only one of a number of important goals. The large size and economic strength of these large companies has, according to managerialism, freed them from the traditional constraints imposed by competition with other firms, the political system, and broader socioeconomic forces. The portrait of the American economy that emerged from this analysis is one of large autonomous corporations run by business diplomats who seek moderation in all things. These "diplomats" avoid dangerous confrontations with all the major political and social actors and cultivate immunity to each other's competition and coercion.

The counterportrait provided in Part I of this volume depends on the sustained attack on this theory which has been carried on for the last two decades. Chapter 1 reviews the evidence against managerialism, resynthesizes this evidence into a critique of its basic conclusions, and offers a different portrait of the dynamics of large corporations in contemporary capitalism. The cornerstones of the argument are, first, the ongoing domination of corporations by the profit motive, and second, the existence of stockholding, lending, and other intercorporate relationships which facilitate important external constraints, and sometimes even domination, over many firms. This second point shows the need to analyze intercorporate relations and suggests the existence of systematic intercorporate coordination. It provides the crucial premise for our argument that such coordination exists and is a significant force in American society.

Chapter 2 catalogs the many different modes of intercorporate coordination and power that exist in late-twentieth-century American big business. The chapter also draws on the recent blossoming of antimanagerial research on the ways corporations influence one another, coordinate their activities (at least in pairs or small groups), influence one another, and on occasion dominate one another's policies. It is these cross-cutting patterns of intercorporate influence and domination that allow for the construction of more systematic and more complete coordination systems across large numbers of firms, and therefore provide the possibility of truly united business action in the face of common enemies and/or in the pursuit of common goals.

Chapter 3 advances the argument still further by demonstrating the role of banks and other financial institutions as the hubs and centers of broad corporate coordination. Specifically, this chapter looks at bank decision making about capital investment—at the process of directing capital flows into promising areas for economic development. It argues that this decision-making power, which resides with the directors of the major banks and insurance companies in America, confers these institutions (and the individuals that lead them) a major portion of the discretionary choices about the direction of the American economy and, by implication, American society as a whole.

Chapter 4 focuses on the makeup of the boards of directors of major banks. These boards include some of the most powerful and respected leaders in industry and finance, a situation that reflects the decision-making position of banks in the economy and the society. In a sense, bank boards serve as a forum in which the "corporate all-stars" arrive at their collective interest and enact that interest through the direction of capital flows.

Finally, Chapter 5 discusses the delicate interface between the institutions that represent the structural foundation of the American ruling class and the individuals who lead them and thus become the personification of the class. This interface is effected through corporate boards of directors, a tricky and vastly understudied and misunderstood institution in American life. Because boards of directors are responsible for directing company policy and making crucial corporate choices, the individuals who sit on the boards of large corporations become crucial actors in the nation's economy. The existence of interlocking directorates, discussed at length in Chapters 2, 3, and 4, means that many of these individuals sit on several boards of directors simultaneously and therefore think in terms not only of the narrow interests of the individual corporation but also of the good of the class as a whole. Similarly, by virtue of their centrality in the economy banks and insurance companies, they tend to pursue policies that are consonant with the class-wide interest.

Hence, individuals with a classwide orientation occupy the positions that determine the policies of financial firms with a classwide interest. This match of people and institutions is the key to the construction of a viable ruling class, since these business diplomats rise above the particular institutions they lead and come to look upon large businesses as tools of their collective political economic interest. In Chapter 5, we first address this interface between institutions and individuals. In Parts II and III we explore the ways in which these same individuals become the bridges between large corporations and other sectors, so that they provide both the coordinating glue among American institutions and the guiding intelligence which determines the policies of these institutions.

NOTE

1. These figures were collated from the following sources: U.S. Internal Revenue Service (1970, pp. 41, 65, 261); Berle (1947, p. 24); Schriftgiesser (1964, pp. 25–26); U.S. House of Representatives (1970, p. 74); Marris (1979, pp. 146–156); 1985 *Fortune's* Directory.

1

Managerialism: Another Reassessment

Mark S. Mizruchi

Between World War II and the early 1970s, most analyses of large corporations in American society were based on the idea that a firm's managers (meaning its leading officers) exercised effective control of its policies free of restraining external influence and that they were increasingly able to mold and manipulate their environments. This perspective, known as managerialism, was the dominant paradigm in most academic disciplines that concern themselves with business behavior, despite the sparse empirical evidence developed by its advocates (see Zeitlin, 1974).

This chapter will present an overview of the managerialist argument, look at some of the now voluminous evidence testing its validity, and analyze the extent to which the data support managerialism or its recently developed alternatives.

The classic statement of the managerialist position was Berle and Means' *Modern Corporation and Private Property,* originally published in 1932. Berle and Means began with the assumption that until the early 1900s, most large American corporations were controlled by the families of founding entrepreneurs, through majority stockholding, or by financial institutions that had provided the loans necessary to create large firms and build huge factories. As these corporations grew in size, however, it became more and more difficult for even wealthy families to maintain their majority holdings.

7

Though it was possible to control a firm with as little as 20 percent of its stock,[1] the proportion of large corporations with a single major stockholder appeared to have declined significantly in the early part of the twentieth century.

According to Berle and Means, control of large corporations rested with "those who have the power to select the board of directors" (1932, p. 66). Legally, this power rests with the stockholders, who elect the board. When stock is widely dispersed, however, stockholders cannot organize themselves as an effective force in corporate policy. Given this situation, Berle and Means argued, the board itself was likely to become a self-perpetuating oligarchy, generally free from the influence of stockholders. Later managerialists pushed this argument a step further, pointing out that most board members were outsiders with little knowledge of the firm's inner workings and little time—given their status as full-time employees of other institutions—to develop into effective overseers of corporate policy. These later theorists concluded that top management—the major operating officers who were in daily command of the company—controlled the firm's policies and selected the outside directors who were supposed to restrain management's actions. (See, e.g., Galbraith, 1967; Mace, 1971; Chandler, 1977; for a critique of this argument, see Mizruchi, 1983.)

Stock dispersion was not the only source of increased managerial independence. At the same time that management was freeing itself from the influence of stockholders, it was also escaping the restraints that derived from corporate borrowing. Huge corporate profits allowed management to repay existing debt and forego further borrowing which might produce renewed lender influence. Thus top management was freed from the second major source of outside control.

The modern corporation, as depicted by Berle and Means and other managerialists, had therefore become a large, powerful bureaucratic organization dominated by insiders, who were free from the dictates of both stockholders and financial institutions. This transformation implied a transformation of behavior, since corporate leadership was no longer subject to the dictates of the capitalist cash nexus. The drive for profits was modulated, and with it the impulse to extract from workers maximum labor for minimum wages (Burnham 1941; Cyert and March, 1963). The relation between business and the large society also became less antagonistic (Bell, 1973; Dahrendorf, 1959; Parsons, 1968; Riesman, 1953).

Most important for this book, the managerial thesis implies that the dispersal of stock and the consequent separation of ownership from control led to the breakup of the capitalist class, and, thus, to the dispersal of its power in society (Dahrendorf, 1959; Bell, 1961; Riesman, 1953). Because each large corporation is independent of outside control, no power exists to weld the corporate world into a unified force capable of dominating social policy. Pluralist political theory (the dominant perspective in the 1950s and 1960s), which argued that American policy formation is essentially democratic, rests firmly on managerialist assumptions (see, e.g., Rose, 1967, Chapter 1).

To support their argument, Berle and Means employed 1929 data on the 200 largest U.S. industrial corporations. Defining management control as a situation in which no individual or family held as much as 20 percent of a firm's stock, they concluded that 44 percent of these 200 firms were management controlled.[2] On closer examination, however, these findings appear to be exaggerated. Zeitlin (1974) has noted that in nearly half of the cases in which Berle and Means defined a firm as management controlled, they had been unable to locate information on the largest stockholder and had labeled the firms "presumably management controlled." Thus, Zeitlin pointed out, by Berle and Means' own criteria only 23 percent of the corporations in their sample could be considered clearly management controlled. This was hardly sufficient to prove that stockholders were not a significant force in corporate behavior.[3]

Although Berle and Means may have overstated their case for the period up to 1930, a much later study by Larner (1970) seemed to provide convincing support for the managerialist thesis. Employing data on the 200 largest U.S. nonfinancial corporations in 1964, Larner lowered the criterion for owner control to 10 percent of a company's stock on the grounds that with increasing stock dispersal, an even smaller concentration of stock sufficed for effective control. Yet, even with this less stringent criterion for owner control, Larner found that 83 percent of the two hundred largest companies were management controlled.

Larner's findings appeared to have settled the issue of stock dispersal and management control once and for all. Even Marxist analysts such as Baran and Sweezy (1966), Miliband (1969), and Herman (1973) accepted the empirical validity of the managerialist thesis.

But there were other empirical studies which contradicted Larner's findings and conclusions. Two such studies used methods similar to those of Larner. A study by Villarejo (1961), little known prior to the 1970s, found owner control in 60 percent of a sample of the 242 largest U.S. industrial corporations, while Chevalier (1970) found a minimum of 60 percent owner-controlled firms among the 200 largest U.S. industrials in 1964. The discrepancies with Larner's results derive from differing definitions of the amount of stock needed for control (see Note 4). Two later studies, by Burch (1972) and Kotz (1978), took different approaches. Burch searched through articles in the business press spanning a 20-year period to locate information on company stockholding. He concluded that at most 40 percent of the 300 largest industrial corporations could be considered management controlled and that as many as 60 percent could be considered owner controlled. Kotz, employing data on bank management of privately held stock, found that as many as 40 percent of the 200 largest nonfinancial corporations could be considered "bank controlled."[4] Since most of these corporations had usually been counted as management controlled in previous studies, this finding was particularly challenging to managerial theorists.

Despite demonstrations by Zeitlin, Villarejo, Chevalier, Burch, and Kotz that managerialists had overestimated stock dispersion, the critics' studies did not show convincingly that stockholding was a prevalant constraint on managerial autonomy. Even with large blocks of stock, share-holders were not necessarily capable of dictating policy to top management. The evidence on stockholding therefore was not sufficient to resolve the question of corporate control.

In many ways, the argument was misplaced, even if huge blocks of stocks could be shown to be the rule in modern corporations. The reason for this is that even possession of a "controlling" interest in a firm's stock is no assurance of actual control. When a nonfinancial corporation is in need of capital, financial corporations can exercise considerable leverage over corporate policy, regardless of the size of the largest stockholding. For example, in the late 1950s, when jets were first introduced into commercial aviation, most airlines purchased these jets through loans from consortia of banks and insurance companies. However, Howard Hughes, president of TWA and owner of 78 percent of the company's stock, was determined to avoid becoming indebted to outside sources of financing, so he attempted to purchase the jets with funds from the Hughes Tool Company, which he also owned. Despite his tremendous wealth, the expenses involved proved to be just too great. In order to complete the purchases, Hughes was forced to go to the lending consortium. Meanwhile, the financial community was furious at Hughes for his behavior and prepared to saddle him with the appropriate sanctions. As a condition attached to the loans, Hughes' 78 percent interest in TWA was set aside in a trust fund controlled by the Chase Manhattan Bank, Equitable Life, Metropolitan Life, and several other financial corporations, which thus had complete discretion over company policy (Fitch and Oppenheimer, 1970; Tinnin, 1973). Mintz and Schwartz (1985) cite a similar case that occurred in 1976, in which E. T. Barwick, founder of E. T. Barwick Industries and holder of over 80 percent of the firm's stock, was removed from effective control by the company's lender banks. In 1985, lenders drove Evans Products into a possibly unnecessary bankruptcy in order to inhibit the freewheeling of Victor Posner, the dominant stockholder of Evans and some 13 other companies (*Business Week,* March 25, 1985, pp. 24–25). Such interventions are commonplace, even among the largest companies (Mintz and Schwartz, 1985, Chapter 4).

The crucial empirical issue here is the extent to which industrial firms actually are dependent on banks and insurance companies for investment capital. Berle and Means had argued that corporations were increasingly able to finance investment with internally generated funds. More recently, Galbraith (1967), Baran and Sweezy (1966), and others have reiterated this claim. But these authors have not presented systematic evidence in support of their argument.

The most definitive study of the issue prior to 1960 was presented in an article by Lintner (1959). Charting the extent of internal and external financing among large U.S. corporations between 1925 and 1955, Lintner found that overall there was no change in reliance on external financing. He concluded that "when one looks at the data, one is impressed by the rather extraordinary stability in the broad patterns of financing used and in the patterns of decision-making behavior which are found" (p. 177). The most definitive study to date, Stearns (1982), reached similar conclusions: dependence on external financing has fluctuated throughout the post–World War II period, with no evidence of long-term decline. These results indicate that a fundamental tenet of managerialism—namely growing corporate independence from financial institutions, resulting from an increased ability for internal financial—has virtually no empirical foundation.

Since the data on stock dispersal fail to convincingly support managerialism, and since the data on outside borrowing actually undermine it, most recent work rejects the portrait of corporate and managerial autonomy that the theory yields.[5]

The most important departures from managerial theory all begin with the insight that each firm is a part of an interorganizational system, that firms are connected by a network of intercorporate ties (Glasberg and Schwartz, 1983; Mizruchi, 1982). Interorganizational theorists have charted various types of ties, each of which in some way binds corporate interests together (see Chapter 2 of this volume). These include joint ventures (Pfeffer and Nowak, 1976), market transactions (Burt, 1983), and, most commonly, interlocking directorates, which occur when an individual sits on the board of directors of more than one company.

Interlocks in particular have been the subject of much antimanagerial research. The exact significance of specific interlocks is, however, difficult to define. While some ties are clearly indicative of control relations and others may facilitate customer-supplier coordination, still others are the result of friendship or family ties or reflect a desire to gain feedback from various segments of society, as when civil rights or women's rights leaders sit on corporate boards. Despite the difficulty in discerning the exact meaning of specific interlocks, if we map out the ties within a network of corporations, specific patterns emerge which can provide a rough indication of the influence of certain firms in the system. And, if the network is traced over a period of time, we can derive a picture of the relative cohesiveness and interdependence of the companies. This logic will be discussed in more detail and applied in Chapters 3 and 4.

Numerous studies of interlocks have found that most large companies in the United States are connected into a single system of ties. Mariolis (1975), for example, found that 722 of the 797 largest companies in 1969 were connected into one continuous network through interlocking directorates. Of these 722, 91 percent were within four steps of any other firm in the system. Bearden et al. (1975) found that 989 of 1131 corporations they studied formed a single graph (see also Mintz and Schwartz, 1985). Every other study of interlocks has also found that most large companies are tied into a single network.[6]

Most interlock studies have analyzed a particular year (or different years which were very close together) and most were based on recent years. There have, however, been several historical studies: Allen (1974), which was based on data from 1935 and 1970; Bunting and Barbour (1971), based on data from several years between 1896 and 1964; Roy (1983), based on data between 1885 and 1904; and Mizruchi (1982), based on data collected by Bunting from seven different years between 1904 and 1974. These historical studies are particularly important because they allow us to test two hypotheses that flow logically from managerialism.

First, according to managerialists, as corporations become controlled by insiders, their dependence on, and ties to, other corporations should have declined. Second, if nonfinancials' dependence on financial corporations has declined, then the dominance of financial institutions in the system should also have declined.

The study by Mizruchi investigated these hypotheses using two concepts from network analysis—density and centrality. The density of a network is the number of actual links between firms, expressed as a proportion of the number of possible links. Centrality is a measure of the degree to which a particular company is interlocked with a large number of other firms which, in turn, are themselves highly interlocked (see Bearden et al., 1975; Mariolis, 1975; Mintz and Schwartz, 1981a, 1981b, 1985).

The historical analysis of density revealed an interesting pattern. Between 1912 and 1935, density declined by nearly 50 percent, from 7.6 to 4.0 percent. This is consistent with the managerialist thesis, and it corresponds with the period about which Berle and Means were writing. However, after 1935, instead of continuing to decline, the density remained basically stable and actually increased slightly. This finding does not support managerialism, and it raises the possibility that the trend pointed to by Berle and Means was a temporary phenomenon. Furthermore, when the distance between the corporations in the network was measured, Mizruchi found that the proportion of firms within three steps of the center remained generally stable over the 70-year period, dropping in 1935 but increasing back to the 1912 level by 1969. These findings on interlocking directorates suggest a high level of cohesion among large corporations and a high degree of continued interdependence within the system.

In analyzing the centrality of financial corporations, it is necessary to distinguish three types of financial institutions: insurance companies, investment banks, and commercial banks. In contemporary American society, insurance companies and commercial banks are the major sources of loan capital, while investment banks are primarily engaged in facilitating mergers and organizing investment portfolios. In the first decades of this century, however, investment banks were also major sources of loan capital and were, in this sense, virtually indistinguishable from commercial banks. Investment banks such as J. P. Morgan and Company, Kuhn, Loeb and Company, White-Weld, and Speyer and Company dominated the economy; Morgan, in particular, was universally recognized as the most powerful firm in the United States, if not the entire world. But by the 1930s, the power of investment banks had declined, and this decline accelerated with the Glass-Steagall Act, which forced banks to choose between investment and commercial banking. Because of their earlier dominance of the economy, the decline of investment banks led many observers to conclude that financial institutions in general had declined in power. Mizruchi's analysis of the relative centrality of corporations in different sectors strongly supports the claims for the declining power of investment banks. From 1904 through 1919, investment banks were on the average 39 percent more central than corporations as a whole. But by 1935 their centrality was 5 percent less than average, and this decline continued steadily to a 1974 level of 66 percent less central than average.

Commercial banks and insurance companies, however, have maintained and even enhanced their importance. As noted above, nonfinancial corporations' use of external financing has not declined since the 1920s, and this has made the nonfinancials dependent on the relative handful of banks and insurance companies that lead loan consortia (Mintz and Schwartz, 1983; Cohen, 1980). Moreover, banks have emerged as major institutional stockholders in nonfinancial corporations. Both these trends suggest that their power has not declined, and this is supported by the evidence on centrality from Mizruchi's study. The relative centrality of commercial banks has been consistently high, dipping in 1919 and 1964, but rebounding in subsequent years to 1904–1912 levels. Insurance company centrality dropped to very low levels in 1912 and 1919, but then, by 1964, increased to levels close to those of commercial banks. Taken as a whole, the centrality of both insurance companies and commercial banks has remained high throughout the century. When combined with the evidence on corporate finance and institutional stockholding, these findings strongly suggest the continuing dominance of financial institutions in the economy, and they undermine managerialist claims of autonomous, independent companies run by unconstrained top management.

Occasionally in social research, particular theories and interpretations are so strongly assumed as true that critical examinations are no longer undertaken. Thus, in the preface to the 1968 edition of *The Modern Corporation and Private Property*, Means stated that "the corporate revolution [i.e., the transformation to management control] is now so widely accepted that statistical evidence is no longer necessary" as proof (p. xiii). Zeitlin, in contrast, used Merton's concept of a "pseudofact" to characterize this situation. And the evidence discussed in the present chapter strongly supports Zeitlin's characterization:

First, although stock ownership has become less concentrated since the early part of the century, it is not at all clear that this development has led to a decline of external control of large corporations. The proportion of stock necessary for control is not as high now as it was in the early part of the century, and several studies indicate that a majority of the biggest companies have a potentially dominant stockholder.

Second, internal financing has not increased since the 1920s and may have even decreased since the early 1960s. This means that corporations' dependence on financial institutions has not decreased.

Third, large corporations remain tightly connected into a system of interlocking directorates. Although the network is not as dense in recent years as it was in the 1904–1919 period, the distances between the corporations have remained virtually equal, and the centrality of banks and insurance companies in the network has remained consistently high, despite the decline in the centrality of investment banks.

The disproof of managerialism has many implications for our understanding of American society, two of which form the basic themes of this book. First, we must analyze and understand how corporate policy is influenced by outside constraints, and, in particular, how these constraints operate at a systemic level to create coordinated action among large or dominant sectors of the business community. Second, we must analyze and understand the degree to which this coordinated action by business constrains and determines both economic trajectories and political decisions in modern America.

In the chapters that follow, we explore these issues in a number of contexts. We can conclude that the largest American businesses are capable of episodic (but nevertheless significant) decison making and coordination, which are critical in determining the areas of development and underdevelopment in the economy, and that the actions become congealed into social and economic structures which constrain future choices inside and outside the economy. Most significantly, these actions often delimit and/or determine the political options available to government, and hence become a major force in the development of government policy.

NOTES

1. Berle and Means reached the 20 percent figure for minimum owner control on the basis of a case in which John D. Rockefeller, Jr., owner of 14.9 percent of the stock in Standard Oil of Indiana, was barely able to muster enough support to oust a recalcitrant president. Berle and Means reasoned that if even one as prestigious as Rockefeller could barely exert control with 15 percent ownership, probably 20 percent was generally necessary for control.

2. Berle and Means identified five types of control: complete owner (virtually 100 percent owned by one individual or family); majority owner (over 50 percent owned by one individual or family); minority owner (between 20 and 50 percent owned by one individual or family); management (no individual stockholder with as much as 20 percent of the firm's stock); and control through a legal device (e.g., pyramiding, in which a company owns a controlling interest in firm A, which in turn controls firm B, which in turn controls firm C, and so forth).

3. Even the 23 percent figure is meaningless in the absence of historical data. Although they argued that a revolution had occurred in corporate organization in the United States, Berle and Means made no attempt to demonstrate that the extent of management control had actually increased (either rapidly or gradually) during the twentieth century. They simply assumed that stockholding had been highly concentrated earlier in the century. In fact, there is evidence that stockholding was already widely dispersed by 1900 (Corey, 1930, p. 284) and even as early as 1850 (Bunting, 1976).

4. As with other studies whose results differed from Larner's, Kotz employed a 5 percent cutoff point for classification as management con-

trolled or, as he termed it, "no identified center of control." Since the Berle and Means study, the exact level of stock ownership necessary for control has been a matter of considerable debate. Larner suggested that 10 percent, not the 20 percent employed by Berle and Means, was probably sufficient for control in most cases. However, others, including the Patman Committee (U.S. House of Representatives, 1968), Kotz (1978), Chevalier (1970), and Burch (1972), have argued that 5 percent (or even less) is often sufficient. These debates have continued to characterize research in this area. But, as is argued here, the issue of stock dispersal may be less relevant to understanding the problem of corporate control than has generally been believed.

5. For reviews of this voluminous literature, see Mintz and Schwartz (1985), Useem (1980), Pennings (1980), and Palmer (1980).

6. Among the most cited studies are National Resources Committee (1939), Perlo (1957), Dooley (1969), Bunting and Barbour (1971), and Allen (1974).

2

Sources of Intercorporate Unity
Beth Mintz
Michael Schwartz

The eclipse of managerial theory has led to a large body of research that describes and analyzes the various mechanisms temporarily or permanently binding large business enterprises to one or other. These bonds may produce coordinated behavior, either through mutually beneficial cooperation or through coercive power which forces one company to serve the other's interest. In this chapter we explore these sources of unity, focusing particularly on the mechanisms that allow one firm to constrain or coerce another. Though these relationships crosscut the corporate world, we shall see in later chapters that their cumulative impact is a quasi-hierarchical arrangement in which major financial institutions are the central actors. We call the decision-making leadership that accrues to the executives of major banks and insurance companies *financial hegemony* (Mintz and Schwartz, 1985).

STOCKHOLDING AS A SOURCE OF INTERCORPORATE POWER AND COORDINATION

The extent to which concentrated stockholding remains an important mechanism in the control of the modern corporation has been at the center of the debate over the validity of the managerial argument (see Chapter 1).

Three different forms of stock ownership are relevant in this context: stock-holding by capitalist families, stockholding by one corporation in another, and institutional stockholding.

Stockholding by Capitalist Families

Traditionally intercorporate planning and coordination were accomplished through the mechanism of stockholding. Ownership of large blocks in multiple organizations allowed an individual or a family to create a coordinated set of policies among otherwise independent companies. This coordination could be achieved either through day-to-day involvement in the affairs of each unit or through the broader method of strategic control, in which the owners dictate general policy for the executive officers to implement (Scott, 1979; Kotz, 1978). In either case, the stockholders may choose to suppress competitive behavior among the firms under their control. They may also suppress supplier-customer conflict or encourage cooperation where there is no other economic incentive to do so.

Obviously, such measures are undertaken only if the owning group feels it can profit from them. Such was the case, for example, in the post–World War II period, when the Dupont family controlled General Motors, holding over 25 percent of the stock, and U.S. Rubber (Uniroyal), holding over 10 percent of that stock. In at least one way they utilized this control to create an otherwise "unnatural" unity between the two corporations. Uniroyal sold tires at cost to General Motors, a policy that effectively transferred profits from Uniroyal to the auto manufacturer, the company in which the Duponts held a greater percentage. Their share of the return from this arrangement was, of course, substantial (Fitch and Oppenheimer, 1970, Part III, pp. 88–92). Moreover, the coordination achieved between General Motors and Uniroyal—in this case at the expense of Uniroyal's balance sheet—implied a unity that prevented interfirm conflict over any of the wide range of economic differences between them. Beyond the exploitative unity on tire prices, they would tend to take consistent positions on access to rubber supplies for Uniroyal or in General Motors' disputes over parts contracts with its other suppliers.

The crucial insight to be gained from this glimpse at common ownership arrangements is that they allow for the coordinated activity of two or more corporations, carried on in the overarching interest of the capitalist family that controls the corporations. For this reason, common family ownership is capable of creating coordination and unity in circumstances in which conflict and diversion might otherwise occur.

Though few analysts dispute the potential power of stockholding by corporate families, managerialists assume that such multiple ownership is no longer prevalent in American business. This claim is exaggerated. A Wharton School study of 1971 stockholding patterns indicated that 0.2 percent of Americans owned about 30 percent of corporate stock and 1 percent owned over half (*New York Times*, December 18, 1972, p. 57). The business press reports a constant stream of examples of corporations whose policies are affected, mediated, and controlled in a variety of ways by their owners. In addition to spectacular cases like Rupert Murdoch's expansion into the communications industry, there are numerous instances of owner-entrepreneurs, such as James Ling, Victor Posner, Charles Mellon Evans, and Carl Lindner, who buy controlling blocks of stock for the express purpose of making the firm a part of their corporate empire. Though, as managerialists point out, many firms do not have dominant stockholders, individual and family ownership remains a prominent feature of the corporate landscape, capable of creating intercorporate unity and suppressing interorganizational conflict.

Stockholding by One Corporation in Another

Intercorporate stock ownership functions in a manner similar to stock-holding by capitalist families. Any firm that holds a controlling interest in another corporation can impose policies which serve its overall interest, even when the target company suffers. In certain cases, the acquiring firm will replace personnel in executive positions in order to guarantee smooth functioning and efficient coordination. At other times, a partially owned company will be allowed to maintain its original management team with broad performance monitored by the owning group.

Outside ownership and control is rarely a matter of intercorporate rape. Consider the following example: Anderson-Clayton, a large cotton export firm, bought a controlling share of United States Marine Steamship Line. This allowed Anderson-Clayton to hire its own ships to transport its products from the United States to overseas customers. Although the economic advantage of this arrangement is quite apparent, it led to a further sort of coordination that is not as obvious. Because it owned its own steamships, Anderson-Clayton found that increasing transport prices no longer affected its economic standing, since the profits made from rate hikes were retained inside the broader corporate unit. The existence of intercorporate stockholding therefore resulted in a change in Anderson-Clayton's political posture: it no longer lobbied against high transport rates, but became an advocate of them (Fitch and Oppenheimer, 1970, Part III, pp. 83–84). Intercorporate stockholding in this case prevented the expression of conflict between two potentially competing interests.

Although the extent of this type of intercorporate ownership is difficult to measure precisely, research suggests that it is widespread (Burch, 1972; Larner, 1970). Even without systematic evidence, however, its importance is incontrovertible, given the persistence of mergers and conglomerate expansion. Between 1960 and 1985 there were three major waves of intercorporate mergers (*Business Week,* November 14, 1977, pp. 176–184; *Business Week,* March 4, 1985, pp. 80–91) and our data show that their effects have been enormous: 150 of the 500 largest industrials of 1962 had been merged into other firms by 1974. When one corporation acquires another, the two companies are brought under common ownership and the constituent parts of the newly merged firm coordinate their activities and suppress their contradictory impulses. Both mergers and conglomerates are therefore institutional incarnations of the sort of control that capitalist families are reputed to have exercised in the early part of the twentieth century. It is ironic that a debate continues over the importance of stockholding when mergers and conglomerates are well-publicized equivalent phenomena.[1]

Institutional Stockholding

Institutional stockholding is a device of recent origin. It grew with the first successes of the Congress of Industrial Organization's (CIO) campaign for pension funding just after World War II, and its importance derives from the ever increasing proportion of investment capital residing in these funds (Rifkin and Barker, 1980; Baum and Stiles, 1965). Pension monies, coupled with the endowments of foundations and universities and the assets of individual capitalist families given over to professional management, have made institutional investors significant actors in the world of big business. These managers, usually located in the trust departments of major banks, make investment decisions for their various holdings. They decide what and when to buy and to sell.

By 1985, institutional investors accounted for an astounding 90 percent of all stock traded on the New York Stock Exchange and 67 percent of all stocks held (*Business Week*, February 4, 1985, p. 61). This concentration has enormous potential for controlling and coordinating the behavior of different corporations:

> As institutions buy and sell ever larger blocks of stock, they develop greater power in corporate affairs—power they occasionally exercise with the impact of a sledgehammer. . . . When institutions sell as a group they can have a devastating effect on a company—squelching financing and expansion plans and sometimes destroying morale. (*Business Week*, July 25, 1970, pp. 53, 55)

The respect shown for this potential is aptly illustrated by the experience of Becton Dickinson, a New Jersey pharmaceutical firm controlled and operated by owner-founder Fairleigh Dickinson. "In 1974, Dickinson voluntarily surrendered the chief executive's post to his handpicked successor, Wesley J. Howe, in a move calculated to assure Wall Street of continued professional management in the company" (*Business Week*, October 3, 1977). The "Wall Street" referred to here was the institutional investment community which held 8.3 million of the 19 million Becton shares outstanding (*New York Times*, January 19, 1978, p. D3). Dickinson feared that his continued leadership would result in a wholesale selling of these shares, which would lower stock prices (making the firm vulnerable to takeover), undermine credit ratings (making the firm less able to finance expansion), and alienate prospective economic allies.

This same power was evident when Ted Turner, owner of Turner Broadcasting, a cable network, attempted to acquire CBS in 1985. The initial bid was altered after one day because it "encountered widespread scepticism by institutional investors and arbitragers, whose ultimate support is crucial if

Mr. Turner hopes to succeed" (*Wall Street Journal,* April 22, 1985, p. 3). Institutional investors held the majority of CBS stock (*New York Times,* April 19, 1985, p. D9).

As *Business Week* commented, "some corporate managements . . . tend to pander to institutional preferences and thus to adopt whatever policies are favored by the money managers in the large investment institutions" (July 25, 1970, p. 54). The policy preferences of large institutional holders, therefore, have become a major force in determining and directing individual corporate policies.

The key to institutional investors' power is not participation in the day-to-day decision making of a corporation but, rather, their propensity to "dump" a firm's stock, thus reducing its price and making it vulnerable to a variety of problems. This stockdumping potential, of course, depends on simultaneous decisions of many institutional portfolio managers. Such decisions have become commonplace when, for example, a company's earning decline:

> These days, institutions commonly dump shares of any corporation that issues a disappointing earnings report. The selling often involves big blocks of ten thousand or more shares at a clip. The phenomenon is so prevalent that investors assume institutional dumping is invariably involved when shares tumble under such circumstances. (*New York Times,* December 17, 1976, p. D2)

Thus, the coordinated trading of large institutional investors has become an accepted part of the American business scene, and its consequences are often devastating. When, despite opposition from bondholders, LTV moved to break up newly acquired Jones and Laughlin Steel, LTV stock declined so precipiticiously as to trigger a corporate crisis culminating in the removal of James Ling, the principal individual stockholder and architect of the giant conglomerate (Brown, 1972, pp. 166, 240). Research Cottrell, a manufacturer of pollution control devices, saw its stock drop from $60.00 to $4.00 because design errors had led to a decline in profits and triggered institutional dumping (*Forbes,* April 1, 1977, p. 78). Even a corporation such as IBM is by no means invulnerable to outside influence. When subjected to mass selling by institutional investors, IBM was forced to purchase its own stock to keep equity prices up (*Business Week,* April 4, 1977, p. 110). Ultimately, this expensive process depleted its cash reserves and led to massive borrowing (*New York Times,* September 30, 1979, sec. 3, p. 1).

Individual, intercorporate, and institutional stockholding are all significant sources of outside influence on the behavior of even the largest corporations. They represent a significant force in constructing temporary or long-term unity among firms with otherwise competing interests.

LENDING RELATIONSHIPS AS A SOURCE OF INTERCORPORATE POWER AND COORDINATION

Although managerialists claimed that outside financing was no longer necessary for the American corporation (see, e.g., Gordon, 1945; Galbraith,

1967), recent evidence reviewed in Chapter 1 demonstrates that this claim is largely unfounded. Since World War II, well over 30 percent of all corporate capital has been borrowed (Stearns, 1982, 1983; Lintner, 1959; Gogel, 1977), while the total long-term debt of American corporations jumped from $49 billion in 1940 to $363 billion in 1970 (Sweezy and Magdoff, 1975, p. 5).

Some firms utilize an almost constant flood of outside financing. American Telephone and Telegraph, one of the most persistently profitable companies in the United States, owed a total of $32.5 billion in 1978 (*Business Week*, November 6, 1978, p. 119). While other companies attempt to expand through retained profits only, they almost inevitably end up borrowing. DuPont lasted 25 years (perhaps a record) between bond issues but finally succumbed; IBM, which had relied almost entirely on internally funded expansion, was forced by stockdumping to borrow $2.5 billion in 1979.

Loans do not necessarily indicate "crises." For DuPont and IBM, they were necessary measures taken by healthy firms. As the IBM analyst for Drexel Burnham Lambert (a top investment bank) told the *New York Times*, "We are pleased at the development. The debt offering tells me that the company will reveal exciting new computer products next year" (September 30, 1979, sec. 3, p. 1).

Lending relationships can be divided into two categories: financing new enterprise and rescuing corporations in crisis. Both may confer upon lenders the power to constrain or coerce the behavior of their customers.

The Infusion of New Capital

In 1978, nonfinancial corporations invested a total of $236.5 billion; $102 billion (43 percent) of this was borrowed, mostly ($71 billion) from lending institutions (*Business Week*, January 30, 1978, p. 62). These loans were not given "automatically." Almost invariably there are more prospective borrowers than available capital, and lenders must choose the best investment by exploring the particulars of corporate planning. The lending officers of banks and insurance companies are in a position to decide which expansion projects will be undertaken and which ones will remain unfunded and, therefore, unexecuted. Consider the 1976 proposal by aircraft manufacturers to develop and market a new airbus, which would "use up-to-the-minute technology, would mean lowest possible noise, enormous fuel savings, and a carefully calculated seating capacity for the most profitable possible operations on intended routes":

> Almost everyone concedes that large new plan programs will only be started with large orders that only United States airlines could be expected to provide. But these airlines' traditional lenders have repeatedly said they cannot provide financing unless the industry's financial health improves markedly, and not just in a one or two year spurt. . . . Conceivably, if the airline recovery continues, the lenders might relent and agree to provide financing. But they are worried not just about short-run profit levels, but also about where the industry is headed in the long run. (*New York Times*, September 3, 1976, p. D5)

Ultimately, despite vigorous lobbying by both airlines and manufacturers, the airbus was not built. The decision by the lenders was a controlling one. In the early 1980s, the reduction of American steel-making capacity and the decision of American auto manufacturers to import Japanese and European cars under their nameplates were in good part a result of the refusal of lenders to fund new product development (Mintz and Schwartz, 1985; Bluestone and Harrison, 1982).

In short, since lenders are constantly faced with choices, they will seek out projects sponsored by economically healthy companies, since their investment is thereby protected. Nevertheless, they must still gamble, since expansion is always based on an unknown future, and economic history is strewn with the demise of apparently invulnerable companies such as International Harvester, W. T. Grant, and the Penn Central Railroad (Mintz and Schwartz, 1985; Glasberg and Schwartz, 1983; Daughen and Binzen, 1971). When large companies collapse, lenders lose more money than their loan reserves can tolerate. For this reason, the projects for which loans are sought are carefully scrutinized and often rejected. Others, even those sought by the soundest companies, are modified before major lenders will accept them. In 1948, General Motors—at that time the richest and largest company in history—was forced to modify its postwar production plans to qualify for needed loans (Sloan, 1965).

Through decisions on which projects to finance, banks and insurance companies lend a degree of orderliness to industrial expansion. They prevent the development of overcapacity and its consequent "destructive" competition, and they channel capital to those firms most capable of utilizing it effectively. At the same time, they create a set of de facto rules which responsible corporate citizens must honor, or risk financial disfavor. Such disfavor might not harm a firm immediately, but during periodic credit squeezes, "the companies most likely to get hurt," according to the financial officer of a major industrial, would be "those companies that have not maintained good relations with their banks" (*Business Week,* January 30, 1978). Occidental Petroleum, for example, found it difficult to borrow money during the early 1970s because the firing of two presidents had undermined bank confidence (*Business Week,* January 10, 1977). American Cyanamid, with no loans outstanding, saved a subsidiary from bankruptcy simply because bankers said they might refuse loans at a later date. The internal affairs of corporations are, therefore, consistently altered—very frequently without explicit directions—to fit within the bounds of the good behavior established by financial institutions. James Ling, the most spectacular and apparently unconstrained conglomerator of the 1960s, told *Fortune:* "Keeping the bankers happy is the most important thing in business" (*Fortune,* June 1973, p. 234).

Lending during Corporate Crisis

Corporations also turn to outside capital sources during times of crisis. In such cases, lenders must avoid "throwing good money after bad"; that is, they must avoid committing further funds if a company cannot be saved. On the other hand, additional loans might save the company and therefore retrieve already committed funds that might otherwise be lost (Glasberg, 1982).

Often, banks and other lenders will dictate certain policies to the troubled company. The classic example of this form of intervention was the removal of Trans World Airlines from the control of Howard Hughes, mentioned in Chapter 1. Beginning in 1939, Hughes had built TWA into a major force in commercial aviation. In the late 1950s, when the first generation of commercial jets was entering the market, he used the airline's dominant position to extract a number of concessions from aircraft manufacturers. The most important privilege he sought was the right to purchase planes in the same way that an ordinary citizen buys a car: the aircraft producer would construct the plane and TWA would pay for it in monthly payments—with interest—after delivery. This arrangement would have forced the aircraft producers to borrow the necessary capital to finance construction, thus adding to the overwhelming debt they had already accumulated in developing the planes.

The manufacturers and their creditors wanted a different payment schedule, one that they had successfully imposed on other, less dominant, airlines, namely prepayment. Under this arrangement, the relatively debt-free airlines would borrow the money and pay it to the manufacturers, which would use it to finance construction. Hughes refused these terms, since the interest he would have paid while waiting for delivery would have reduced his profits. His market position allowed him to insist on delivery before payment and, for two years, he managed to impose this arrangement on the aircraft industry.

During the 1959 recession, however, Howard Hughes' other major holding—the Hughes Tool Company—was unable to repay a $25 million loan to several major New York banks. Under ordinary circumstances the loan would have been "rolled over" and repaid at a later date. In this instance, however, the lenders threatened foreclosure unless Hughes placed the 78 percent of TWA stock that he owned into a voting trust under their control. Once this demand was granted, the immensely successful Hughes management team was ousted and the new leadership quickly renegotiated the airplane purchase agreement. Ultimately, Hughes was forced to sell his shares in the company (Tinnin, 1973).

This episode, despite the dramatic conflict involved, demonstrates the enormous capability for suppressing capitalist competition which resides in the concentration of finance capital, even if this resulted in the weakening or bankruptcy of one or more of the major aircraft manufacturers. Such competition is traditional capitalist behavior and is supposedly the mechanism that prevents the establishment and maintenance of unity and coordination within the world of big business. Bank intervention in this case, therefore, was enormously significant. It revealed the existence of a power capable of overcoming these competitive tendencies and, thus, a potential mechanism for establishing intercorporate unity.

Of course, we must ask how frequently creditors are in a position to exercise this sort of control. Hughes' case was an exceptional one, but it is by no means unique. Less dramatic lender interventions are part of the everyday life of the corporate world because this is the best method that banks have of conserving their capital investment in a troubled organization (Mintz and Schwartz, 1985). Moreover, financial institutions often see such interventions as the only alternative to a wave of bankruptcies. One banker explained the intervention in Great Southwest Corporation (GSC) thusly:

> If GSC was a unique situation, we'd push them under. But if we did that to all companies in the same boat, we'd throw the economy for a loop. In any case, some interest is better than none. It gives the company a real opportunity to come out of its troubles, and it stretches out future losses for us. (*Business Week,* April 25, 1977)

Banks do not intervene every time they disagree with corporate policy. They have neither the opportunity nor the desire to do so. Intervention occurs only when opportunity and inclination intersect, as in the ouster of Colgate's chief executive officer:

> David Foster's fall was largely caused by a series of long running differences of opinion with key [bank] members of the Colgate board over his managerial style and acquisition of policies. So long as all went well, Foster was safe, but once some trouble began to surface, he was vulnerable. (*Fortune,* September 24, 1979)

While loose management style contributed to the fall of David Foster, tight management led to the 1977 ouster of Franklin Jarmon as president of Genesco, a firm his family had controlled for 70 years. Just as the company was emerging from a crisis the board, led by major creditors, brought in three outsiders to replace him because "the constant second guessing, unnecessarily harsh controls on how capital outlays and operating budgets should be spent, and a general practice of requiring too much approval for even such things as leasing needs, strapped the company" (*New York Times,* January 4, 1977, p. 37).

In 1985, the banks pushed Evans Products into what may have been an unnecessary bankruptcy, because its owner, Victor Posner "had a penchant for takeovers":

> "A lot of people" says a Wall Street investment banker with evident delight, "are out to get him". . . .
> "A number of people thought there were some proposals that might have worked short of bankruptcy" says a banker at a major Evans lender. They were rejected, this banker adds, because many banks "don't feel warm and fuzzy toward Mr. Posner". Says a blunter source close to Evans: "The banks hate him". (*Business Week,* March 25, 1985, p. 24).

Such episodes are regularly reported in the business press; one incomplete survey uncovered 50 cases, among the top 500 companies in a 7-year period (Mintz and Schwartz, 1985). This frequency has led many researchers—most notably Menshikov (1969) and Fitch and Oppenheimer

(1970)—to view lending relationships as a principal mechanism for welding the corporate world into a united, coordinated whole.

Typically, of course, direct intervention in the affairs of a corporation is a temporary procedure used in an exceptional situation. Nevertheless, direct intervention, combined with the ability to define the lending environment within which corporations operate, gives financial institutions considerable influence over corporate policy and makes them a major force in accomplishing intercorporate coordination.

JOINT VENTURES AS SOURCES OF INTERCORPORATE POWER AND COORDINATION

For many years, General Motors and Exxon jointly owned the Ethyl Corporation, which produced lead additives for gasoline, and this joint venture was an ongoing point of contact and cooperation between the parent firms (*Moody's Industrials,* 1963; *Forbes,* May 29, 1978, p. 85). While such a joint effort was unusual before the 1960s, it has become commonplace. An incomplete survey of the 1974 *Moody's Industrial Manual* uncovered over 200 joint ventures among corporations in the Fortune 500 listings. This prevalence of joint ventures makes them an important focus in intercorporate conflict reduction (Pfeffer and Sanancik, 1978; Pfeffer and Novak, 1976).

The conflict-reducing potential of joint ventures is nicely illustrated by the initial response of American steelmakers to cheaper, better foreign steel—mainly Japanese and German—which became a market force in the 1970s.[2] Many American companies had established joint ventures and partnerships with their overseas competitors and would thus be competing with themselves if they modernized. They were further deterred from modernizing by the difficulty of obtaining loan capital. The industry sought tariff and legal barriers that would produce sufficient profits to finance conversion, but when these efforts failed, the steel companies abandoned the fight altogether.

This abandonment was premised on the ability of Big Steel to diversify into other industries quickly and profitably. The diversification was accomplished through purchases of nonsteel companies and through joint ventures. U.S. Steel, for example, combined its expertise in industrial production with Texaco's experience in petroleum chemistry. This combination provided a solid foundation upon which to build a one-billion-dollar investment in the development, manufacture, and marketing of high-density polyethylene. So successful was this initial venture that after one year, the two companies doubled their investment and began to diversify (*Business Week,* November 26, 1979).

Without joint ventures, the steel industry might have been forced to modernize and compete with foreign products or it might have pursued its political fight for import barriers. The availability of joint ventures facilitated the suppression of this potential conflict and saved the issue from the mediation of the state.

The potential of joint ventures for creating unity is also illustrated in the creation of the uranium cartel in the mid 1970s.[3] During the great buildup of nuclear power as an alternative form of energy, the nuclear industry developed joint exploration and marketing ventures for its fuel. Over the years, the many small firms merged and grew into a few large, oligopolistic companies which were managerially and economically inter-married. This intimacy seems to have been a crucial factor in the creation of the uranium cartel, which by 1977, had raised the price of nuclear fuel to 10 times its 1970 level; an escalation even greater than the highly publicized price increases of the oil producers. Thus joint ventures helped bring about the necessary unity among otherwise dispersed and potentially competitive corporations, and this unity, in turn, wrought fundamental changes in the economics of nuclear energy.

Lending Consortia

The business press contains daily announcements of lending arrange-ments between major industrial corporations and consortia of large financial institutions. For example:

> The Standard Oil Company (Ohio) of Cleveland announced . . . that it had entered into a $500 million revolving credit and term loan agree-ment with the Manufacturers Hanover Trust Company, as agent, and 18 other banks, to help pay for tankers that would transport its Alaskan crude oil and to develop its Alaskan north slope reserves at Prudhoe Bay. (*New York Times,* October 1, 1976, p. D12)

Loan consortia have become normal operating procedure in both the financing of new ventures and the refinancing of troubled corporations. They are necessary because even the very largest banks cannot individually pro-vide the huge amount of capital needed for corporate use. Moreover, a large loan, of say $500 million, to a single enterprise would make a bank's financial and economic well-being contingent on the health of that single firm. Such a risk is always unwise, particularly when the borrower is in financial trouble, as is the case with many large loans. Banks and insurance companies therefore divide up both the risk and the benefit in major lending endeavors.

Lending consortia are joint ventures which impose cooperation on their members (Mintz and Schwartz, 1985). Since it is very difficult for even a single lender to withdraw, the needs of each bank are tied to the collective enterprise. The consortium must, therefore, develop and maintain devices for creating and enforcing common policy.

The normal procedure is the establishment of a lead bank—usually the institution with the largest percentage of the loan and the longest ongoing relationship with the corporate borrower. The lead bank is responsible for broad supervision of the loan and for insuring that the borrower does not pursue policies that endanger the investment of the consortium.

We see from this basic structure of corporate financing the potential for united action by a large group of banks. Since the number of major commer-cial lenders in the United States is actually quite small,[4] the existence of large consortia imposes upon the financial community a united policy vis-à-vis any particular corporation. Thus, if a firm finds itself in ongoing financial difficulty, it usually cannot seek out alternate funding sources. Since the original loans were probably supplied by a consortium, all banks of sufficient size to re-fund the debt are already members of the lending group.

This circumstance is perhaps most pointedly illustrated by the bankruptcy of W. T. Grant, the 16th largest retailer of 1974. During the crisis preceding the bankruptcy, Grant borrowed from a consortium of 129 banks and insurance companies. Almost every major and minor commercial lender was involved. As the crisis deepened, the consortium attempted to protect its collective investment by controlling Grant's everyday activities. The consortium ultimately decided that bankruptcy was the least costly alternative. Because the lenders recovered more of their investment than the credit groups—suppliers, customers, stockholders, and employees—this episode became the subject of a major lawsuit, and it underscored the potential power that derives from the unity of commercial financiers (Glasberg, 1982).

By standardizing decisions about capital flow, consortium-produced unity reinforces the potential for financial hegemony. Consortia also help to crystallize power relations among lenders. Since the consortium must reach unity, the interplay of different interests must be resolved in some internal fashion. Most often, these divisions are minor and do not create problems. In some circumstances, however, the differences are major and the consortium becomes a forum within which differential power is exercised; inevitably some firms are forced to adopt and support financial policies that they do not desire.

One example of such interbank power involved the near bankruptcy of the many real estate investment trusts (REITs) in the early 1970s.[5] These companies, many of which were often owned by major banks, had been established to facilitate commercial construction (malls, office buildings, etc.). They borrowed very large sums of money in the late 1960s, and during the collapse of the real estate market in the early 1970s, most REITs fell into grave financial difficulty. The major commercial banks were placed in an unusual bind: if the REITs went bankrupt, their stock would become worthless, but if they maintained them in business, their loans from bank consortia would have to be renegotiated at very low (and unprofitable) interest rates, since the trusts were incapable of repaying the debt at the appointed rates and times. For the banks that owned REITs, the latter course was preferable; for the other institutions, with only loans outstanding, bankruptcy and sale of assets was a much better arrangement.

The overt conflict that resulted was resolved in favor of the New York money market banks, which protected their equity investment. Using their position as lead banks in the consortia—as well as their dominance in the economy—the New York banks were able to engineer the renegotiations of loans at interest rates as low as 1 percent. The lesser lenders were unable to resist this development.

Lending consortia have also created a foundation upon which international financial planning has been constructed. In the 1970s, loans to underdeveloped countries were organized in the following way. The major New York banks, which were inevitably the lead banks in the financing of developing countries, established a lending limit for each nation. Corporations wishing to invest—or the governments of these countries themselves— approached the banks with proposals for particular industrial or commercial development. The decisions about which loans to grant rested with the lead banks, which then created a consortium of interested lenders (*Business Week*, December 10, 1979, p. 31). In this manner, centralized planning and decision making were established in this crucial sector of lending.[6]

Lending consortia, therefore, have immense potential for creating economic coordination. They contribute to financial leadership in the corporate world in three significant ways:

1. The negotiation of a loan between a large corporation and a consortium of lenders implies and creates a unified financial posture toward that company. In subsequent loans, if the firm is financially pressed, it may not be in a position to shop around for a lending arrangement which offers it maximum flexibility and minimum control. The consortium therefore creates unity of financial institutions vis-à-vis corporate borrowers, making lender control all the more feasible.

2. The prevalence of loan consortia imposes a decision-making process upon the lenders that activates and consolidates power relations among them. This implies the forced resolution of interbank conflict and creates an opportunity for the exercise of interbank power.

3. The necessity—in the broadest sense—of interbank consortia creates a framework within which broad decision making about the flow of capital can proceed. Since large-scale lending inevitably takes place within the framework of consortia, consortia encourage a consistent policy toward specific areas of investment as well as a unified posture toward particular industrial sectors or corporate entities.

Lending consortia, then, take their place as the most significant form of joint ventures and the most important to analyze if we are to decipher the lines of influence, cooperation, and power within the corporate community. They are one of the crucial mechanisms through which capital flow decisions are standardized and thus are instrumental in establishing the environment in which the modern corporation operates.

CUSTOMER-SUPPLIER RELATIONSHIPS AS SOURCES OF INTERCORPORATE POWER AND COORDINATION

The firm that borrows money is in need of a resource that banks and/or insurance companies can supply, and this dependency is sometimes translated into the leverage that lenders use to influence, alter, or transform corporate policy. A similar leverage can develop when one firm purchases goods, raw materials, or finished products from another

Obviously, a large corporation that purchases its typewriters from IBM could never be brought under IBM's control. When, however, the relationship becomes crucial to the economic well-being of one of the companies, the circumstances are entirely different (Pfeffer and Salancik, 1978). In the 1970s, the Kellwood Company, an apparel manufacturer, sold over 50 percent of its output to Sears (*Moody's*, 1974). The potential for control in this circumstance is apparent: Sears could use the threat of purchasing its clothing line elsewhere to directly intervene in the affairs of the dependent supplier. (There is no evidence that Sears has exercised this power.)

The American economy is laced with interindustry dependencies of this sort. The auto industry is dependent on the steel industry; steel depends on coal; the garment industry depends on both the chemical fiber industry and textile manufacturers. The chemical industry depends on oil. And so on and so forth. These broad interdependencies are the environment in which individual corporations operate. Each firm must find a way to control and regularize its supply of raw materials and the markets for its products.

Recent research has demonstrated the importance of these interdependencies (e.g., Pfeffer and Salancik, 1978; Burt, 1983). Asymmetrical dependency as in the Kellwood example, can be translated into direct intervention in the affairs of a target company either through operational management or strategic control. Alternatively, it can lead to a looser, hegemonic, relationship, in which the actions of the dominant firm force a specific type of reaction from the subject company.

Customer-supplier relationships, therefore, vary in their potential for intercorporate coordination, and they may work in tandem with or in contradiction to other dependencies. A single firm may be involved in several resource dependencies, as well as lending and stockholding relationships, at the same time. The resulting profile of constraint, intervention, and dominance can be complex and problematic.

INTANGIBLE SOURCES OF INTERCORPORATE POWER AND COORDINATION

The kinds of ties discussed thus far have all had tangible economic and monetary foundations. Recently, interorganizational sociologists have begun to analyze a number of less tangible resources. Although these have not yet been fully explored, it is useful to consider how they, too, may serve as sources of intercorporate power and coordination.

The clearest example of nontangible intercorporate resource is information. A great deal of the internal energy of many large organizations is devoted to developing and processing the mass of information necessary to make and implement the crucial decisions that face modern enterprise. The entire research and development effort of industry can be seen as a matter of processing information about technical aspects of the production process.

To understand the potential for intercorporate power which derives from information, consider the role of Moody's and Dun and Bradstreet in rating corporate bond issues. Since low credit ratings not only imply higher interest rates, but may also exclude the corporation (or government agency) from the lending market entirely, Moody's and Dun and Bradstreet may under certain circumstances, dictate corporate policy (*Wall Street Journal,* October 10, 1976, p. 1; *Business Week,* October 16, 1978, pp. 90–100).

> One midwestern company, for example, learned with dismay that Moody's was giving it an A rating on a private placement, although the company had all the appropriate ratios for a double A. The problem was its high dividend policy. If dividends continued to grow at the past rate, said Moodys, projected capital expenditures of the company would increase its debt ratio to a level above the double A norm. The company and the underwriter then sought to persuade Moody's that in fact no such outcome was likely, for management was planning to reduce the rate of dividend increase. After two days of negotiations, the company agreed to include a dividend covenant, and persuaded Moody's to come across with a Double A. (*Fortune,* April, 1976, p. 141).

Corporate rating services, therefore, occupy a special position in terms of interorganizational control. In certain cases, they can directly intervene in the affairs of a corporation, as illustrated by the above example. In a broader sense, however, they offer another instance of hegemonic control—an asymmetrical dependency which forces the rated firm to alter its policy as a reaction to a decision by the rating agency. "Some companies are brought to believe that if they are not in a particular rating category now, they are not precluded from it if they mind their P's and Q's" (*Fortune,* April 1976, p. 141).

Control of information therefore offers still another basis for corporate control, although the extent of its application is probably quite limited.

THE BROADER SYSTEM OF INTERCORPORATE RELATIONSHIPS

The relationships described above intersect in every possible way. A company dependent on another for resources may hold controlling stock in that firm and thus reverse the direction of leverage. A loan relationship between a bank and a nonfinancial organization may be congruent with institutional stockholding or may coexist with bank holdings in a competing firm. The possible permutations of these relationships are limitless. Two examples will illustrate the complex intercorporate relationships that may underlie particular events.

Given our knowledge of intercorporate relations, it seems difficult to imagine circumstances under which an industry—or a corporation in a given industry—could dictate another sector's labor relations policies. Yet in 1980 U.S. Steel negotiated the bituminous coal industry's union contract:

> U.S. Steel Corporation, long critical of the coal industry's conduct of labor negotiations, will soon get a chance to see if its approach can work any better. Directors of the Bituminous Coal Operators Association, the industry's labor relations arm, voted on January 14 to reorganize the group's bargaining structure along lines that U.S. Steel had demanded. (*Business Week,* February 22, 1980, p. 42)

This development, although remarkable at first glance, is made almost mundane when we follow the chronology of events that preceded it. We begin by noting that coal is a crucial ingredient in steel production. Therefore steel corporations had long sought to stabilize their supply of coal. U.S. Steel, for example, had begun buying coal companies in the 1960s, and by 1980 it was the third largest bituminous coal producer. Other large steel companies were similarly situated.

The bituminous coal industry had always maintained unity in its labor relations through Bituminous Coal Operators Association (BCOA). An organization of approximately 130 firms, the BCOA had come to play such a dominant role in labor policy that the constituent firms were no longer equipped to negotiate on their own. Moreover, the industry found itself in poor financial condition in the late 1970s. The intersection of cross-industry stockholding, economic difficulty, and joint labor bargaining resulted in tremendous leverage for U.S. Steel and other steel companies, which threatened to withdraw from joint negotiations and bargain separately. This would have resulted in disunity and, in all likelihood, a major strengthening of the union position. For U.S. Steel and its allies—whose economic well-being depended only partially on their coal operations—disunity would be a problem but not a tragedy. For less diversified members of the industry, however, the negotiation of an unfavorable contract could have produced a major economic disaster. U.S. Steel's threat was therefore made credible and powerful by the cross-industrial nature of the relationship and by the fact that the coal company was only a small part of its larger economic interest. The other operators agreed to U.S. Steel's bargaining strategy in order to keep the BCOA unified.

This example illustrates the complex combination of several different processes discussed above: customer-supplier interdependency, the creation of intercorporate stockholding arrangement, the interdependence that flows from the creation and maintenance of joint ventures, and the broader economic resources available to the much larger steel company. In this case the forces were arranged congruently: most of the leverage lay in the hands of the steel companies, and they came to dominate the labor policy of the coal industry.

Consider, however, the case of Leasco's attempted takeover of Chemical Bank.[7] Leasco had grown dramatically through a series of acquisitions in the 1960s; by 1968 it was a large, but not giant, conglomerate. That year, Leasco's chairman, Saul P. Steinberg, decided to acquire Chemical Bank of New York, one of the nation's largest and most powerful commercial banks. The strategy was to exchange Leasco stock worth $120 for each share of Chemical, then selling at $80. When enough shares were accumulated, Steinberg hoped to take over the leadership of Chemical Bank. Once in control he would revamp "outmoded" policies and revolutionize foreign operations to make Chemical more profitable.

Initially, this was a straightforward attempt to translate intercorporate stockholding into operational management. But it very rapidly was transformed into a dramatic illustration of multilayered intercorporate coordination:

1. Institutional investors began dumping Leasco stock, causing a dramatic drop in four weeks. This, by itself, frustrated the acquisition effort, since the reduced value of Leasco stock offered was not sufficient to make the exchange profitable.

2. Leasco's lead bank, Continental Illinois, opposed the acquisition effort and indicated that it would not look favorably on future loan agreements.

3. Leasco's investment bankers, Lehman Brothers and White Weld, informed Steinberg that they would not participate in a Leasco tender offer for Chemical.

4. Major customers of Leasco announced their intention to refuse renewal of contracts with the company if the merger attempt continued.

5. The management of Chemical threatened to resign if the merger succeeded and indicated that major depositors would withdraw their funds.

6. U.S. senators introduced a congressional bill that would make Leasco's plan illegal.

7. Nelson Rockefeller, governor of New York, called for a bill at the state level that would make the acquisition illegal.

In a very short period of time, Chemical Bank had been able to rally to its cause the main institutional holders of Leasco stock, Leasco's investment banks, Leasco's lenders, and many of Leasco's major customers. It had also demonstrated its influence over government at both the federal and state levels. In sum, the tentacles of intercorporate cooperation were extensive and readily mobilized in this instance.

We cannot, of course, extrapolate from this one example to the general structure of intercorporate relationships in American business. However, this case suggests that—at least under special circumstances—intercorporate coordination and unity can be readily mobilized into a visible and powerful force. More important, however, it suggests that particular mechanisms of intercorporate control function well in particular situations but not in others. Even stock ownership is not always effective, as the Howard Hughes fiasco at TWA showed.

The existence of various sources of intercorporate unity and different forms of corporate control does not undermine the notion of a more ordered set of intercorporate relationships that define the environment in which these affairs are played out. Sometimes the needs of dominant stockholders prevail. At other times bond-rating services exert the ultimate influence. At still other times joint venture commitments are primary. The modern corporation is subject to multiple influences and tied to differing interests. Nonetheless there is an overarching pattern to these arrangements. In the next chapter we will begin to analyze this pattern, which demonstrates the centrality of lenders in establishing coordination among different corporate actors.

NOTES

1. Some managerialists have argued that intercorporate stockholding is not the same as "family" ownership unless the overall entity

(controlling firm, merged firm, or conglomerate) is family controlled (Berle and Means, 1932; Larner, 1970). Although many conglomerates are, in fact, controlled by owner-entrepreneurs (e.g., Ling, Simon, and Riklis), even in the absence of ultimate owner control, the potential for conflict suppression remains.

2. This account is based on the following sources: *Business Week,* September 19, 1977, pp. 66–86; October 10, 1977, p. 39; November 14, 1977, p. 48; November 28, 1977, p. 34; January 23, 1978, p. 25; May 1, 1978, p. 31; September 11, 1978, p. 60; September 18, 1978, p. 29; October 9, 1978, p. 56; *New York Times,* June 12, 1977, p. D1; September 8, 1977, p. D3; September 15, 1977, p. 57; November 15, 1977, p. 57; *Forbes,* March 6, 1978. See also Bluestone and Harrison (1982).

3. This account is based on the following sources: *Business Week* January 31, 1977, pp. 60–66; February 7, 1977, p. 8; December 26, 1977, p. 33; *New York Times,* February 17, 1977, p. 57; March 31, 1977, pp. D1, D12; June 9, 1978, sec. 3, p. 1; January 31, 1980, p. D1.

4. Eight major New York commercial banks provide over 50 percent of all industrial financing; 50 banks account for over 70 percent.

5. This discussion is based on the reports in the *New York Times* (March 2, 1975, p. E1; July 1, 1975, p. 4) and *Business Week* (April 4, 1972, pp. 114–116). It is interesting and significant to note that while the REIT repayment schedules were being renegotiated, the banks were refusing to loan money to New York City at a tax free 10 percent level. This suggests that banks follow their own financial interest even when this may mean driving city government and city services into disarray.

6. See also Mintz and Schwartz (1986, 1985). A quite spectacular example of intraconsortium power-wielding occurred during the 1979–1980 Iran-American confrontation. In the early part of this crisis, American lenders sought to default loans that Iran held with American banks. These loans were international in nature, however, and European bankers opposed the move for a wide range of reasons related to the differing interests of the United States and Europe. Nevertheless, because of the discipline imposed by lending consortia, the American banks were able to vote through a major default despite the fact that the Iranians had never failed to pay the interest and principal on their debt. The vote was seven American financials—Chase Manhattan, the lead bank, Bank of America, Banker's Trust, Chemical Bank, Citibank, Manufacturers Hanover Trust, Morgan Guarantee Trust—against four foreign banks—Swiss Bank Corp., Union Bank of Switzerland, Toronto Dominion Bank, and National Westminster Bank. Thus, the United States banks forced the other consortium members to participate in a default operation they did not support. This subsequently triggered an international controversy (*Business Week,* December 10, 1979, pp. 30–31). For an excellent analysis of international bank consortia, see Fennema (1982).

7. For a complete discussion of the remarkable developments in the Leasco takeover effort, see Glasberg (1981, 1982). For other accounts see *Business Week* (July 25, 1970) and Austin (1973).

3

Corporate Interlocks, Financial Hegemony, and Intercorporate Coordination

Beth Mintz
Michael Schwartz

Though the needs of large corporations may often be consonant, major conflicts of interests do exist within the American business community. Companies vary by sales, capital intensity, product line, supplier dependence, and the like; and these differences produce different reactions to a changing economic climate. Labor shortages, for example, are less troublesome to the highly automated petrochemical industry than to labor-intensive mining. High interest rates affect some industries more than others. Changing technologies often transfer profits from one sector to another.

To be a ruling class, the corporate elite must transcend these differences and act in concert often enough to insure that its collective interests are not severely undermined. A ruling class cannot be comprised of autonomous actors; it must act in concert with sufficient regularity to maintain its position against frequent institutional challenges and collective insurgencies.

In Chapter 2, we reviewed some mechanisms of intercorporate unity, and in this chapter we look at the overall structure and process these mechanisms produce at the systemic level. To accomplish this broad portrait, we study patterns of interlocking directorates,[1] which symbolize and materialize the underlying unity and disunity of the corporate world. We conclude that American business structure is most profoundly influenced by a handful of the largest banking institutions of the country. Located mainly in New York and including such giants as Chase Manhattan Bank, Morgan Guaranty, Citibank, Bankers Trust, and Chemical Bank, these companies achieve a loose coordination that usually constrains nonfinancial firms into conformance with the orderly process of economic life and with specific interests of the financial firms themselves.

We call this "hegemonic power," a term borrowed from Antonio Gramsci (1971). Bank hegemony is rooted in the control of capital flows (described in Chapter 2), which amounts to the selection of those industries and firms which will receive infusions of loan monies for rescue and expansion. Such decisions are often made without direct intervention by lenders into the affairs of either the selected or the rejected applicants for loans. Consequently, the corporate coordination traced by the structure of interlocking directorates is loosely constructed and based on the ongoing capital needs of modern industry.[2]

In this chapter, we will review the evidence which leads to our contention that financial institutions function to transform individual corporate leaders into a unified ruling class. We will then offer a more detailed sketch of the institutional structure of American business.

BOARDS OF DIRECTORS AND THE ROLE OF INTERLOCKING DIRECTORATES

In the United States, the board of directors of a corporation is the legal governing body of the firm, and its members are responsible for the performance and the functioning of the organization. Individual directors, however, are not necessarily involved in the day-to-day administration which ultimately determines corporate performance. Although some members are top-ranking officials of the firm—president, chief executive officer or, perhaps, an executive vice-president—most have other full-time jobs and maintain these directorships as a small part of their everyday work life. These outsiders manage companies of their own, occupy prestigious positions in the noncorporate world, or represent ownership interests in the company in question. They are briefed on the details of operation and consulted at times of major change. Thus, the official decision-making body of the modern corporation brings together the specific knowledge of insiders, and the broad business experience of outsiders.

Consider the case of General Motors. In 1962, G.M.'s board comprised 27 seats, of these, twelve were occupied by insiders, including John F. Gordon, president of the company, and Louis Good, executive vice-president. The remaining 15 seats were occupied by outsiders—a broad assortment of business figures, including Henry Alexander of Morgan Guaranty Trust, Richard King Mellon of Mellon National Bank, Lewis Douglas of Mutual New York Life Insurance, William Whiteford of Gulf Oil, and Howard Morgens of Proctor and Gamble.

This practice of recruiting decision makers from outside of the organization raises some very interesting questions about intercorporate relations. The presence of Henry Alexander on the board of General Motors created a tie between G.M. and Morgan Guaranty, while that of William Whiteford created a relationship between G.M. and Gulf. Interlocking directorates, in short, create ties between companies (Palmer, 1980, 1983a; Di Donato et al., forthcoming).

Since the turn of the century, this sort of leadership overlap has been viewed with suspicion. As early as 1914, for example, Justice Louis Brandeis (1914), in a now famous attack on interlocks, argued that "no man can serve two masters," that "the practice of interlocking directorates is the root of many evils. It offends laws human and divine" (p. 51). Study after study sponsored by the government echoed this concern.[3] Nevertheless, the practice continues with little change in its overall scope (Mizruchi, 1982).

If director interlocks reflect and create intercorporate interaction, it should not be surprising that interlock may serve a range of different functions.[4] In fact, interlocks imperfectly trace all the relationships reviewed in Chapter 2. Some interlocks insure the availability of necessary economic resources.[5] Other links establish channels of communication.[6] Others reflect ownership interests.[7] Still others primarily reflect friendship networks: corporate leaders may call on business acquaintances, friends, or members of their clubs to fill vacant board seats (Koenig et al., 1979; Palmer 1980, 1983a 1983b). In such a case, the interlock may at least initially have very little meaning as an intercorporate measure (though it may produce intercorporate relations at a later date).

This variation suggests that for our purposes, interlocking directorates are best considered on the aggregate level, rather than as indicators of one-to-one relationships between firms (see Chapter 5). Analyses of director interties can identify what types of corporations typically interact and what types of firms are the most active in the intercorporate world. They allow us to discern general patterns of interactions—to identify those firms most immersed in the corporate world and therefore best placed to coordinate intercorporate interaction.

We undertook such an analysis by looking at corporate interlocks in 1962. We drew on *Fortune* magazine's annual listing of the largest publicly owned American companies for our list of companies and, for each firm, obtained director names from *Standard and Poor's Register of Corporations, Directors and Executives, Dun and Bradstreet's Million Dollar Directory, Moody's Manuals,* and *Directory of Directors for New York.* As a result, a total of 1,131 companies with 15,073 board positions was recorded, an average of 13.2 directors per firm. We were then able to analyze the interlocks.

Table 1 presents some of our data for corporate types (banks, insurance companies, utilities, etc.). It lists the average number of interlocks maintained by each corporate type in 1962, as well as the average number of ties maintained by the five largest companies in each group. Two major points emerge from these data. First, financial institutions maintained more inter-

Table 1

INTERLOCK FREQUENCIES BY CORPORATE TYPE, 1962

Corporate type	Number of firms	Average number of ties	Average number of ties for 5 largest firms in group
Commercial banks	66	25.9	47.0
Insurance companies	55	13.9	39.4
Transportations	73	11.3	26.8
Utilities	59	10.9	23.2
Industrials	689	8.8	22.8
Retailers	65	8.4	15.0

ties than other organizational types: commercial banks tied to an average of 25.9 different firms, life insurance companies to an average of 13.9 firms. At the other extreme, industrials linked to 8.8 firms on average, and retailers to only 8.4. Second, within each type the number of interlocks for the five largest corporations was nearly two to three times greater than the average. The five largest commercial banks linked to 47 companies on average; among the five largest retailers an average of 15 ties was maintained. These data indicate that it is the largest firms that are most involved in intercorporate relationships. Such firms are not isolated, as managerial theorists once claimed.

These findings are underscored by Table 2, which presents a list of the 20 most interlocked corporations of 1962. Note that major financial institutions dominate. Equitable Life, the third largest insurance company in the United States, was the most heavily interlocked firm, sharing 75 directors with 62 different organizations.[8] Morgan Guaranty, the fifth largest commercial bank, was the second most interconnected firm, maintaining 72 interlocks with 59 companies. Of the 20 most intertied firms, 17 were financial institutions; of the top 15, 14 were financials.

These results suggest that although both size and type are major predictors of corporate interlocking, type is consistently more important than size. Many of the largest industrial companies—General Motors, Exxon, Ford, etc.—are conspicuous in their absence from the list of 20, underscoring the importance of financial institutions in the systems of interlocking directorates.

Since we are using patterns of corporate interaction to identify those firms that are the potential organizing units of the business world, we must search for companies tied, not only to the greatest number of firms, but also to major corporate actors. We therefore need to measure the importance of each company on two dimensions, evaluating both its outreach (the number of interlocks) and the density of its environment (the number of interlocks maintained by its partners). To do this, we use centrality analysis, a technique that assigns each company a score based on: a) the number of corporations with which the firm interlocks; b) the number of ties it maintains with each interlock partner; and c) the centrality of the corporations

Table 2

TWENTY MOST INTERLOCKED CORPORATIONS, 1962

Rank	Name	Type[a]	Fortune Rank[b]	Number of Interlock
1	Equitable Life Assurance	Ins	3	75
2	Morgan Guaranty Trust	Bank	5	72
3	Chemical Bank of New York	Bank	6	70
4	First National City Bank	Bank	3	69
5	Chase Manhattan Bank	Bank	2	66
6	New York Life	Ins	4	61
7	Mellon National Bank & Trust	Bank	14	59
8	Manufacturers Hanover Trust	Bank	4	59
9	Bankers Trust	Bank	8	55
10	Harris Trust & Savings Bank	Bank	23	54
11	First National Bank of Chicago	Bank	10	52
12	Insurance Company of North America	Div	c	52
13	Metropolitan Life	Ins	1	51
14	Southern Pacific Railroad	Trans	2	50
15	First National Bank of Boston	Bank	17	49
16	Pennsylvania Railroad	Trans	1	49
17	International Harvester	Ind	21	48
18	Irving Trust	Bank	12	48
19	Penn Mutual Insurance	Ins	14	48
20	Continental Illinois Bank	Bank	8	46

[a] Bank = commercial bank; ind = industrial; ins = life insurance company; trans = transportation company; div = diversified investment company.

[b] *Fortune* ranks all corporation within types. Thus, in 1962, Equitable was the third largest insurance company (in terms of assets), while First National City was the third largest commercial bank (in terms of assets).

[c] Diversified investment companies were not ranked by *Fortune* in 1962.

with which the firm interlocks.[9] Those companies that are most central are the most deeply immersed in intercorporate affairs.

Table 3 presents a list of the 20 most central corporations of the 1962 network of interlocking directorates. We note that the same highly interlocked banks dominate this list. The giant New York money market institutions—Morgan Guaranty Trust, Chase Manhattan Bank, Equitable Life, Chemical Bank, Citibank, Metropolitan Life, and Bankers Trust—are all among the most central. These findings serve to eliminate any possibility that bank interlocks concentrate on small or isolated firms. Rather, they suggest that financial institutions are centrally located in the interlock network, that they tie to major firms, and that their boards bring together important directors who sit on other highly central boards (see Chapter 4).

Note, however, that Table 3 excludes several corporations that appeared in Table 2: First National Bank of Chicago, 11th in interlocks, was 26th in centrality; Continental Illinois Bank, 20th in interlocks, was 34th in centrality; First National Bank of Boston, 15th in interlocks, was 78th in centrality; Penn Mutual Insurance, 19th in interlocks, was 36th in centrality; and International Harvester, 17th in interlocks, was 24th in centrality. Four of these five firms were financial institutions and they are replaced, in the analysis of centrality, by nonfinancial corporations (AT&T, General Electric, U.S. Steel, Westinghouse, and Phelps Dodge). We note that the demoted financial firms were regional banks, and we interpret this pattern as indicating important differences between national and local financials: regional banks appear to interlock with industrial firms in their area, many of which are loosely tied to the larger network. The differences between Table 2 and Table 3 suggest, then, that the largest banks connect to large, heavily interlocked companies, while smaller banks have a much different, less dominant, profile. And we can conclude that major New York financial institutions, which control many capital investment decisions, are key actors in the corporate world.

While the financial companies listed in Table 3 were the most important financials in the country, whether importance is measured in terms of deposits, dollar amount of loans granted, percentage of institutional stockholding controlled, or other criteria,[10] the nonfinancials are a more heterogeneous lot. It is true that most—although not all—were among the largest

Table 3
TWENTY MOST CENTRAL CORPORATIONS, 1962

Rank	Corporation	Type[a]	Fortune Rank	Interlock Rank	Number of Interlocks
1	Morgan Guaranty Trust	Bank	5	2	72
2	Chase Manhattan Bank	Bank	2	5	66
3	Equitable Life Assurance	Ins	3	1	75
4	Chemical Bank of New York	Bank	6	3	70
5	New York Life	Ins	4	6	61
6	First National City Bank	Bank	3	4	69
7	Metropolitan Life	Ins	1	13	51
8	Southern Pacific Railroad	Trans	2	14	50
9	Mellon National Bank & Trust	Bank	14	7	59
10	Manufacturers Hanover Trust	Bank	4	7	59
11	American Telephone & Telegraph	Util	1	30	43
12	Pennsylvania Railroad	Trans	1	15	43
13	Insurance Company of North America	Ins	b	11	52
14	Bankers Trust	Bank	9	9	55
15	General Electric	Ind	4	33	40
16	United States Steel	Ind	6	42	37
17	Westinghouse Electric	Ind	17	28	44
18	Irving Trust	Bank	12	17	48
19	Harris Trust & Savings Bank	Bank	23	10	48
20	Phelps Dodge	Ind	164	55	33

[a] Bank = commercial bank; ins = life insurance company; trans = transportation company; util = utility; ind = industrial.

[b] Not ranked by *Fortune* in 1962, due to its diversified nature.

firms in their sectors: AT&T among utilities; Penn Central and Southern Pacific among railroads; U.S. Steel among steel producers; and General Electric and Westinghouse among electrical equipment manufacturers. Nonetheless, the exclusion of leaders in other industries is striking. General Motors (34th in centrality), Exxon (273d), IBM (49th), General Dynamics (170th), and Dupont (539th) would all seem to be as good, if not better, choices for inclusion. In a similar vein, New York Central Railroad, the third largest transportation company and a close second to Southern Pacific in terms of assets, ranked 520th in centrality. Bethlehem Steel, the second largest steel company, had no interlocks at all.

We interpret these results as evidence for two important propositions about intercorporate relations. First, the enormous overrepresentation of financial companies, especially banks, among the most central firms is indicative of the preeminence of financial capital in determining and shaping intercorporate affairs. Second—and more profound in our view—the processes that produce financial centrality appear to be different from those that produce centrality in nonfinancial institutions. Whereas the network location of banks appears to be a straightforward consequence of their role in capital flows, nonfinancial centrality appears to be only partly a function of economic importance. We see this as consistent with arguments that capital is a very special resource, as well as with our viewpoint that capital flows create ongoing dynamic relationships among corporations.

Although financial institutions dominate the interlock network, the prominence of banks and insurance companies may reflect the dependence of financiers on the productive sector, since capital is, in fact, created by industry and distributed by the financial world. Since commercial banks, especially, depend for their deposits on large industrial firms (and the capitalist families connected to them), financial centrality in the intertie system may reflect industrial surveillance of financial institutions.

A glance at director composition of a major bank gives credence to this notion. Citibank's board in 1962 included Amory Houghton of Corning Glass, John Kimberly of Kimberly-Clark, Roger Milliken of Deering-Milliken, and Reginald Taylor of the Taylor-Pyne interest, all of whom also were leading members of propertied families. It also included executives of General Foods, Metropolitan Life, NCR, United Aircraft, and Exxon. The boardroom of Citicorp might have functioned as a meeting place for these members of the corporate elite, where business policy in general could be considered and intercorporate coordination planned. If the companies represented on the board had invested much of their available capital in the bank, their presence on the board of directors could reflect a monitoring of these investments. The existence of extensive links to powerful organizations, which elevated Citicorp's network position, would thus reflect not financial hegemony, but just the reverse.

We will consider the significance of the composition of bank boards more fully in Chapter 4. In this context we wish to test whether the network position of the major financials is a result of bank dependence on industrial firms by considering the origin of each interlock. We assume that a director represents his or her corporation of primary employment, and that a tie which places an officer of Corning Glass on the board of Citibank implies that Corning, as an institution, will be represented in Citibank's decision-making process.[11] In our analysis, we credit the company that sends such an interlock and discount the importance of the company that receives one.

If financial overrepresentation in the interlock network were the result of bank domination by representatives of industrial corporations, banks and insurance companies would be less central when directional interlocks are considered. As Table 4 demonstrates however, the reverse is true. Of the nine corporations appearing in both Tables 3 and 4, eight are financials. Included among these are J. P. Morgan, Chase Manhattan, Equitable Life, Chemical Bank, New York Life, and Citibank—money market firms prominent in our previous analyses. Table 4 also includes some important regional financials— Mellon, First National Bank of Chicago, and Continental Illinois.

These results indicate that major financial institutions send directors to other firms which, in turn, send their leaders to still other companies. Their network position, therefore, reflects both the presence of important outsiders on bank boards and the presence of bank officers as outsiders on the boards of other companies. This result is inconsistent with a notion of industrial domination; it supports the argument that banks (and some insurance companies) are central actors in intercorporate affairs.

This impression is further supported by the disappearance of six of the seven nonfinancials that were among the most central in Table 3: whereas six of nine banks and two of four insurance companies appeared in both lists, of the nonfinancials only AT&T reappeared in Table 4. In our view, this is a consequence of financial hegemony, as can best be seen by analyzing two further results from Table 4.

First, we note that certain regional banks appear to be more central in the directional network than the larger, national financials. Mellon National, a Philadelphia area bank, was the most central firm in the directional system; and the two largest Chicago banks, First National Bank of Chicago and Continental Illinois, were both more central than the money market institutions.

Second, the nonfinancial firms among the most central tend also to be regional in character. Commonwealth Edison, International Harvester, Inland Steel, Quaker Oats, and Marshall Field were all Chicago area companies. Corning Glass and Pacolet Industries were both regional companies. National Distillers, while located in New York City, maintained a strong Virginian base. Of the ten nonfinancials, only At&T and Sears were national firms.

Regional commercial banks receive a large proportion of their total centrality from ties to a small number of major nonfinancials headquartered in their locale (see Table 5). Mellon National, the dominant financial in the Pittsburgh area, received over half (55 percent) of its centrality from ties to Gulf, Consolidation Coal, and Westinghouse Electric—all area firms. Sim-

Table 4

TWENTY MOST CENTRAL CORPORATIONS, 1962: DIRECTIONAL ANALYSIS

Rank	Corporation	Type[a]
1	Mellon National Bank & Trust	Bank
2	Sears[b]	Mer
3	First National Bank of Chicago	Bank
4	Continental Illinois Bank	Bank
5	Chase Manhattan Bank	Bank
6	First National City Bank	Bank
7	Commonwealth Edison[b]	Util
8	International Harvester[b]	Ind
9	Inland Steel[b]	Ind
10	Quaker Oats[b]	Ind
11	Bankers Trust	Bank
12	Equitable Life Assurance	Ins
13	Chemical Bank of New York	Bank
14	Morgan Guaranty Trust	Bank
15	American Telephone & Telegraph	Util
16	Corning Glass[b]	Ind
17	National Distillers & Chemicals[b]	Ind
18	Marshall Field[b]	Mer
19	Pacolet Industries	Ind
20	New York Life	Ins

[a] Bank = commercial bank;   Mer = Merchandiser retailer or wholesaler;   util = utility; ind = industrial; ins = life insurance company.

[b] Not among the most central corporations of the 1962 full interlock network.

ilarly, 56 percent of First National Bank of Chicago's centrality derived from three Chicago-based companies, as did 48 percent of that of Continental Illinois.

The interlock patterns of national banks are considerably different. We saw that the local banks received between 48 and 56 percent of their centrality from their top three industrials. For the national institutions this range fell to 23 to 42 percent. Furthermore, national commercial banks interlocked with a geographically diverse set of companies. The largest suppliers of Chase Manhattan's centrality came from New York (AT&T), Saint Paul (Great Northern Railway), and Pittsburgh (Westinghouse Electric). Citibank's top three were located in Neenah, Wisconsin (Kimberly Clark), Dayton (NCR), and Chicago (United Airlines).

Hence we can conclude that commercial banks achieve their position in the interlock system from direct ties to a wide assortment of different companies, whereas regional financial prominence results from a limited number of links to highly central, locally based firms. The regional banks are the crucial actors in their local economies, while the money market banks tie the various regions into a coherent national network.

Insurance companies contributed another form of cohesion to the interlock network by simultaneously interlocking with several money market and/or regional banks. Sixty-seven percent of Equitable's centrality derived from ties to three commercial banks, First National Bank of Chicago, Chase Manhattan, and Chemical. Links with Morgan Guaranty and Chemical contributed 41 percent of New York Life's centrality. Thus insurance companies created unity within the financial community.

The lives of major companies are punctuated by periods of rapid expansion and of corporate crisis. At these junctures, outside financing is both inevitable and necessary, and therefore even the largest firms maintain and cultivate ties to capital sources. There are few major loans that do not involve the eight largest banks and/or the five largest insurance companies, and this concentration is reflected in the interlock network.

As we demonstrated in Chapter 2, recent cases of corporate crisis indicate that financial institutions may decide the fate of faltering companies, but these dramatic episodes are less important than the responsiveness of perfectly healthy firms to the needs and desires of those institutions which control capital. The example of American Cyanamid, which invested further in a failing subsidiary simply to maintain good relations with credit sources, may be prototypical of the way in which financial power pervades the system on a daily basis. But the process is much more varied and subtle, and before we attribute to banks a vast discretionary power in which they decide the fate of American business and society, we must dissect the nature of constraints on the power they wield.

Commercial banks, insurance companies, and other capital centers are not free to spend their money as they choose. The market and competitive mechanisms that impose profit maximization on other firms operate on them as well. Financial institutions could not pursue whimsical investment strategies, resulting in less than the highest possible returns. Such policies would reduce interest rates paid to investors and dividends paid to stockholders, and would result in drops in stock prices, the migration of capital to other banks with better rates of return, and vulnerability to takeover and bankruptcy. Therefore, decisions as to whether to fund particular companies or ventures are not simply matters of choice, but rather of careful fiscal planning which seeks to maximize return on investment.

But these constraints do not lessen the impact of financial institutions on the corporate world. Although there is much controversy over the extent to which financial-industrial interests diverge (Hilferding, 1910; Lenin, 1917; Perlo, 1957; Menshikov, 1969; O'Connor, 1968, 1972; Fitch and Oppenheimer, 1970; Sweezy, 1972; Herman, 1981), there can be little doubt that substantial differences of interest exist. In many circumstances, a prudent policy for lenders (e.g., refusal of new loans) may be dangerous or even devastating for borrowers. Given these conflicts, whose interest will prevail? The answer is traced by the corporate network and reinforced by the daily financial news: financial firms hold the dominant position in this contradiction and their interest finds dominant expression. This does not imply that they will inevitably win every confrontation—quite the contrary. The pursuit

Table 5
SOURCES OF CENTRALITY OF THE 20 MOST CENTRAL CORPORATIONS:
DIRECTIONAL NETWORK, 1962

Nonfinancials	Headquarters	Percentage Derived from top 3 financials	Top 3 financials
Sears	Chicago	54	First National Bank of Chicago, Continental Illinois Bank, Chemical Bank of New York
Commonwealth Edison	Chicago	44	Continental Illinois Bank, New York Life, Nortrust
International Harvester	Chicago	56	Continental Illinois Bank, First National Bank of Chicago, Harris Trust and Savings
Inland Steel	Chicago	48	First National Bank of Chicago, Continental Illinois Bank
Quaker Oats	Chicago	48	First National Bank of Chicago, Northern Trust
American Telephone and Telegraph	New York	60	Chase Manhattan Bank, Morgan Guaranty Trust, Metropolitan Trust
Corning Glass	Corning, N.Y.	58	First National City Bank, Morgan Guaranty Trust, New York Life
National Distillers & Chemicals	New York	45	First National Bank of Chicago, Chemical Bank of New York
Marshall Field	Chicago	78	First National Bank of Chicago, Harris Trust & Savings
Pacolet Industries	Spartenburg, N.C.	35	First National City Bank, Irving Trust

of profit forces nonfinancial firms to constantly strain at the tethers of financial constraint, to find ways of obtaining funds for expansion and acquisition at the lowest possible cost and despite lender resistance. Often these efforts are successful, but control of capital leads to long-range processes that favor banks.

But what of the myriad other sources of constraint discussed in Chapter 2? Resource dependency and joint ventures produce intercorporate unity, which is often fitted into the hegemony of finance capital. If the Big Three auto manufacturers dominate the auto supply industry, the flow of capital to the auto industry will simultaneously dominate the parts manufacturers. If major steel companies acquire their coal suppliers, their reliance on capital infusions will confer lender influence on both industries simultaneously.

There is, therefore, no inconsistency between financial hegemony and the widest array of intercorporate interdependency and power. It is for this

Banks	Headquarters	Percentage Derived from top 3 Non-financials	Top 3 nonfinancials
MA			
Regional			
Mellon National Bank & Trust	Pittsburgh	55	Gulf, Consolidation Coal, Westinghouse Electric
First National Bank of Chicago	Chicago	56	Sears, Marshall Field, Inland Steel
Continental Illinois Bank	Chicago	48	Commonwealth Edison, International Harvester, Esmark
National			
Chase Manhattan Bank	New York	23	American Telephone & Telegraph, Great Northern Railroad, Westinghouse Electric
First National City Bank	New York	24	Kimberly Clark, NRC, United Airlines
Bankers Trust	New York	42	American, General Foods, International Business Machines
Chemical Bank of New York	New York	32	National Distillers, Associated Dry Goods, Uniroyal
Morgan Guaranty Trust	New York	23	Campbell, Johns Manville, Panhandle Eastern

Insurance companies	Headquarters	Percentage Derived from top 3 ties	Top 3 ties
Equitable Life Assurance	New York	67	Chase Manhattan Bank, First National Bank of Chicago, Chemical Bank of New York
New York Life	New York	56	Morgan Guaranty Trust, Chemical Bank of New York, Otis

reason that the interlock network contains and reflects both financial and nonfinancial interdependencies. The inevitable antagonisms are by and large absorbed into a broader unity.

At the same time, the looseness of the relationships within the network implies a considerable degree of discretion for each company. The interest of banks and other financials in maximizing return on investment does not imply a full-fledged understanding of the best procedure by which to do so.

Industrial leaders therefore operate with a considerable discretion, choosing from a relatively broad range of options in seeking to advance the interests of the corporations they lead.

But as has been emphasized, this discretion is by no means unlimited. Most companies, even the most profitable, must fit their expansionary trajectory into the capital flow decision making of financial executives. This constraint arises because loan consortia choke off what appears to be interbank competition. A financially healthy borrower could, in principle, seek to play one financial source off another, but this does not happen, because a single bank could not supply its needs. Moreover, the cumulative effect of a multitude of consortia is the creation of similar loan portfolios among major banks. An investment that might unbalance the investment profile of a particular financial institution would also hurt another bank with similar outstanding loans.

The portrait which emerges is that of a loosely structured system which follows the dictates of the market but under the leadership of the money market commercial banks. Control of capital, the material base of hegemony of financial institutions, allows for episodic coordination in a context of substantial corporate autonomy.

NOTES

1. An interlocking directorate occurs when one individual sits on the board of directors of two or more companies. See Chapter 1.

2. For documentation of the continuing capital needs of American business, see Lintner (1959), Sweezy and Magdoff (1975), and Stearns (1982, 1983). For a more complete development of hegemony theory, see Mintz and Schwartz (1985).

3. See National Resources Committee (1939), Federal Trade Commission (1951), and U.S. House of Representatives (1965, 1968).

4. For discussions of the meaning of interlocks, see Chapter 5 of this volume, Palmer (1980, 1983a), and Mintz and Schwartz (1985).

5. See, for example, Aldrich and Pfeffer (1976), Aldrich (1979), Pfeffer and Salancik (1978), and Burt (1983).

6. See, for example, Mokken and Stokman (1974, 1979), Scott (1979), and Useem (1984).

7. For example, when Rapid American owned 62.5 percent of McCrory's, this was reflected by a series of interlocks between the two firms (Moody's Industrial Manual, 1963).

8. Since two companies may share more than one director, they can maintain more than one interlock. Both the total number of interlocks and the number of different companies to which a firm is tied are therefore of interest.

9. For details of this measure, see Bearden et al. (1975), Bonacich (1972), Mariolis (1975), Mariolis et al. (1979), and Mintz and Schwartz (1985).

10. Note the absence of Bank of America—the largest commercial bank—among the most central financial institutions. Although the richest

bank in terms of assets, in the 1960s it was not a major money market institution. It derived its size from retail banking with individuals, not corporations. It has, however, grown in this regard in the 1970s, and this is reflected by its greater centrality at later dates.

11. For a full discussion of the technical details of directional analysis, see Bearden et al. (1975), Mariolis et al. (1979), and Mintz and Schwartz (1985).

4

Financial Hegemony, Social Capital, and Bank Boards of Directors

James Bearden

In Chapter 3, Mintz and Schwartz argued that the centrality of financial firms, especially banks, in networks of corporate interlocks reflects their involvement in critical capital flow decision making and, ultimately, their leadership in the corporate community. This chapter further explores the hegemony of financials, by looking more closely at the nature of social capital and at the makeup of bank boards of directors. This closer look allows us to take Mintz and Schwartz's arguments one step further.

SOCIAL CAPITAL

Since the late nineteenth century a basic feature of capitalism has been the formation of larger and larger corporations (Chandler, 1977). Indeed, such corporations provided the basis for Berle and Means' managerial argument, in that they are rarely owned by a single individual or family (see Chapter 1). They are called public corporations because their shares are bought and sold in the stock market. Even when a dominant stockholder appears, he or she may hold as little as 5 percent of the stock, the remainder being traded in the market among a large number of people and institutions who, however, usually represent a small—less than 10 percent—proportion of the population. This form of ownership contrasts dramatically with the owner-entrepreneur we associate with developing capitalism, has been called *social capital* (Marx, 1967, Vol. III, p. 440) because it is a form of collective ownership.

Important differences exist between the modern large companies and their smaller ancestors, albeit not those that managerialists painted. For our analysis the most important such difference is that social capital is not as securely tied to a particular sphere of production as is private capital: social capital is more mobile. When the rate of profit in a particular firm or industry drops below the average rate of profit, outside investors can easily pull out and move their money to higher paying sectors. An owner-entrepreneur cannot do this.

There are two key mechanisms involved in the transfer of social capital. The stock market partially accomplishes that transfer: a low profit (expressed, perhaps, by a lower dividend or simply by a report of poor earnings) results in sales of a company's stock, which lead to a decline in stock price. The company or sector in question experiences increased difficulty in raising money through stock sales, since it must sell many more shares to reach a needed figure. Other companies, or often other sectors, therefore, receive the capital that would have been used to buy the stock.

The loan market is the other key mechanism transferring social capital from low- to high-profit companies and/or industries. Highly profitable companies or sectors can afford to pay higher interest for loans, since their profit margin is higher. They therefore "bid up" the interest rate and attract the available capital. Less profitable firms and industries, therefore, are squeezed out because the high interest rates make their expansionary project uneconomical.

The pervasiveness and impact of social capital transfers can readily be shown by means of examples. During the late 1970s, the high rates of profit in the energy sector (especially oil) diverted capital from many other sectors. While many companies in other sectors could not finance necessary replacement of obsolete equipment, oil companies invested huge amounts in expensive exploration and multibillion dollar acquisitions (*Business Week*, June 1, 1981, pp. 68–71). In the mid 1980s, many high technology companies that had been the foundation of American economic recovery had difficulty obtaining needed capital because the higher profits of overseas competitors attracted social capital (*Business Week*, March 11, 1985, pp. 56–68).

Ultimately, financials make the major decisions regarding both stock market investment and major loans (Chapters 2–3). Thus they have become the institutional embodiment of social capital. Though a firm can acquire capital in a variety of forms—shares of common stock, long-term bonds, medium-term loans and short-term loans—these are largely interchangeable. More significantly, stocks, bonds, and loans are now sold almost exclusively through or to financial institutions, and even more significantly, there are major forces that push financial firms into a unified stance toward a particular company or industry (see Chapter 2; Mintz and Schwartz, 1985). Bank leadership in essence decides whether companies and industries will be nurtured with new investment or starved by disinvestment. Their unique structural role and tendency to take a unified stance underly the power that banks wield in the American economy.

BANK BOARD OF DIRECTORS

The unique role of banks is reflected in and explains the significant number of differences between bank boards of directors and the boards of nonfinancial corporations. Some of these already emerged in the discussion of interlocks in Chapter 3; let us look at some of the other differences and characteristics of bank boards.

Bank boards notoriously attract "corporate all-stars," key chief executives. Because of their firsthand involvement in major sectors seeking investment, these outsiders provide a critical resource in bank decision making: the understanding of the possible short- and long-term profitability of the range of industries to which investment could be committed. They thus help safeguard against major blunders. Though nonfinancial firms also utilize outsiders in this way, they do not require, nor can they attract, the broad range of executives which banks recruit.

One of the most obvious differences between financial boards of directors and those of nonfinancial firms is size. The breakdown for particular types of companies in 1972 based on a larger study of interlocks in that year (Bearden, 1982) is given in Table 6. On the average, banks and insurance companies have six to eight more board members than do nonfinancial corporations. The large size of a financial company's board of directors can be explained by two factors. One is that it permits representation from a wide range of industries, a feature we will explore below. The second is that the quality of participation by individual board members changes as the quantity of board members increases. In part, this process is a general one, which applies to any group. A larger group requires more complicated decision-making processes; this makes it more likely that a subgroup will in fact take command. In the case of boards of directors, size is particularly likely to have an impact, because of an imbalance that exists between officer directors and nonofficer directors. Officers, who work full time for the company, have greater knowledge of the corporation's affairs and generally control the flow of information to the nonofficer directors (Mace, 1971; Chandler, 1977). Most nonofficer directors, moreover, are fully employed elsewhere and have little time or energy to reach beyond the information offered to them by management. Except in a crisis situation, outside directors are unlikely to have more than a superficial role in corporate decisions (Taylor, 1978; Bearden, 1982).

The importance of large boards in reducing the influence of outsiders is illustrated by the actions of Peter Grace, the chief executive officer of W. R. Grace & Company, when the board came within one vote of rejecting his plan to change the company dramatically. After surviving this crisis, Grace worked to fill the board with his friends and to increase the size of the board, which finally contained 30 members. His explanation for such a large board

Table 6

SIZE OF BOARD OF DIRECTORS FOR VARIOUS CORPORATE TYPES, 1972

Type of company	Mean number of directors per board	N
Banks	22.0	20
Insurance Companies	20.6	20
Oil, gas and refining	13.5	19
Machinery and transportation equipment	14.5	31
Materials, metals, and chemicals	14.9	29
Food, tobacco, textiles, etc.	15.5	21
Transportation	14.6	20
Utility	13.6	20
Merchandising	14.8	20

was straightforward: "the larger the group, the more difficult it is for it to work effectively" (*Forbes*, May 15, 1976).

W. R. Grace's board was unusually large for a nonfinancial corporation, but not so unusual for a financial. Without implying that bank managers have the same sort of manipulative attitude toward their boards as Peter Grace did, it is apparent that the larger size of bank boards works against, not in favor of, outside directors taking control of the bank. In the 1970s, only one instance of bank board intervention made its way into the business press, the ouster of Philip Abboud as chief executive at First National Bank of Chicago (see Herman, 1981 and Mintz and Schwartz, 1985).

Another key difference between bank boards and nonfinancial corporation boards is that bank directors are less likely to hold substantial blocks of stock in the company. In my study (Bearden, 1982), I considered shares held personally by directors together with shares owned by relatives or other entities (such as corporations and foundations) with which the directors were associated.

Of the complete complement of 3180 directors in my study, half held less than 0.03 percent of the company's stock. Clearly, a great majority of all directors represent only token amounts of stockholdings. Defining a substantial stock representation as any percentage of shares that was equal to or greater than .25 percent, I went on to classify directorships accordingly.[2] As shown in Table 7, banks, along with utilities, are much less likely than other types of companies to have directors who represent a substantial shareholding. This discrepancy is important for two reasons. First, it indicates that few bank directors achieve their status because of major stockholdings, and it therefore supports the argument that bank directors do not tend to dominate policy. Second, the absence of stockholders supports the proposition that bank outsiders play a different role.

Bank boards are also notable for the wide variety of principal affiliations their members have. Chemical New York Corporation, which had 18 outsiders and 5 insiders in 1972, presented a typical pattern (see Table 8). As can be seen from Table 8, all but one of the bank's outside directors came

Table 7

PERCENTAGE OF DIRECTORS HOLDING SUBSTANTIAL BLOCKS OF STOCK
FOR VARIOUS CORPORATE TYPES, 1972

Type of company	Percentage of directors representing substantial shareholdings
Banks[a]	3.6
Oil, gas, refining	7.7
Machinery and transportation equipment	6.6
Materials, metals, and chemicals	12.4
Food, tobacco, textiles, etc.	13.6
Transportation	10.3
Utility	4.4
Merchandising	18.6

[a] Insurance companies are not included because many of them were mutual companies that had no shares.

from well-known large companies. (Robert G. Goelet, the exception, represented a substantial shareholding—.89 percent—in Chemical New York). Moreover, as a group, they represented most major business sectors except agriculture. Still further, Chemical had no directors whose principal affiliations were with law firms, foundations, universities, and other banks. Though banks occasionally have such nonbusiness directors, the predominant pattern at large banks is to have a very wide spectrum of business spheres represented on the board, and virtually no one else except the bank's management.

This tendency of bank boards toward broad representation is indicated by Table 9, which gives the sectoral affiliation of board members for firms in the various sectors. Banks had the highest proportion of manufacturing representatives by almost 20 percent (58.2 percent compared to 40.2 percent for utilities, the second highest category), nearly twice as many circulation industry representatives as other sectors had (22.8 percent to an average of less than 10 percent), almost no financial representation (only 5.3 percent compared to an average of over 25 percent), and the lowest proportion of nonbusiness members (only 13.7 percent compared to an average of over 30 percent).

Taken together, these differences are striking evidence for the unique role of the bank board as a source of expertise on capital flow decision making. This role explains the concentration of basic manufacturing and circulation industries, the virtual absence of financial and nonbusiness members, and the marked contrast with other industries.

As already mentioned, banks appear to attract directors with considerable personal prestige in the business community. This is indicated by Table 10, which records the number of directors again for 1972, who sit on at least one other board (leaving aside, of course, their principal affiliation). Since invitations to sit on outside boards are good indicators of an individual's standing in the corporate community, this is a useful way of comparing the prestige of directors in various sectors. As Table 10 shows, bank directors are far more likely to serve on multiple boards than are other directors. The evidence for the "all-star" nature of bank directorates thus appears to be strong.

Another pattern of interest is that banks attempt to preserve the representative nature of their boards, by replacing departed directors with others who represent the same company or industrial sector. In my study, I compared board composition in 1962 and 1972 for a group of 48 corporations, consisting of the 10 largest banks, the 19 largest manufacturing corporations, and 19 of the largest other corporations. The results are reported in Table 11 (the percentages in each column include the percentages in the preceding columns). In the first column, it can be seen that the percentage of outsiders in 1972 that had been on the board in 1962 remains constant across types of corporations. Given that most directors are not elected to other companies' boards until late in their careers, it is impressive that such a high proportion of individuals had served for 10 years. In the second column, the difference between bank boards and other boards emerges. For bank boards 43 percent of the links with other corporations still existed as opposed to only

Table 8
PRINCIPAL AFFILIATION AND MAJOR INDUSTRY OF OUTSIDE MEMBERS OF THE BOARD OF DIRECTORS OF CHEMICAL NEW YORK CORPORATION, 1972[a]

Outside directors	Principal affiliation	Major industry of company
H. I. Romnes	American Telephone & Telegraph	Communication
Richard K. Paynter, Jr.	New York Life	Insurance
Robert G. Goelet	Real estate and investments	Real estate
Lammot DuPont Copeland	DuPont	Chemicals
Henry L. Hillman	Hillman Company	Investments
J. Irwin Miller	Cummins Engineering Company	Machinery
George T. Piercy	Standard Oil of New Jersey	Oil
Rawleigh Warner	Mobil Oil	Oil
James W. Button	Sears, Roebuck & Company	Retail chain
George R. Vila	U.S. Rubber	Rubber
Robert C. Tyson	U.S. Steel	Primary metal
J. Wilson Newman	Dun & Bradstreet	Business service
W. Thomas Rice	Seaboard Coastline Railroad	Railroad
Lewis P. Seiler	Associated Dry Goods	Retail chain
T. Vincent Learson	International Business Machines	Business machines
G. Keith Funston	Olin Corporation	Chemicals
Augustine R. Marusi	Borden	Food products
Howard C. Harder	CPC International	Food products

[a] Outside members are those members of the board who were not full-time employees of Chemical New York.

Table 9

TYPE OF PRINCIPAL AFFILIATION AMONG OUTSIDE DIRECTORS FOR VARIOUS
CORPORATE TYPES, 1972

	Percentage of outside directors whose principal affiliation was in:			
Type of company	Manufacturing	Circulation industries[a]	Financial	Noncorporate and unclassifiable
Banks	58.2	22.8	5.3	13.7
Insurance	26.7	13.9	18.0	41.3
Oil, gas, and refining	37.2	3.5	20.6	38.7
Machinery and transportation equipment	38.5	11.4	25.4	24.7
Materials, metals, and chemicals	27.0	9.7	26.9	26.3
Food, tobacco, textiles, etc.	28.7	8.8	29.4	33.1
Transportation	38.7	6.3	25.0	30.0
Utility	40.2	9.4	23.1	27.4
Merchandising	18.4	10.1	32.3	39.2

[a] Transportation, utility, communication, merchandising.

34 percent for manufacturers. The third column reinforces this finding: industrial sector representation is also more stable for banks than for other companies.

These above results reflect the determination of banks to maintain contacts in the range of industries about which they must make capital flow decisions. By consistently including prestigious individuals from a broad spectrum of sectors, banks obtain first hand expertise and are in a better position to make capital investment decisions. In short, a large number of outsiders on bank boards does not reflect outside domination, as might appear at first glance, rather, it reflects the crucial institutional power that accrues to capital flow decision making.

The Case of Franklin National Bank

Not all bank boards have the characteristics analyzed above. The difference between national banks and regional banks has already been attended to in Chapter 3. Regional banks, which loan money mainly in the area of the country near their main office and/or join syndicates organized by major banks, tend to draw outside directors from important regional corporations rather than from the nation as a whole. Thus, if the regional economy is concentrated in certain industries, the board does not exhibit the breadth or diversity of the large national and international money center banks.

The difference between the two sorts of banks can be clearly seen in the case of Franklin National Bank of New York, a regional bank that tried and failed to become a money center bank.[3]

Franklin National Bank was a suburban bank on Long Island, New York, which had its greatest growth during the 25 years after World War II, when Long Island became a major part of the New York metropolitan area. Ranked by assets, the bank was 1,231st in 1940 and 20th in 1972. This growth was based primarily on suburban development. Franklin's main source of funds was the checking and savings accounts of individuals. Almost all of Franklin's loans were to relatively small companies and individuals in the Long Island area.

Franklin grew in the boom years because the large New York City banks were prohibited by New York law from expanding into the suburbs. The enormous increase in population and commerce (markets, malls, and other retail activity) offered the growing company privileged access to huge numbers of prosperous depositors and borrowers. But, although Franklin grew rapidly in terms of both deposits and loans, it was rarely the recipient of large corporate deposits nor was it a leader in major industrial or commercial loans. Long Island's largest companies. Grumman and Levitt, continued to do their business with Chase Manhattan, Citibank, and the other New York money market institutions.

In 1962, though Franklin was already the 25th largest bank in the country, its board was not at all like those of the money market banks. The board was not large: it had only 15 members. It was not dominated by outsiders: directors were full-time employees of Franklin. It was not free of ownership representation: Arthur Roth, the chief executive officer, was the dominant stockholder. The board did not represent a wide range of industrial and commercial sectors: even Long Island industries (e.g., aerospace) were conspicuously absent. Industry leaders were scarcely represented: only two Fortune 500 corporations (LILCO and Johnson and Johnson) were represented among the eight outsiders. And the outside directors were not prestigious members of the business community: none held outside boardships

Table 10

PERCENTAGE OF DIRECTORS WHO WERE MEMBERS OF BOARDS OF ONE OR MORE OTHER COMPANIES, 1972[a]

Type of company	Mean percentage making any link
Banks	52.9
Insurance	28.3
Oil, gas, and refining	28.4
Machinery and transportation equipment	42.5
Materials, metals, and chemicals	38.9
Food, tobacco, textiles, etc.	25.0
Transportation	28.6
Utility	28.7
Merchandising	18.5

[a] Membership in the firm of principal affiliation is, of course, discounted.

Table 11
STABILITY IN BOARD REPRESENTATION, 1962–1972

		Mean percentage of outside directors who:	
Type of company	On board in 1962	Had the same principal affiliation as someone on the board in 1962	Had a principal affiliation in the same industry as a 1962 director
Banks	30	43	56
Manufacturers	27	34	44
Other corporations	28	33	43

in top companies and none were listed in *Who's Who* or other indexes of prominent people.

These differences are not surprising, in light of Franklin's economic profile. Because it had few dealings with major industrial and commercial enterprises, it had little need to access the expertise and influence of executives in these sectors. Franklin's board composition expressed its role as a retail service bank in the Long Island region.

In 1961, New York law was changed and the big city banks began to compete for Franklin's Long Island business. While the money market took nearly a decade to move into Long Island, Franklin's managers anticipated the inevitable competition by boldly counterattacking, seeking to break into major commercial lending. They sought major regional and even national corporate deposits, and competed for industrial loans. They entered the international money markets and invested in foreign currencies.

Franklin failed to establish itself as a major money market bank. In fact, it failed entirely. In 1974, the company went into bankruptcy. The collapse was precipitated by speculation in the foreign exchange markets and some shady deals engineered by Michele Sindona, who had purchased a controlling interest in the bank in 1972. The losses in the foreign exchange markets and Sindona's shenanigans were not, however, the basic cause of the failure. Franklin, together with a number of other weak banks, succumbed to a general financial crisis that developed worldwide.[4]

Franklin was vulnerable to the crises for two connected reasons: the managers of the bank did not have the knowledge and experience to manage a money center bank, and more importantly, Franklin was entirely unable to attract important corporate customers. Nonfinancial corporations do not break their banking ties very readily, and Franklin had little to offer them by way of incentives. It was forced to take high-risk loans that other banks had shunned and to offer better terms. It even had to fight to participate in syndicated loans organized by the major banks. Franklin's managers hoped to establish a place in wholesale banking, but were shut out completely by the major banks.

The size and composition of Franklin's board of directors in 1972 show clearly that the bank had failed in its objective. Franklin's board had not grown; it comprised only 14 members. Of these six were officers of Franklin.

Two others were Michele Sindona, who held a controlling block of stock, and Carlo Bordoni, his associate. Yet another was Lawrence Tisch, who had recently sold Sindona the controlling stock and who would leave the board within a year. Thus, only five board members were genuine outsiders; and as before, none of these were officers or directors of major companies.

If Franklin Bank had succeeded in attracting corporate customers, its board would not have been barren. It could have attracted major executives, whose careers and companies would have benefitted from the prestige, influence, and information that membership on a major bank board confers. If Franklin had attracted major executives, it might have broken into the money market. The influence and information of its directors would have facilitated its search for corporate customers. Its failure, therefore, in demonstrating the differences between regional and major banks, also demonstrates the intersection between capital flows and interlocking directors.

FINANCIAL HEGEMONY

We have seen that the appearance of corporate all-stars on bank boards both reflects and facilitates the role of banks in determining the magnitude and direction of capital flows. The high prestige and sectoral diversity of bank boards of directors enable them to collectively represent the economy as a whole and to provide a classwide perspective (Chapter 10)[5] that will direct investment into the most profitable sectors, even at the expense of important industries with major capital needs. The composition of boards of directors is therefore consonant with the lenders' role as the instrument of collective decision making over investment.

This role is perhaps most neatly expressed when banks are faced with crises in client firms which force them to choose between risky infusions of new capital and refusal to lend further funds. In the decade following the 1974 recession, a systemwide shortage of capital forced banks to put "the squeeze on borrowers like never before," to press for drastic cutbacks in investment, to remove chief executives, and to shutter marginal plants or subsidiaries" (*Business Week*, June 22, 1981). In these circumstances sharp contradictions of interest arose between banks—which acted as representatives of social capital—and large industrial firms—which sought to protect their own economic health.

Consider as an example the case of International Harvester. Lenders insisted on policies that would maximize debt repayment, including the sale of healthy subsidiaries and the abandonment of investment programs designed to upgrade the company's productivity and introduce new technology. In this context *Business Week* commented, "For Harvester, the key issue is whether the banks will be providing enough financial cushion to support realistic hopes of turning the company around" (June 22, 1981; Mintz and Schwartz, 1985). The cushion was not provided and, ultimately, the company fell into bankruptcy. Even after bankruptcy, Harvester was forced by lenders to press for cash to repay debts. In 1984, it was forced to sell its agricultural equipment business to Tenneco to accumulate $200 million for

debt service (*Business Week*, December 10, 1984, pp. 41–45). These developments were certainly unfortunate ones for International Harvester, but they
may have been the least damaging course for the lenders, since the farm
machinery industry was suffering through a major market contraction.
Other companies—including, for example, John Deere and Company and
Caterpillar—were also in trouble, and restoring Harvester's competitiveness
might have triggered other crises and therefore further problems. In this
context we see how banks represent the system as a whole. Contraction of
the farm implements industry was functional for the health of the economy,
and lenders were thrust into the powerful (and unenviable) position of
choosing which firms to nurture and which to abandon. They were, in short,
representatives of social capital.

In the late 1970s, Continental Illinois Bank, one of the leading lenders
to farm machinery companies, including Harvester, had representatives of
both Harvester and John Deere on its board. Here again we see the expression of the bank's unique role in the economy: the contradiction of
interest was expressed simultaneously in the presence of competing interests on the bank's board and in the bank's choices about whether to advance
further funds to Harvester. The bank therefore became the institutional
umbrella for addressing fundamental economic conflicts.

One could argue that Continental Illinois and the other banks were
acting merely as financial institutions, protecting themselves against loan
losses, rather than as genuine representatives of social capital seeking the
best result for the capitalists as a whole. Such an argument would appear to
be supported by the 1984 financial crisis experienced by Continental Illinois
itself, caused largely by loan losses. But this connection between bank action
and the profit motive merely underscores the decision-making role of financial leadership. Ultimately business leaders and government investigators
judged the Continental Illinois crisis as a failure of the bank's leadership to
realize that critical investments were not viable and to redirect investment
elsewhere. This judgement produced both executive turnover and the mass
resignations of outside board members, who accepted at least partial responsibility for these errors (*New York Times*, December 8, 1984, p. D1; *Business
Week*, December 17, 1984, pp. 33–34). This judgement expresses the role of
banks as the decision makers of the economy. Bank leaders are expected to
make sage judgments about which sectors to nurture, and bank failure is
judged as a failure in leadership.

Banks and insurance companies are not inevitably placed in this position of choosing options and enacting them. There are large areas of shared
interest among large corporations, which produce united action without
bank mediation, such as their common desire to maintain the social and
political conditions conducive to expanded production. And there are many
conflicts that are handled without bank mediation. Most significantly, there
are many conflicts over which lenders cannot exercise decisive leverage,
conflicts that no institutional structure can completely overcome. Nevertheless, the most persistent and respected integrative force is the control over
capital flows which collectively resides with financial institutions. As one

major industrial executive commented, "You cannot put into operation any large project without the help of the New York banks" (Katona, 1957).

NOTES

1. A 1973 study (Conference Board, 1973), using a much larger sample, found an average of 24 members on bank boards and only 11 members on the boards of nonfinancials.

2. Though this may appear to be a low figure, it should be kept in mind that 5 percent stockholding may be sufficient to dominate corporate decision making and 1 percent may confer considerable influence. In this context four directors, each with only 0.25 percent of the stock, could represent a formidable ownership interest.

3. This account is taken from Bearden (1982, pp. 50–77), based on business press coverage.

4. For descriptions of other, similar failures, see Mintz and Schwartz, (1985).

5. For impressive evidence of the existence of this classwide perspective among prestigious individuals with multiple directorships, see Useem (1984).

5

The Dual Nature of Corporate Interlocks
Donald Palmer

KINECON-BASED INTEREST GROUPS

Corporate decision making is necessarily a matter of judgments—even guesses—made in a context of interests pushing toward quite different choices. Under these circumstances, corporate leadership may seek to base its choices on external criteria, that is, criteria beyond the narrow interests of the particular company involved. This may give rise to intercorporate coordination.

Early researchers of intercorporate coordination attempted to identify "interest groups." Interest groups restrict competition among member firms (often to the detriment of some individual firms) in order to maximize profits of the group as a whole. Most earlier researchers believed that kinship (i.e., relationship by marriage or birth) or close business associations (i.e., financial partnerships) among the major stockholders of different corporations were the basis for interest group formation. Traditionally, researchers used the shorthand term "family" to describe these units (Lundberg, 1937; Rochester, 1936). Zeitlin et al. (1976) have introduced the more accurate term "kinecon group" (meaning kin-based economic group).

Kinecon groups may use three different devices to create intercorporate coordination. First, a person-corporation connection arises when a person owns stock or occupies a bureaucratic position in a firm (Berle and Means, 1932; Larner, 1970; Burch, 1972). Kinecon groups can use person-corporation connections to facilitate intercorporate coordination when one of its members owns stock and occupies leadership positions in two firms sufficient to control them. Two firms with the same principal stockholders and top managers and directors are subject to the same locus of control. For example, one might expect that in the 1960s, the Kaiser family was capable of coordinating the activities of Kaiser Aluminum and Chemical Company and Kaiser Industries because various members of this family were major stockholders of both companies and E. F. Kaiser was chairman of each.

Second, corporation-corporation connections arise when two companies establish interorganizational boundary-spanning structures with one another, often allowing one, considered the dominant firm, to gain some measure of influence over the other. Kinecon groups can use these devices to direct coordination in an interest group if (*a*) members of the kinecon group determine the policies of the interest group's dominant firms, and (*b*) these dominant firms own controlling blocks of stock in the interest group's other firms. Although, in principle, the kinecon group may choose any of the firms in its interest group as its power center, many researchers believe that most often they choose financial institutions (especially commercial banks) for this purpose. This choice reflects the institutional leverage of financial institutions, as discussed in Chapters 2–4. For example, one might expect that in the 1960s the Mellon family was capable of coordinating the activities of Gulf Oil Corporation and Aluminum Company of America because Mellon National Bank, which the Mellons were believed to control through the possession of stock and leadership positions (Burch, 1972), owned a substantial amount of stock in and placed representatives on the boards of both Gulf Oil and Aluminum Company of America (Kotz, 1978).

The third device is person-person connections, which arise when two individuals establish social bonds with one another. Kinecon groups can use such connections to accomplish intercorporate coordination if (*a*) the two individuals own stock and occupy leadership positions in different corporations, and (*b*) the bonds between the individuals are strong enough to cause them to adopt complementary policies for their respective firms. In such cases, two firms are subject to related loci of control. Two types of person-person connections are generally cited as strong enough to cause owners or senior executives and directors from different firms to adopt compatible corporate policies: kinship relations and close business associations. Business associations may emerge as the product of a series of alliances forged over the course of individual business careers (Knowles, 1973) or as the result of the operation of formal and informal mechanisms for the intergenerational transmission of family wealth (Dunn, 1980). For example, one might expect that in the 1960s the Allen family was capable of coordinating the activities of American Bosch Arma Corporation (an industrial) and Allen and Company (an investment securities firm) partially because F. William Harder, a director and substantial stockholder of American Bosch Arma, was a close business associate of Charles Allen, Jr., a principal stockholder and partner in Allen and Company. Harder was an official of Allen and Company and sat on the board of at least three other large industrial corporations with Allen (Burch, 1972).

The three types of connections must be considered simultaneously if intercorporate coordination is to be fully understood. This point can readily be grasped by considering Figures 1–4, which diagram the connections linking a hypothetical set of firms. Figures 1–3 present each type of connection separately. When we consider only person-corporation connections (Figure 1), we see three different interest groups (firms A and B, C and D, and L and P). When we consider only corporation-corporation connections (Figure 2), we see four different groups (firms E and F, D and H, K and L, and M and N). When we consider only person-person connections (Figure 3), we see a larger group, consisting of firms A, B, C, D, F, and N. Only in Figure 4, which diagrams *all* three types of connections simultaneously, do we get the full picture of two interest groups, one consisting of three firms controlled by a single individual, the other consisting of nine firms controlled by a kinecon group.

Reflecting the above insight, traditional studies tried to include the simultaneous analysis of all three types of connections in an attempt to elucidate the structure and impact of interest groups in the American economy. Although these studies often covered different periods in American history, their results were remarkably consistent. They depicted an American economy divided into 8–12 interest groups headed by prominent capitalist kinecon groups. Kinecon groups exercised control over firms in these interests groups through a central core of financial institutions (Rochester, 1936; Lundberg, 1937; Sweezy, 1953; Perlo, 1957; Menshikov, 1969). Further, Knowles (1973) demonstrated that firms that were members of the "Rockefeller financial group" competed with one another less than did a comparable group of firms that were not in an interest group.

An important 1974 article by Maurice Zeitlin (the same one cited in Chapter 1), however, pointed out two limitations of this research that compromised its conclusions. First, Zeitlin argued that methodological problems associated with the way in which early researchers identified kinecon-based interest groups raise questions about the accuracy of their findings. Systematic data on the three types of connections through which kinecon groups organize intercorporate coordination are often difficult, if not impossible, to collect. While top management and board of directors lists are available for the vast majority of firms, stockholding evidence is usually incomplete, and information on kinship and business associations is extremely scarce. Thus many interest group theorists proceeded unsystematically to search for data supporting their hunches (e.g., evidence of stockholding among suspected interest group members), overlooking data that contradicted them (e.g., evidence of stockholding between firms believed to be in different interest groups).

Second, Zeitlin maintained that early researchers ignored many types of corporation-corporation and person-person connections that may facilitate intercorporate coordination but are not necessarily established to further

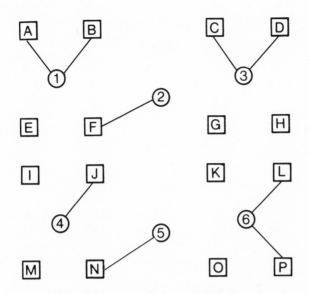

FIGURE 1: Person-corporation connections. In Figures 1–4, circles represent people, boxes represent corporations, and lines represent connections. Thus in this figure the line between circle 1 and box A indicates a person-corporation connection between person 1 and corporation A. The person-corporation connections depicted here establish three groups, each consisting of two firms: A and B, C and D, and L and P.

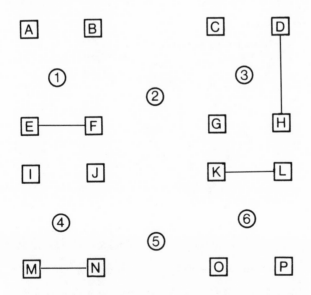

FIGURE 2: Corporation-corporation connections. The corporation-corporation connections depicted here establish four groups of two firms each: firms D and H, E and F, K and L, and M and N.

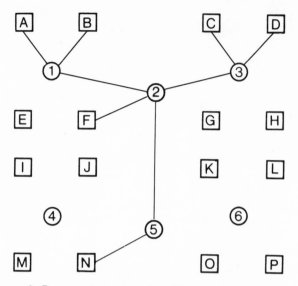

FIGURE 3: Person-person connections. The person-person connections depicted here (between persons 1, 2, 3, and 5), if considered in conjunction with the person-corporation connections drawn in Figure 1, establish one group, consisting of firms A, B, C, D, F, and N.

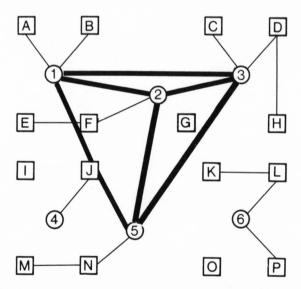

FIGURE 4: All three kinds of connections. If we simultaneously consider all the connections depicted in Figures 1–3, we can conclude that these firms actually compose two groups. One consists of firms A, B, C, D, E, F, H, N, and M, while the other consists of firms K, L, and P. And persons 1, 2, 3, and 5 may be considered a kinecon group.

kinecon group interests. The need to exchange resources efficiently and effectively may lead two firms to formally coordinate their behavior, negotiating long-term contracts, engaging in joint ventures, or even purchasing each other's stock (see Chapter 2). Further, the need to unify the capitalist class as a whole may lead the managers and directors of two firms to informally coordinate their firms' behavior, each elite independently guiding its firm within the boundaries of the same capitalist code of conduct (see Chapters 9 and 10).

Zeitlin called for a multidimensional study, and his article in fact inspired two major approaches: the interorganizational and intraclass paradigms. Specifically, researchers turned their attention to "interlocking directorates," which arise when one person simultaneously sits on the board of directors of two firms. Researchers were initially attracted to this type of evidence for two reasons. First, complete data on interlocking can be obtained relatively easily from publicly available sources such as *Moody's Industrial Manual* and *Standard and Poor's Directory of Corporations and Executives*. Second, interlocks can reflect the full range of each of the three types of connections discussed above. A single person may sit on the board of two firms because (*a*) he/she is a stockholder (perhaps a principal stockholder) and manager (perhaps the leader) of both, (*b*) he/she is a representative of one and this firm exercises some measure of influence perhaps through stockholding over the other, or (*c*) he/she is a representative of one and maintains social bonds (perhaps kinship or business associations) with the directors of the other. Despite this initial motivation, however, researchers began to emphasize either the second, corporation-corporation, *or* the third, person-person, aspect of interlocking, to the exclusion of the first, person-corporation, aspect. Further, they tended to deemphasize the role kinecon-group-based stock ownership and kinship/business associations might play in interlocking. Thus the fully multidimensional approach Zeitlin advocated failed to materialize.

INTERORGANIZATIONAL PARADIGM

In the interorganizational paradigm, one of the two approaches inspired by Zeitlin's article, corporations are actors that possess interests, and managers and directors are their agents. The interests of specific corporations derive from their relationships to other corporations. Corporations obtain the resources they need for survival from other corporations. Because a focal firm requires a sufficient supply of resources to achieve its policy goals, it experiences the external control of these resources as a source of uncertainty in its policy-making. It is generally thought to be in the interests of the focal firm to reduce this uncertainty, because to do so increases its planning capacity. Corporations may reduce uncertainty derived from interdependence with other firms in three ways—through adaptation to, management of, or elimination of the source of uncertainty. Management of uncertainty often involves establishing corporation-corporation connections, some of which facilitate formal coordination (Pfeffer and Salancik, 1978; Burt, 1983).

Interlocks can facilitate such corporation-corporation connections in two ways: cooptation and infiltration. One firm coopts another by electing a representative of the other firm to its board and then attempting to gain the commitment of the elected director to its policies (Pfeffer and Salancik, 1978). A firm infiltrates another through the opposite process: by placing one of its representatives on the board of another company and thus potentially influencing that company whenever the board acts (Bearden et al., 1975; Pennings, 1980). Thus, once it is known which firm an interlocking director represents and which type of device an interlock facilitates, one can determine the balance of power between two firms.

In order to function as a cooptive or infiltrative device, however, an interlock must be created by an individual who is principally affiliated with (i.e., is an executive or major stockholder of) one of the firms. Otherwise, the individual is not likely to be able or willing to act as a representative of one of the firms he/she connects. Interlocks created by directors who *are* principally affiliated with one of the two firms they connect, labeled "directional interlocks," account for about one-third of all interlocks. Interlocks created by directors who *are not* principally affiliated with either of the firms they connect (i.e., who are officials of a third company in the network or of nonbusiness organizations such as universities or law firms) account for the other two-thirds (see Chapter 3). For example, an individual who was the chief executive of company A and a director of firms B and C would create two directional interlocks; one between A and B and one between A and C. He or she would, however, create a nondirectional interlock between B and C, as well.

Two kinds of interlock studies are commonly performed from the interorganizational vantage point. The first uses the network of interlocks among firms to determine the structure of corporation-corporation connections that facilitate formal coordination in the economy. The analysis reported by Mintz and Schwartz (Chapter 3) in this volume is an example of this type of study. These studies invariably find that more than 90 percent of the firms in their population are joined together in a single interconnected group. Within this large group, interlocks are geographically clustered. Further, within each cluster, financial institutions are prominent nodes around which nonfinancial firms are organized. These patterns are especially apparent when only directional interlocks, those most likely to facilitate cooptation or infiltration, are included in the analysis (Mariolis, 1975; Bearden et al., 1975; Dooley, 1969; Allen, 1978; Mizruchi, 1982; Bunting and Barbour, 1971; Mintz and Schwartz, 1981a, 1981b, 1985). Researchers infer from this that corporation-corporation connections that facilitate formal coordination are extensive, geographically ordered, and dominated by financial institutions. Further, the interorganizational approach suggests that these patterns reflect the geographical segregation of resource exchanges and the importance of capital as compared to other resources (Allen, 1974; Mintz and Schwartz, 1985).

The second kind of study attempts to validate the assumption which underpins the first—the assumption that interlocks represent corporation-

corporation connections that facilitate formal coordination. Most of these studies support hypotheses, derived from the interorganizational paradigm, that predict relationships between interdependence, interlocking, and corporate performance. For example, Pfeffer and Salancik (1978) and Burt (1983) have demonstrated that interlocks tend to arise between firms that compete or are likely to transact with one another. Further, Burt has presented evidence suggesting that such interlocking increases corporate profits. Studies distinguishing between directional and nondirectional interlocks found that such statistical associations were stronger when only directional interlocks were included in the analysis.

There is, however, a serious gap in the interorganizational line of research. No one has estimated the percentage of interlocks representing corporation-corporation connections that facilitate formal coordination. An estimate of this kind is very important. If a majority of interlocks trace such corporation-corporation connections, then the structure of the network of interlocking directorates presents a clear description of organizationally motivated intercorporate coordination. If only a minority of interlocks trace such connections, however, then the significance of the interlock network's structure is unclear. It may be that interlocks do not trace any kind of relationship among corporations or their leaders, in which case the structure does not reflect intercorporate coordination at all. Or it may be that interlocks trace other kinds of relationships, such as person-person connections, in which case the structure may reflect intercorporate coordination of a different kind.

To assess the proportion of interlock ties representing corporation-corporation connections that facilitate formal coordination, I collected a sample of 238 interlock ties that joined two large firms in 1962 but were disrupted between 1962 and 1964 because the individuals creating them died, left business for government, or retired (Palmer, 1980, 1983a, 1983b; Palmer, Friedland, and Singh, 1986). Then I monitored subsequent continuity, or lack thereof, during the period 1964–1966. Two companies that use interlocking directors to formally coordinate their activities should not allow their tie to be discontinued when a director departs for one of the reasons outlined above. Such events are "accidental" from the standpoint of the firms involved, in that they are not stimulated by changes in the firms' interorganizational strategies. Tie discontinuity might precipitate a costly interruption of the firms' jointly planned activities. If multiple interlocks join two firms at the time of an accidental break, the two may "maintain" their tie by simply retaining those interlocks not affected by the accidental break. If no other interlocks join the firms at that time, however, they must "reconstitute" their tie, by creating a new interlock. Thus, reconstitution of a tie indicates that an interlock represents a corporation-corporation connection that facilitates formal coordination, and failure to maintain or reconstitute a tie indicates the opposite. Further, it follows that the proportion of reconstituted or maintained ties among a sample of disrupted ties is an upper bound estimate of the proportion of interlocks that trace such corporation-corporation connections.

The interorganizational view of intercorporate coordination assumes that a majority of all ties should be reconstituted, because it interprets the interlock network structure as an accurate reflection of corporation-corporation connections that facilitate formal coordination in the economy. It also suggests that ties composed of directional interlocks should be reconstituted more frequently than those composed of nondirectional interlocks, because the former are better suited to act as cooptive or infiltrative devices. Finally, the interorganizational view suggests that when directional interlocks are reconstituted, they should be reconstituted in the same direction as the recently broken interlock; that is, they should be reconstituted by a new interlocking director who is principally affiliated to the same firm as the recently departed interlocking director. The direction of an interlock indicates the balance of power between two firms, and an accidental break should not allow this balance to be altered.

The results of my study provided only partial support for the interorganizational view. On the one hand, ties composed of only nondirectional interlocks were almost never reconstituted or maintained. This suggests, consistent with the interorganizational view, that directional interlocks are more likely than nondirectional interlocks to represent corporation-corporation connections that facilitate formal coordination. On the other hand, only about 31 percent of even the directional ties were reconstituted or maintained. Further, about one-half of these were reconstituted by nondirectional interlocks or directional interlocks arranged in the opposite direction of the original tie. This suggests, contrary to the implicit assumption of the interorganizational view, that only a small proportion of all interlock ties actually represent corporation-corporation connections that facilitate formal coordination. It also suggests that an interlock's direction is not indicative of the balance of power between the firms it joins.[1]

Thus, the interorganizational paradigm's view of intercorporate coordination adequately accounts for at most one-third of all directional interlocks. The remaining two-thirds of the directional ties and virtually all of the nondirectional ties must be explained in some other way if we are to adequately understand both the nature of interlocking directorates and the structure of intercorporate relations. With this in mind, we now turn to the second major theoretical approach suggested by Zeitlin's (1974) article.

INTRACLASS PARADIGM

In the intraclass paradigm, business elites (i.e., managers and directors) are actors and corporations are their instruments. The interests of specific business elites are derived partially from their relationship to other business elites. All business elites are members of the capitalist class, which is in opposition to other classes in society (e.g., the working class). The capitalist class is unified through the membership of its constituents in elite social clubs and public policy-making groups—the organizational settings in which the capitalist class culture that guides business elite behavior is developed and transmitted (Domhoff, 1967, 1970a, 1974, 1979, 1983).[2] The capitalist class is also internally differentiated into complementary and competing segments. The most important segment, called the "inner group," consists of those business elites who belong to the capitalist class's most influential social and political institutions, such as the Bohemian Grove and the Business Roundtable (Zeitlin et al., 1974; Useem, 1978, 1979a, 1980b, 1982, 1984).[3]

The ranks of the inner group tend to be filled by the most powerful and prominent business elites, those who sit on the board of a large financial institution and/or the boards of many large industrial corporations.[4] Capitalist social institutions seek individuals who have upper class origins, because such persons are likely to be socially and ideologically cogenial. Capitalist political institutions seek individuals who are well known and have access to a wide range of economic resources, because such persons are likely to command influence over other corporate leaders. Financial institution and multiple industrial corporation directors tend to exhibit these characteristics (Soref, 1980; Useem, 1979a).

Further, inner group members are more likely than other capitalists to act on behalf of the capitalist class as a whole, rather than the more narrow interests of the firms to which they are principally affiliated (see Chapters 9 and 10). The directors of large firms are more sensitive to the necessity of preserving general capitalist prosperity, because the firms they command have easily recognizable effects on nationwide, and in some cases worldwide, economic conditions. The directors of multiple industrial corporations are likely to represent social capital, because they must be concerned with the welfare of several firms (see Chapter 9; Useem, 1979a, 1984). Finally, the directors of financial institutions are more cognizant of the imperatives of the capitalist system as a whole, because they are directly exposed to the needs and logic of capital flows which underpin the system.

Business elites pursue their interests as members of the capitalist class or one of its segments by establishing person-person connections that facilitate informal coordination between the firms they command. Interlocking directorates provide a means to establish such connections. When the director of one corporation sits as an outside director on another firm's board, he or she comes into regular, in some cases frequent, contact with the managers and inside directors of that firm. Outside directors can use such contact to socialize and socially control the managers and inside directors of a firm. They can convey the norms, values, and beliefs of the capitalist class to these managers and directors. Such cultural transmission is especially important for regulating the behavior of those managers and directors who have only recently been appointed to their board positions. Outside directors can also discipline managers and inside directors who knowingly violate the tenets of capitalist class culture. Dismissal is the ultimate act of discipline. Outside directors can precipitate a manager's or inside director's dismissal directly—by firing him or her—or indirectly—by relinquishing their seat on his or her board, thus calling his or her competence into question. In some cases, outside directors may even facilitate formal coordination between two firms, although such coordination will only be pursued if it is in the interests of the capitalist class as a whole (Koenig and Gogel, 1981). The person-person connections facilitated by interlocking directorates are a particularly important means by which the inner group segment of the capitalist class pursues its interests. As noted above, inner group members tend to hold multiple board positions. Thus they are more capable than other directors of performing the functions attributed to outside directors in general (see especially Chapter 10; Useem, 1979a, 1984).

This intraclass view of interlocking directorates as vehicles of intercorporate coordination differs dramatically from the previously outlined interorganizational one. The managers and directors of different corporations pursue roughly compatible courses of action, because they interact with other members of their class, especially the most prominent, powerful, and forward-looking inner group members. This interaction allows for the transmission and enforcement of a common "capitalist" code of corporate behavior. Only occasionally does this process lead to formal coordination of the type emphasized by the interorganizational paradigm. Essentially the process creates a loose, but nonetheless very real system of coordination in which firms are instruments of inner circle policy.

Two kinds of interlock studies are commonly performed from the intraclass vantage point. The first focuses on the structure of the interlock network. Some researchers restrict their attention to the geographically segregated bank-centered interlock patterns found in previous studies. Such patterns are believed to reflect the fact that the conflict between capital and labor in the United States is highly decentralized. In the United States, decisions that affect the price of labor and other inputs to production are made at the local as opposed to the national level. Thus, business elites, especially bank directors who most directly control the use of capital within a region, must organize themselves to influence local rather than national government policy (Friedland and Palmer, 1984). Other researchers have demonstrated that the individuals who are most responsible for creating the interlock network—those who hold the most corporate board seats—are also the most likely to possess inner group status—to belong to many social clubs and public policy-making groups (Domhoff, 1975).

The second, much less developed, kind of study focuses on the effects of a firm's position in the interlock network (where position refers to the extent to which a firm's outside directorships are held by inner circle members). The role interlocks play in socializing corporate managers and directors is suggested by preliminary evidence on mergers and acquisitions. Those forms most likely to attempt unfriendly takeovers in the 1960s, when such acts were considered "deviant," appear to have maintained few interlocks with other large corporations (Palmer and Friedland, 1986). The role interlocks play in the social control of corporate directors have been documented by Mark Mizruchi (1982), who reported numerous instances in which the dismissal of a top manager was precipitated by the actions of outside directors. Finally, a series of impressive studies by Richard Ratcliff (see Chapter 10) indicates how interlocks may facilitate intercorporate coordination in the interests of the capitalist class as a whole. Financial institutions tend to promote investment in the locales in which they are situated, partially because doing so improves their long-term chances of success (Palmer, Friedland, Jennings, and Powers, 1986). Ratcliff shows that the extent to which financial institutions depart from this tendency and lend capital to firms situated outside their locale is positively related to the extent to which their directors are inner group members who sit on the boards of several national corporations.

It is interesting to note that the intraclass view of interlocking directorates *is* consistent with precisely those aspects of the previously discussed broken ties study with which the interorganizational view *is not* consistent. Contrary to the interorganizational paradigm, most broken interlocks are not maintained or reconstituted. This is exactly what the intraclass paradigm would predict. Interlocks, in this view, represent relationships between a specific interlocking director and the other members of the boards on which he or she sits. When he or she dies or retires, those relationships are irrevocably severed; that is, they cannot be reestablished by placing a different person on the same boards. Similarly, contrary to the interorganizational paradigm, over half of the reconstituted directional interlocks were not reconstituted in the same direction as the original interlock. This also is exactly what the intraclass paradigm would predict. In this view, interlock direction does not signify the balance of power between firms engaged in formal interfirm coordination, because interlocks function, not to allow one firm to influence another, but rather to allow the interests of both firms to be subordinated to those of the capitalist class as a whole. In addition, the intraclass paradigm might predict that those directional interlocks reconstituted in the wrong direction would be reconstituted by inner group directors, because they are the directors most able and willing to represent the interests of the capitalist class as a whole. A closer examination of the reconstituted directional interlocks revealed this to be true. In almost every case, the director who reconstituted a directional interlock in the wrong direction was also a director of a large financial institution.[5]

CONCLUSIONS

Thus, recent research suggests that interlocking directorates have a dual significance for corporate decision makers.[6] Some represent corporation-corporation connections that facilitate formal coordination. Financial institutions play a central role in organizing such connections. Others represent, at most, person-person connections that facilitate informal coordination. Inner group members play a central role in organizing such connections. The relationship between this recent research, which emphasizes general organizational interdependencies and class commonalities, and the earlier research, which emphasizes more specific kinship and business associations, remains to be examined. It is likely that kinecon groups still play a role in shaping interfirm coordination. Kinecon groups may be the motivating force behind the financial institutions that dominate regional clusters. As much as 50 percent of the largest U.S. commercial banks may be family controlled (Burch, 1972). Further, membership in a prominent kine-con group may be a prerequisite for obtaining inner group status. Substantial economic resources are still necessary for elite university attendance and social club membership.

Uncovering the role kinecon groups play in the contemporary U.S. economy, though, is likely to be difficult. Information on individual stock-holding and wealth remains hidden from the public domain. Regardless of the outcome of such future research, however, it is clear from the studies already completed that corporate decision makers must exercise discretion in the command of their firms. Further, this discretion is exercised within the bounds of organizational, class, and family constraints.

NOTES

1. Several other researchers (Koenig, Gogel, and Sonquist, 1979; Ornstein, 1982, 1984) have conducted similar studies and found essentially the same results.

2. C. Wright Mills (1956) was the first modern theorist to focus attention on the social relations among the corporate elite.

3. Though we often refer to the inner group as an entity with well-defined boundaries, it is more accurately perceived as a network within which an individual can be more or less central.

4. This pattern is so striking that some researchers base a person's inner group status solely on whether or not he or she (*a*) sits on the board of a financial institution or (*b*) holds multiple industrial corporate boardships (Useem, 1979a, 1984). (For this reason, inner group members are also sometimes called finance capitalists—see Chapter 10; Soref, 1980.) It is important to stress that membership in the inner group is not guaranteed to any individual who holds a seat on a financial institution's board or holds multiple industrial corporate boardships. Membership is an interaction of corporate and individual status. This can be illustrated if we consider the corporate control factors that lead a focal firm to choose a person as an outside director. The management of a particular company will often choose outside directors with whom it maintains strong social relationships, because such directors can be expected to defend management against threats to its position of leadership in the company (Mace, 1971). The friendships between the management of a firm and outside directors may have arisen as a result of common membership on elite social club, civic, government advisory, and/or business policy-making institutions. In this way, social relations created outside the corporate world may be translated into multiple corporate board memberships and thus into formal inner group status.

5. It should be noted that we have elaborated and evaluated only those portions of the interorganizational and intraclass views of interlocking directorates that pertain to intercorporate coordination. Both paradigms also detail the conditions under which and the manner in which interlocking directorates may facilitate informative exchange between corporations and their elites. The interorganizational paradigm allows that interlocks represent corporation-corporation connections that facilitate information exchange between interdependent firms (see Burt, 1983). The intraclass para-

digm allows that interlocks represent person-person connections that facilitate information exchange between knowledgeable directors (see Useem, 1984). One would not expect broken interlocks that facilitated such relationships to be reconstituted.

6. Breiger (1974) was the first academic researcher to note the importance of this duality. See also Mintz and Schwartz (1985) and Bearden and Mintz (1986).

PART II
American Government and the Expression of Capitalist Interest

Introduction

On April 10, 1962, Roger Blough, chairman of United States Steel, announced a general rise in steel prices. The other "Big Five" steel companies quickly followed suit. This action, in direct contradiction to the wage-price guidelines set by John F. Kennedy and honored by the United Steelworkers Union, led to immediate action by the president. After publicly denouncing the move as ruinous to the program for containing inflation, Kennedy utilized all legitimate tactics at his disposal to defeat the increase. The next few days witnessed a flurry of activity as big government and big business fought out their differences in public. When Inland Steel, a Chicago-area producer, resisted the price rise and Bethlehem Steel, the second-largest firm, rescinded its increase, the Kennedy administration emerged victorious. The other giants, faced with the prospect of losing business to Inland and Bethlehem, were forced to lower their prices as well.[1]

This small episode seems to go against the Marxist assertion that American government expresses the interest of the business elite and, therefore seems to undermine the general analysis of capitalism presented in this book. It would appear that government intervened on behalf of the people and prevented big business from abusing its power. In fact, Arnold Rose, a highly respected political sociologist, used the steel crisis of 1962 to make this very point, that Kennedy would "not hesitate to use coercion to force businessmen to conform to the economic policies [he] favored" (1967, p. 100). In Rose's view, the steel crisis therefore demonstrated the validity of his portrait (and that of many other scholars) of American government as a neutral arbitrator of diverse interests.

These conclusions, however, miss some subtleties of the episode and of the processes of American government generally. According to Grant Mc-Connell, the major analyst of this incident, Kennedy himself felt he was acting in the interests of the steel companies, not against them. First, in Kennedy's view, the defeat of the price increase insured expansion of foreign trade, which more than offset lower profits per unit (McConnell, 1962, pp. 41–45, 68). Second, Kennedy was not primarily concerned with guarantee-ing low prices per se. In convincing steel workers to accept his wage-price guidelines the previous year, Kennedy had promised that there would be no price increases. He feared that the increase was occurring too soon after the wage settlement and that it would provoke wildcats and other strikes, which would obliterate the very profitability of the price hike while endangering his whole program of inflation control, which was very much in business's interests. According to McConnell, Kennedy would not have opposed the increase if his role in the wage settlement had been secret, since the price rise could then have been presented as compatible with the wage-price guidelines (McConnell, 1962, pp. 21–22). The first quoted response of a high-ranking White House official was "My God, what will labor do?" (McConnell, 1962, p. 53), reflecting the president's overarching fear of resistance by steelworkers. The next year, after the threat of strikes had subsided and foreign trade was less volatile, the price increase went through without any complaint from the president (Rose, 1967, p. 107).

We conclude, therefore, that while Kennedy did act as a mediator between labor and management, he was neither a neutral arbiter nor a representative of inarticulate interest groups such as consumers. He saw himself as an ally of business in general and the steel companies in par-ticular, and he feared that they were making a mistake that would hurt their interest and his image. When neither were at stake a year later, he made no fuss at all.

There is, however, a much deeper insight to be culled from this example. We are accustomed to assuming that government is omnipotent—that it can, if it wishes, impose its will upon other institutions in society. At first glance, this incident seems to exemplify this omnipotence of govern-ment; but a second look reveals that government's only power was that of "persuasion and publicity" (McConnell, 1962, p. 94). This power of persua-sion convinced Inland Steel to "hold the line"; but if Inland had not done so, all Kennedy's activity would have been futile. It was Inland's action that created the economic pressure that first pushed Bethlehem and then forced the others among the "Big Five" to rescind the increase. In McConnell's judgment, the appearance of presidential power in this controversy was nothing but "a tribute to the Kennedy administration's skill in public rela-tions" (p. 103).

The steel example thus suggests that government had neither the power to control business nor the inclination to defend the interests of workers and consumers against the needs of large corporations.

As this example also shows, however, government is not simply "controlled" by business. Rather, as we shall argue in these chapters, it is constrained by the consequences of business decision making and consequently acts in business's broad interest, though not necessarily according to its overt demands. The steel companies could have preferred an immediate price increase, but Kennedy recognized that workers might not accept this without disruptive and costly strikes. Kennedy's actions produced a proindustry settlement of the crisis that was actually imposed upon most of the steel industry. Thus, though the president responded to the needs of business, he was clearly not simply an instrument of the will of the steel industry.

Business therefore does not rule at its own whim, and we cannot understand the dynamics of government activity through an isolated analysis of the actions of the business elite. Such an analysis could not satisfactorily account for the many significant examples of social reform. Conflict and change in American society are in good measure a reflection of the constant tension between the needs of business and the potential and actual power of popular dissent, made effective through the ability of the working population to disrupt the normal functioning of business or government.

Despite this popular power, however, the sides in this struggle are by no means equal. It means a great deal to say that the business elite is the "ruling class." Because of the factors explored in the first part of this book, business is able to structure the activities of government so that its interests are built into the policy-making process. Business interests have become institutionalized within the very organization of government to the degree that it almost seems "unnatural" for government to oppose the vital interests of the corporate elite. It is in this sense that we employ the phrase "business hegemony over government" to describe the relationship between the two.

The relations between business and government are conditioned by the same underlying processes that we reviewed in discussing the relations among large businesses. In part the actions of businesses, especially decision making over capital flows, constrain the activities of the state apparatus and make it impossible for local, state, and federal governments to execute policies that explicitly contradict the needs and desires of a united business community. The operation of these constraints is sometimes quite subtle and at other times overt, as the evidence in Chapters 6–9 makes clear. Though these constraints circumscribe and limit potential decision making, those who lead the American government nonetheless make many choices that impact significantly on the fate of large corporations, either individually or collectively. The choices made in government, constrained as they may be, are therefore of the utmost significance to the corporate world. For this reason, most large corporations individually and collectively attempt to influence discretionary decision-making power at various levels and in diverse sectors of government to insure that their interests will be represented when these choices are made.

Many government policies reflect both the restrictions of choices created by already enacted business decisions and the elaborate structural arrangements that provide corporate leadership with access to government agencies. In this section we discuss the intermingling of these processes.

Chapter 6 looks in detail at electoral reform. The Federal Election Campaign Act of 1971, requiring disclosure of campaign contributions, is considered by many scholars to be the most significant recent attempt to segregate business interest from the process of American politics. Yet in fact, as the chapter shows, this electoral reform both was constrained by already existing electoral structures, which reflected business interests, and was actively shaped by representatives of the business elite. Thus, paradoxically, but not surprisingly, its impact was to consolidate and regularize the connections between the business elite and the American government.

Chapter 7 catalogs the relationships by which government and business are connected. The chapter both underscores the processes of constraint, by which government finds itself incapable of acting in certain ways, and describes the processes by which active relationships with business insure that many viable options are not pursued because they would infringe upon the collective interest of the business elite.

Many critics have argued that our view of corporate hegemony constitutes a theory of government by conspiracy (see Domhoff and Ballard, 1968). This accusation is particularly plausible in our emphasis on personnel transfers, which bring business people into government as decision makers, advisors, and overseers and which bring politicians into business or into contact with business. This process is not, however, a conspiracy—though much is secretly accomplished. Rather, it is for the most part enacted by an open set of relationships and justified by an ideology that legitimates the cooperation of government and business.

Chapter 8 reviews the history of the relationship between industries involved in transportation and government transportation policies. This complex story again shows the broad range of business-government connections, from subtle constraint to flagrant intervention. The horse-drawn trolley's replacement by the electric trolley and the latter's ultimate replacement by the gasoline bus were major political-economic events involving the influence in the public sector of private sector concerns, including real estate interests, electric utilities, and the automobile, steel, and rubber industries. A related development with many implications—namely, the decline of public transportation and the predominance of the automobile—was, contrary to popular opinion, far from inevitable. Like the developments within public transportation, it reflected the influence of private investment decisions on public policy. The recent rebirth of urban rail transit is yet another chapter in this long interactional history between public policy and private industry.

NOTES

1. The best account of these events appears in McConnell (1962). A slightly different, and much less accurate, account appears in Rose (1967, pp. 104–109). See also Schlesinger (1965, pp. 634–640).

2. On page 68, McConnell documents Kennedy's argument that the price rise would lower sales and hurt profits. On page 94, McConnell argues that the increase was recognized to be economically unsound by Inland Steel, which accounts for Inland's unwillingness to go along with it. McConnell argues, however, that Inland would not have resisted without Kennedy's urging.

3. For a detailed discussion of JFK's motives, see McConnell, pages 82–83. Kennedy would not have opposed the rise if his role in holding down steel wages "had been secret," because then he would not have feared that the rise would be seen as a betrayal by workers. However, his public role meant that acceptance of the price rise could result in rank-and-file repudiation of union leaders, "more determined" bargaining by membership, and perhaps strikes. Actually, this incident resulted in the ouster of the president of the United Steelworkers Union in the next election.

4. See pages 83–85 and 102–104 of McConnell, for a careful discussion of why no other powers of government could be effectively used. Schlesinger states that Kennedy "had, in fact, *no* direct authority available against the steel companies. Instead he mobilized every fragment of quasi-authority he could find and, by a bravura public performance, converted weakness into strength" (1965, p. 639).

5. For a more complete discussion of this crucial point, see Balbus (1971).

6

Business Support for Disclosure of Corporate Campaign Contributions: An Instructive Paradox

Tom Koenig

The Federal Election Campaign Act of 1971 has made it possible for the first time in American history to compile reasonably accurate records of the funding sources tapped by presidential candidates. Under this law all campaign contributions or loans of more than $100 must be reported to the General Accounting Office (GAO). Various subterfuges, such as contributing under someone else's name, have been explicitly prohibited, and campaign committees are required to report receipts from ticket sales, mass collections, and sales of political materials. With this information researchers can detect any instances in which committees are spending substantially more than they claim to have received. The GAO has been empowered to compile this datum and make it available to the public. Thus, although there are still numerous cracks in which to hide funds, the public now has access to generally reliable information about the sources of major contributions in presidential elections.

The basic argument advanced in this part of the volume is that the state, although it has some autonomy from business, ultimately supports the interests of the capitalist class as a whole. This view derives from the arguments about business structure developed in Part I. The structure of relationships among major corporations results both in a consonance of interest and in a set of mechanisms that allow for coordinated action. Simultaneously, business structure produces and empowers an inner circle of leaders who adopt classwide economic and political strategies and who seek to enact these strategies as social policy. The power of informed consensus and the coordinated action of the inner circle combined with the nation's need for a prosperous economic climate are the basic ingredients of business leverage over government.

If all this is true, why would Congress pass, and the president sign, this contribution disclosure law? It has been common practice for corporate heads to provide money and other campaign resources to congresspeople who will be framing legislation relevant to their interests and industries. Even if such gifts are not indirect bribes but merely expressions of ideological similarity, the public is likely to take a cynical view of the practice and its practitioners. Thus, it seems odd that business leaders, if they dominate the government, would allow the enactment of a law revealing the extent of their political involvement. On the surface, passage of this law seems to argue against the positions taken in this book and, conversely, to support the pluralist perspective, according to which government is not an agency of a united business elite.

THE PLURALIST PERSPECTIVE

The nation's elite, in the pluralist view, comprises the leaders of a wide range of organized interest groups. Since the leaders of these various groups compete with one another (both for control of scarce resources and because of ideological differences), they cannot achieve real unity. There is intense dispute at the top rather than a ruling alliance of the powerful. The representatives of each group must therefore struggle, compromise, and logroll with a myriad of other leaders in order to get the policies they desire approved by the government. Some groups are more powerful than others, but no group can win without allies, and no alliance stays together long enough to dominate the political scene. In the words of William Frenzel, a congressman from Minnesota:

> The assertion that the political process is dominated by the wealthy, vested interests to the exclusion of the public interest is misleading and an oversimplified view of the realities of our democratic process. While there are numerous examples in which heavily financed interest groups have obtained tax loopholes, subsidies and other governmental favors, there are also many instances where these interest groups have been frustrated in their interests or unable to block legislation that was unfavorable. (1973)

This is a powerful argument. If other interest groups are as successful as the capitalist class in getting state cooperation, then the position argued in this book collapses. For the business elite to be a ruling class, it must be able to defeat its opponents on the great majority of important issues. How it is possible for a capitalist minority to do this will be explored in this chapter.

Conflict theorists have tended to respond to the pluralists by arguing from two positions (see Introduction; Gold et al., 1975). The first, instrumentalism, asserts that the government is directly influenced by the inner circle of the business elite, who either become state officials or use their power to dominate those who are. The second, structuralism, asserts that the government is constrained to serve the interests of large corporations by the economic, ideological, and political underpinnings of capitalism (by the "structure" of American society), regardless of the intentions of government officials or the machinations of business leaders. There have been caustic debates between these two perspectives, but they are not actually contradictory. By applying them both to the origins of the Federal Election Campaign Act of 1971, we can show how this legislation actually illustrates the processes which guarantee that most policies ultimately serve the interests of big business. This will demonstrate how these two perspectives together can illuminate the broader analysis of policy-making presented in this book. The following descriptions of the instrumentalist and structuralist positions have been somewhat overdrawn in order to make the logic clear to the reader and to show that each perspective seems a little mechanistic without the insights provided by the other.

THE INSTRUMENTALIST POSITION

During the past one hundred years, the federal government has enacted numerous measures apparently designed to limit the power of the business community. Thus, during this period, regulatory commissions were set up to serve as government watchdogs over most major industries, unions were given legal protections, antitrust legislation was enacted, and a variety of other governmental regulations have eroded the freedom of action that big business enjoyed in more laissez-faire days. Pluralists have no trouble accounting for this governmental interference in the economic sphere: reformist interest groups gained popular support, providing liberals with enough electoral power to rein in the "robber barons." Thus extensive governmental regulation, pluralists claim, has been achieved despite substantial opposition from the affected industries. The pluralist business historian Theodore Levitt (1960), for example, argues that "ever since 1887, when American business had its first important experience with governmental regulation in the form of the Interstate Commerce Act, business has been a persistent and predictable loser in all its major legislative confrontations with government and with the voting public" (p.51). Populist political power has triumphed over the corporate rich according to this viewpoint.

Gabriel Kolko (1963) and James Weinstein (1968) have each examined turn-of-the-century politics from an instrumentalist perspective and perceive an entirely different scenario. Big business, they claim, was beset by a number of serious problems. Like the pluralists they note that there were important protests by numerous groups of reformers, including Progressives, Grangers, Populists, muckrakers, trade unionists, and socialists. These groups demanded state intervention into the economic sphere in order to protect the citizenry from business abuses. However, unlike the pluralists,

Kolko and Weinstein examine two other threats to the prosperity of the giant firms.

First, the large corporations found themselves under serious challenge from smaller competitors. This was a period of rapid technological change, and, in some industries, the giant firms proved too lethargic to keep up. By the time their leaders realized what was happening, key patents and new locations were controlled by relatively tiny but fast-growing rivals. U. S. Steel, for example, "failed to alter the location of its facilities sufficiently or improve its technology at a time when its competitors were rapidly moving ahead" (Kolko, 1963, p. 38). The value of its shares fell from $55 in 1901 to a low of $9 in 1904.

Second, the absence of any mechanism for enforcing a code of ethics was hurting the largest firms in many markets. For example, the giant meat-packing companies were distributing so much diseased beef that European meat importers refused to buy from America. Yet no individual firm was willing to adopt sanitary codes, since the extra expense would allow them to be undersold in America by less scrupulous rivals.

Business leaders therefore needed a way to refute their radical critics, to control dangerous competition, and to introduce enforceable codes of fair practice. All of this was done, Kolko and Weinstein conclude from their examination of historical documents, by encouraging governmental regula-tion of the economy. Big business, which wanted to stabilize social and economic conditions so that long-run profits could be made more secure, succeeded in part by duping the leftist opposition into supporting corporate-sponsored solutions for the problems of industry. The reformers, Kolko ex-plained (1963), were easily coopted because they "could not tell the dif-ference between federal regulation of business and federal regulation for business" (p. 285).

Thus, government regulatory commissions were imposed on the firms with the secret blessing of the companies themselves. Although they publicly resisted, the leaders of the giant firms saw a number of different advantages to this form of governmental interference:

> The mere existence of [a] commission served . . . as a buffer against public antagonism toward business, but most of the earliest [business sector] advocates of a commission had also conceived of it as an agency that could give business legal advice and create predictability for their economic actions. (Kolko, 1963, p. 271)

The giant firms that dominated the commissions used them both to coordinate activities and to put smaller firms at a competitive disadvantage. Rules requiring the federal inspection of meat, to return to our example, allowed the European market to be regained, with the government bearing the expense of providing the inspectors. At the same time certain sanitary requirements proved such a financial burden for the smaller firms that many were forced out of business. In short, contrary to the pluralist interpretation, the corporate rich had triumphed.

Instrumentalist theorists see this pattern as prototypical of corporate relationships with the U.S. government over the last one hundred years. Big business frequently does not attempt to keep the state out of the economic sphere; rather, it encourages government regulation (even while sometimes publicly resisting it) because such regulation in fact works to the advantage of industry. Bowles and Gintis (1976), for example, explain the expansion of free education by demonstrating industry's growing need for a more literate labor force. They argue that the corporate rich backed public schools so that this need could be met at public expense. Although Piven and Cloward (1971) do not explore who or what is responsible, they argue that welfare programs are enlarged when there is a labor surplus. In this way, a pool of potential laborers is stored at taxpayer expense until needed by the large corporations. Income support payments make unemployment more bearable, thereby undermining radical movements. When the firms need more workers, cutbacks in welfare pressure people to take undesirable jobs. The reforms we have discussed therefore all serve a dual purpose for the business elite: they simultaneously raise long-term corporate profits and reduce protest.

In looking at the enactment of the Federal Election Campaign Act, the instrumentalist would be quick to notice that members of the business elite may be counted among the early supporters of this legislation. Only one month after the 1968 federal election, the Committee for Economic Development (CED)—a policy-planning group composed of two hundred top corporate leaders as well as a smattering of university presidents (Domhoff, 1983, pp. 88–89)—published *Financing a Better Election System,* a book containing a series of proposals for change in American political financing laws. The second recommendation made is particularly germane to our discussion:

> Stringent disclosure requirements on every aspect of political financing must be imposed and enforced, both at the national and state levels. All candidates, political parties, associations, and other organizations engaging in election activities should be required to file full disclosure statements quarterly, as well as 20 and 10 days before each primary and general election. Receipts and pledges by source, expenditure, debt, and all other commitments should be reported in detail. Moreover, each person who contributes more than $500 for all political purposes in any one year should be required to file a statement listing donations with the appropriate governmental agency. . . . All these statements ought to be open to examination and publication. (1968, p. 21)

This CED suggestion is quite similar to the provisions of the disclosure law that was adopted three-and-one-half years later.

The composition of the CED gives special significance to the fact that the committee came out in favor of these changes four years before the Watergate scandals focused public attention on the need for campaign contribution reforms. Its members are primarily corporate heads, and its positions are generally reflections of the thinking of the inner circle (see Chapter

7). In Useem's (1984) words "[it] seems almost always to require inner-circle status [to ascend] into the leadership of the Committee on Economic Development" (p. 73). Domhoff (1967) has shown that many governmental policies have been successfully championed by the CED. If big business leaders guide governmental policy-making, such leaders should be found among the most active members of the CED.

The obvious question raised by the CED proposal is why an organization of the corporate rich should urge the government to keep track of and publicize large political contributions. Since the recommendation does not come from a group of elite rebels, but from what is generally regarded as a hardheaded and farseeing group of corporate moderates, it seems reasonable to hypothesize that such disclosures were somehow perceived by the inner circle as serving their interests.

The CED's own explanation for its position is brief, and it must have seemed to most readers in those pre-Watergate days unconvincing:

> Contributions made for political purposes are sometimes intermingled with a candidate's personal funds. They are readily channeled to campaigns other than that intended by the donor. Individual contributors have a right to know how their money is used, and voters are entitled to a complete and accurate report on each candidate's campaign financing. (p. 18)

To answer our question, then, we must look elsewhere. We start by looking at the fund-gathering tactics of Richard Nixon before he became president.

Business leaders had reason to fear fund-raising abuses by Richard Nixon well before they published their recommendations for contribution reform. For example, lobbyist Robert Winter-Berger (1972) reports the following exchange between Nixon and Gerald Ford which occurred when he presented Ford's campaign fund with a substantial donation in 1966 (Nixon's opening reference is to a contributor from General Electric who had also given money to the Democrats):

> Nixon said: He's a smart boy. He can't lose. But I don't play like that. When I'm watching a football game or a baseball game, I get my biggest thrill by betting on one team at a time.

> Ford said: Bob [Winter-Berger], here, obviously agrees with you. He's only betting on the Republican team.

> Nixon seemed pleased. He said: That's the best way, although it isn't always the most effective way to play the game in Washington. But I'll tell you how I feel about these things. I am a man of strong loyalties, and for better or worse I will always back up to the nth degree those who have helped me financially when I really needed it. Bob, I will never forget you and your efforts on Jerry's behalf. (p. 240)

This appears to have been a staged interchange designed to scare contributors away from the Democrats. Winter-Berger got the message, adding in his book, "it was . . . good to know how Nixon operated" (p. 240). However, those business leaders who had traditionally assured their political influence through contributions to both sides were not likely to have been pleased by the implied threat in Nixon's message. As the president of American Airlines was later to tell the Senate Select Committee studying Watergate: "A large part of the money raised from the business community for political purposes is given in fear of what would happen if it were not given" (U. S. Senate, Select Committee, 1974, p. 451). Business leaders were quite aware of their vulnerability to an aggressively partisan president such as Nixon.

Nor were Nixon's threats and promises empty; consider first the punishments and their likely effects. A brief examination of contributions from the largest governmental contractors in 1968 and of contracts awarded them in 1968, Johnson's last year, and 1969, Nixon's first, gives the impression that if Richard Nixon did not use his office to aid corporations whose directors and officers funded him, he at least used his power to damage the business interests of those who supported the Democrats. *Congressional Quarterly* (1974, p. 85) collected information on recorded contributions by officers and directors of the 60 firms that the federal government listed as among the 25 largest contractors for either the Defense Department, the Atomic Energy Commission, or the National Aeronautics and Space Administration during 1968.[1] Forty-nine of these companies had at least one donor on their boards of directors or among their top executives. Of these 49 corporations, 7 were sources of more money for the Democrats than for the Republicans, while 41 gave more to the Republicans, and 1 gave the same amount to both sides.

Nixon's initial awarding of contracts was not likely to have pleased either his corporate supporters or opponents. The mean Republican-supporting firm received $36.2 million less in contracts during the first year of President Nixon's term than in the final year of Johnson's presidency, while the mean Democratic firm lost almost twice as much—$71.9 million. Firms whose leaders gave more to the Democrats than to the Republicans tended to receive less money from government contracts (less than .02), while those whose leaders backed Republicans showed no consistent pattern of contract gains or losses. It appears that as early as 1969, the Nixon administration moved to punish those who had supported the Democratic party without, however, providing increased rewards for loyalists. Even if the relationship is mere coincidence or the result of firms backing a candidate committed to the weapon systems they produced, it was likely to create paranoia in corporate boardrooms, particularly as Nixon already had a reputation for intense partisanship.

Nixon's fund-raising tactics during his 1972 campaign further confirmed that this reputation was well founded. The funding disclosure laws did not take effect until April 7, 1972, and the Nixon campaign organization worked hard to collect as much as possible from big contributors before the donations would need to be revealed. President Nixon raised at least $19.9 million (almost one-third of his total funds) in large contributions before the April deadline. More than $5 million of this was gathered during the final 48 hours before the new law took effect (Alexander, 1976, pp. 72–73). Were it not for the work of Common Cause, which forced disclosure of these records by arguing in the courts that the early fund raising was merely a transparent device to evade the disclosure rules, the sources and amounts of these gifts would still be secret.

Safe from the public eye, Nixon's staff did not approach the rich as humble supplicants. Their manner was aggressive, with the implied threat of punishment for those who did not give enough. A quote from Richard "Racehorse" Haynes, a prominent Texas attorney, in Woodward and Bernstein (1974) will serve to illustrate:

> "Maury [Stans, finance chairman of the Committee to Re-Elect the President] came through here like a goddamned train," said Haynes, "he was really ballin' the Jack. He'd say to the Democrats, the big money men who'd never gone for a Republican before, 'You know we got this crazy man Ruckelshaus, [head of the Environmental Protection Agency] back East who'd as soon close your factory as let the smokestack belch. He's a hard man to control and he's not the only one like that in Washington. People need a place to go, to cut through the red tape when you've got a guy like that on the lose. . . .'"
>
> . . . The message was indelible, said Haynes. "Maury's a right high-type fellow; he would never actually threaten any of those guys. Then he'd do his Mexican hat dance, tell them there'd be no danger of the Democrats or their company's competitors finding out about the contributing, it would all get lost in Mexico. . . . If a guy pleaded broke, Maury would get him to turn over stock in his company or some other stock. He was talking 10 percent, saying it was worth 10 percent of some big businessman's income to keep Richard Nixon in Washington and be able to stay in touch."

It doesn't really matter whether this kind of extortion was as blatant and widespread as Woodward and Bernstein's sources claimed. What does matter is that intimidating pressure was used and that it was serious enough to make even some top corporate executives insecure. Business executives were not being politely asked for help. They were being systematically approached by people who were demanding exorbitant sums in return for protection from government officials. Clearly it is not in the interests of big business to allow any president such power.

In short, Nixon's campaign tactics were coercive and were perceived as such, and once in power Nixon seems to have backed up his threats with action. To a large degree, Nixon's tactics, in evidence as early as 1966, help resolve the apparent paradox of the early support of the Committee for Economic Development for contribution disclosure.

Skeptics might argue that even with disclosure the power of the presidency can be used to coerce contributors. This is undeniably true; yet publicity does provide the corporate rich with some counterpower. Disclosure allows the corporate chief executive to get together with rivals and agree that all firms will give only a certain amount (or nothing at all) without having to worry about some untrustworthy company secretly breaking the agreement. When executives had no way of knowing how much others had given, they found themselves forced to contribute in self-defense. If one corporation was suspected of donating a large sum to gain leverage with public officials, this put immense pressure on rival firms to contribute generously. Thus, companies found themselves competing with one another, with corrupt politicians the only long-run beneficiaries.

It might also be argued that even if corporations did have this motivation for supporting disclosure, they stood to lose far more than they gained. After all, during both Nixon administrations, some corporations received in return for secret campaign gifts favors worth hundreds of millions of dollars, in the form of high milk support prices, low oil import quotas, generous depreciation and capital tax policies, etc.

The response to this argument is based on the concept of the inner circle, whose members, as has been argued here, are concerned not so much with the benefits to a particular corporation as with classwide interests. While these indirect bribes may have been profitable for some individual corporations or groups of firms, they were bad for the corporate rich as a class. First, contribution scandals do much to delegitimate the American socioeconomic order: If secret deals became public knowledge, as some tend eventually to do, confidence in the social order would be eroded, and this erosion is particularly likely and dangerous in times of social upheaval such as the late 1960s.

Second, payoffs were bad for the corporate establishment because they tended to rob government officials of the ability to do the kind of planning needed to assure the long-term health of the economy. The world situation is far too complex and fluid to have governmental officials more concerned with the prosperity of some firm or industry than with the health of the U.S. economy as a whole. To illustrate, the high tariffs desired by the American shoe and textile industries to protect them from third world competition would make it impossible for many Latin American nations to repay their debts to American banks. If such countries were deprived of their U.S. markets, their standards of living would fall sharply, which would in turn strengthen Marxist and anti-American movements. The resulting decline in U.S. power (combined with the damage to the U.S. banks, which might not be repaid) would have far more serious repercussions for the American economy than would the decline of the domestic shoe and textile industries. Thus, the best situation for big business as a class is to have officeholders who are sympathetic to business needs but who are not corrupt. The honest supporter of the system will do better for the giant firms in the long run than will the cynical favor seller. Presumably the leaders of the CED recognized this.

There is yet another way in which the concept of the inner circle provides an answer. Although with mandatory disclosure top executives lost much of their freedom to use secret contributions to influence government officials, this is not a serious handicap for members of the inner circle. Such individuals, and the giant corporations with which they are associated, retain a number of alternative channels through which to persuade political leaders (see Chapter 7). They can still command a great deal of leverage through interchange of personnel with the government (especially with regulatory bodies), through possession of expertise, through prestige, contacts, resources, efficient organization, and because the government carries out much of its work through private firms. Unlike most smaller companies, the top corporations are always in a position through lobbying, job offers, the building of plants, and other mechanisms to do many favors for officeholders (and to receive favors in return). In short, the largest firms have alternative channels and resources that enable them to give up the extra leverage gained through secret campaign contributions.

The Federal Election Campaign Act of 1971 can be seen therefore as a typical example of the kind of corporate-sponsored reform that the instrumentalists look for—a law that appears to seriously hamper the corporate rich but actually benefits them. It increased the power of the corporate elite by helping to alleviate public discontent and by restoring some legitimacy to the American political system. The danger from Nixon-style power-hungry politicians was reduced because under its provisions elected officials had less ability to extort money from firms through the threat of political reprisals. Individualistic large corporations found it far more difficult to use contributions to buy political favors; smaller firms were weakened because the legislation deprived them of their major source of political leverage. Insofar as such companies were rivals, the inner circle and its corporations were strengthened. In short, an apparent defeat for the inner circle, the passage of political contribution disclosure legislation was actually a significant victory.

THE STRUCTURALIST POSITION

The instrumentalist perspective has been criticized by structuralists for overemphasizing the power of conspiratorial groups and underestimating the importance of "structural" factors which force the state to uphold capitalism. In the words of Magrass (1981):

> By focusing upon direct ties between the state and corporation, we may fail to ask if there is a logic embedded within the capitalist state which forces it to act in the ultimate interests of the capitalist class regardless of who controls its bureaucracy. If we ignore this question, we risk implying the state is an essentially neutral agency which can be used according to the needs of whichever groups happen to have resources to influence its personnel. (p. 33)

Structuralists point to a wide range of "structural" factors: the need of any government to preserve social order, accumulate capital, maintain stable international relations, maintain its legitimacy in the eyes of its citizenry, and so forth. To review all the ways that structural factors supported the passage of this legislation is beyond the scope of the present chapter. Accordingly, we shall focus on what is perhaps the most subtle of the major structural forces: the role of American ideology or, expressed more technically, the cultural hegemony of classical liberalism. We shall see how a structuralist would argue that the pervasiveness of classical liberalism insured both that the CED's contribution disclosure proposal would not meet with much opposition from more conservative members of the business community and that other elements of the population, in particular reformist groups such as Common Cause, would actively support the legislation.

First we need to state explicitly a point that is implied in the immediately preceding lines, namely, that "classical liberalism" encompasses not only New Deal, Fair Deal, and Great Society "liberals," but also Goldwaterite and Reaganite "conservatives." A number of social historians and political scientists (e.g., Greenberg, 1977; Hartz, 1955; Lowi, 1969; Wolff, 1971; Young, 1973) have described this perspective as the dominant ideology throughout U.S. history. It is a measure of the pervasiveness of the classical liberal paradigm that individuals most Americans think of as occupying opposite ends of the political spectrum actually hold many basic notions in common. Compared even to the nations of Western Europe, the United States has an amazingly narrow political spectrum.

Classical liberalism as it is defined by these intellectual historians is a complex doctrine with its roots in John Locke, John Stuart Mill, and Adam Smith. Its major provisions that are relevant to the issue of political contributions can be roughly outlined as follows:

1. People, whether as individuals or joined together in groups, will work toward their own (generally selfish) interests.

2. There is only a limited obligation of individuals toward the community as a whole. We should follow the rules of the game (e.g., be good citizens), but beyond that we are expected to look out for ourselves.

3. Despite this emphasis on following one's own interests and desires, the social system will tend to be good for the people as a whole, because the "invisible hand" assures the survival and perpetuation of those projects that bring progress.

4. Power corrupts; therefore, no individual or organization should be allowed to gather too much power. It is competition that keeps groups serving the public good.

5. The government should be limited in its power, particularly its power in the economic sphere, since it, too, is composed of selfish individuals and groups which would become despotic if given too much authority.

These ideas are so pervasive that most Americans consider them self-evident and unchangeable because embedded in human nature.

Liberalism was traditionally a doctrine of laissez-faire. Competition with little planning or coordination brought the fastest progress. However, over time Americans found that there were cases involving monopolies, social welfare, national emergencies, pollution, as well as political and economic instability, which called for substantial governmental intervention into the private sector. Different positions on the use of this power have led to the popular division of classical liberals into "liberals" and "conservatives." In the words of E. K. Hunt (1972):

> The flaws in the system were thus seen as minor and ephemeral. An enlightened government could correct them and free the invisible

hand once again to create the best of all possible worlds. There did develop, however, an inability to agree on the extent and significance of the flaws. Those who believe them to be fairly widespread and quite significant have, during the course of the twentieth century, become known as liberals. They have sometimes advocated fairly extensive government intervention in the economic system, but most have continued to use neoclassical economic theory as an ideology to defend the private ownership, capitalist market, economic system. (p. 99)

"Conservative" in contrast became the label for those classical liberals who felt that their ideal could best be achieved through the open economic and political competition arising from minimal state intervention. Thus, Reaganites and liberal Democrats like Edward Kennedy share certain basic assumptions, although they differ significantly in the conclusions about the use of government power that they draw from them.

We now turn from discussing the hegemony of classical liberalism to exploring how this hegemony served as a structural factor facilitating passage of a contribution disclosure act such as that proposed by the CED. As noted earlier, the CED represents politically moderate firms. Other elite policy-planning organizations associated with this group are the Council on Foreign Relations, the Rockefeller Foundation, the Carnegie Foundations, and the Brookings Institution. There is, however, a second major grouping within the corporate community, "led by the ultraconservative wing of the power elite as exemplified by the Hoover Institution and the American Enterprise Institute. Its economic base is in highly conservative, often smaller, and often less international corporations" (Domhoff, 1983, p. 144). These conservatives tend to be quite suspicious of calls for government action issued by "corporate liberal" groups like the CED. In addition, conservative business leaders by and large viewed campaign reform as an undesirable intrusion upon their autonomy. Nonetheless, they quite clearly did not go all out to oppose passage of the campaign reform legislation. We will first examine the reason for this and then look at why liberal support for the legislation was essentially guaranteed.

The Conservative Business Perspective on Corporate Political Contributions

Conservative business leaders tend to see corporate political contributions as an attempt by industry to protect itself from governmental interference. Business executives, they argue, sometimes expect a quid pro quo for their money, but for the most part corporations want—or at least should want—governmental officials to return to their proper sphere and to leave the company alone. It is dangerous to the capitalist system when corporations begin to want more state aid, which becomes inevitable if the role of the government is allowed to expand. Levitt (1960) expressed this fear when he wrote that

> involvement in politics can lead only to corporate inefficiency and possible ruin. The corporation that becomes deeply involved in party

politics will necessarily dilute its basic profitmaking function. The politically active corporation will have to become less seriously profit-minded. When that happens, it will cease to deliver the goods abundantly and efficiently. (p.50)

Industry does quite well in producing goods and services, and it must stick to that job, according to the conservative perspective.

As business and government intermesh, conservatives argue, the nation will develop a power elite centered around the president. Government intervention thus undermines the freedoms that come from a multiplicity of interest groups. Worse, power raises counterpower. Increasing unity between industry and the state may well lead in turn to increased militancy by the labor unions and socialist groups. This will tend to polarize society into classes. Because of such dangers, conservatives are not happy with corporate leaders who give large contributions to political candidates. However, they place most of the blame on the government. The expansion of state economic power makes the presidency such a source of potential rewards and punishments that industrial leaders cannot afford to stick to business.

The cure is to force government to cut back on domestic interference. Once firms are not so vulnerable to state regulation, business will not waste its money on electoral campaigns. From this perspective, contribution laws are of little value because they do not touch the root of the problem: the overexpansion of governmental power. If the government insists on regulating business, it is only fair that business be allowed to use its wealth to protect itself.

Conservative business leaders feel that they are on the defensive and are reluctant to sacrifice any political leverage. Still, they feel uncomfortable with the notion of firms taking the active electoral role implied in making large political donations (Silk and Vogel, 1976). Their mixed feelings with regard to corporate contributions hampered their ability to organize effectively to block contribution reforms. Thus, the emphasis in the classical liberal model on dividing power and especially on limiting governmental power undermined the resistance of the corporate conservatives, even though this legislation reduces corporate freedom of action in the short run.

The Liberal Perspective on Corporate Political Contributions

The liberal version of classical liberalism leads to serious concern about the potential for corruption arising from large contributions. Like the conservatives, liberals believe in the classical liberal ideas that people are motivated by self-interest and that power corrupts. At the same time, in contrast to conservatives, liberals also believe the government must actively control the economy. If the government plays such a role, then the people around the president will inevitably be making frequent decisions involving tens or even hundreds of millions of dollars in corporate profits. Given this situation, it would be remarkable indeed if firms did not attempt to ingratiate themselves with political decision makers. Thus, political contributions are likely to be used as direct or indirect bribes. And whereas conservatives tend to see campaign reform as an undesirable intrusion into business autonomy, the liberal version of classical liberalism does not object to such intrusion. To the liberals publicity is a valuable check on the greed of both politicians and the corporate rich. This is an example of the way the state can and must be employed to maintain a balanced division of power among interest groups in order to keep the system legitimate and operating smoothly.

Not only did members of the CED believe this, so did the leadership of the most active mass-based group of liberal reformers, Common Cause. John Gardner, the head of Common Cause, has been called the individual most responsible for the passage of the election financing reforms (Caddy, 1975, p. 17). For this reason a brief review of his political views is useful for understanding the classical liberal assumptions that underlay the support by nonelite groups for the 1971 federal election campaign act. Gardner outlined his position in his book *In Common Cause* (1972). First, he took pains to dissociate the policy-makers leading Common Cause from the radicals:

> We are also part of "the system." Most of us are members of one of the major parties. . . . Many are involved in special-interest groups. . . . What we share is a concern for the public interest. We share a recognition that no one of us will prosper for long if the community deteriorates. If the nation fails, we all fail. (p. 22)

Gardner made clear that he was principally concerned with the exchange of money (and other considerations) for governmental favors—"the system in which too many of our 'public servants' work out their terms in servitude to big donors" (p. 19).

This cycle of favors between the wealthy and government officials was, in his view, largely made possible through contributions: "Only very impatient or stupid men give or take cash bribes any more. It is dreadfully old fashioned. The preferred mode of corruption today is either the campaign gift or circuitous and hard-to-trace business favors" (p. 38). The campaign reform laws were therefore, in Gardner's view, a key step in insuring that ethical individuals would be elected. Unlike Marxist theorists, Gardner did not see the American social order as fundamentally undemocratic. Rather, in the best classical liberal tradition, he was attempting to get everyone to honestly live up to the rules of the game, thus guaranteeing socially responsible representative government. Even though Common Cause and the CED often sought different short-term goals, the shared belief in the liberal variant of classical liberalism created a common perspective. Both the CED and the liberals like John Gardner wished to use the state to guide America toward the classical liberal ideal under which the capitalist class would prosper. Thus, nonelite support for the act was not a case of naive reformers being manipulated by Machiavellian big business but, rather, of unity made plausible by a shared view of reality.

In summary, all three major pressure groups were operating out of the same ideological framework, one that assumes that people are naturally selfish and that decentralization of power is the best solution to the problems produced by this unfortunate psychological reality. In this way, ideology acts as a "structural" force that shapes policy decisions. The structuralists maintain that big business wins most American political struggles not because of skillful maneuvering by the corporate rich but because such structural forces uphold the capitalist system.

We have seen that the apparent paradox of business support for disclosure of corporate campaign contributions can be explained by taking a perspective that combines structuralism and instrumentalism. This combined perspective, together with the concept of an inner circle, enables us to understand both why many business leaders supported the legislation and how the legislation was passed.

The instrumentalist view focuses on the fear of Nixon-style tactics and of their possible repercussions at home and abroad as motives. Members of the inner circle were more concerned with class interests than with the interests of their particular firms, and they had access to important channels of influence other than campaign contributions. Hence it is not surprising that the CED was an early proponent of legislation requiring disclosure of campaign contributions.

The structuralist view focuses on the role of underlying structural factors such as shared ideology. The classical liberal ideology not only was a further factor motivating the inner circle position and proposal, but it also insured that conservatives within the business community would not oppose the legislation and that liberals in nonelite organizations like Common Cause would actively support it.

Taken separately, the instrumentalist and structuralist views would provide only a partial, ultimately insufficient explanation for passage of the act. That is, it would be misleading to attribute the act's passage solely to active efforts on the part of the business elite or, alternatively, to view it as an inevitable result of the operation of structural factors. The instrumentalist perspective alone tends to overstress the foresight, political subtlety, and unity of the inner circle, sometimes leading to mechanistic "conspiracy" theories. On the other hand, the structuralist position by itself tends to underrate the importance of specific groups and individuals. By combining the two perspectives, however, we arrive at a far more realistic and compelling picture, in which the business elite was successful in obtaining its goal in large part because structural forces operated in its favor. We have every reason to believe that this picture obtains not just in this instance but in many others as well.

NOTE

1. Since this was before the disclosure laws, the accuracy and completeness of this contributions data are open to question.

7

The Ties That Bind Business and Government

Laura Anker
Peter Seybold
Michael Schwartz

Chapter 6 explored the consonance that exists between business interest and government action and analyzed two types of forces producing this consonance: the structural constraint on government and the direct application of influence to government officials. In this chapter we focus on the latter type of forces, looking at specific mechanisms through which direct business influence on is exerted. But before looking at these mechanisms, let us first consider the general nature of and reasons for the ties between business and government.

THE INTERDEPENDENCE OF BUSINESS AND GOVERNMENT

Every important public activity requires the mobilization of substantial corporate resources. A war, for example, is fought only partly in the battlefield. The other half—the battle of production—is fought behind the lines, where armaments, equipment, and supplies are produced, where air bases and other military installations are constructed, and where combatants and materiel are transported to the battlefront. In World War II, the government created over 11,000 advisory councils, consisting almost entirely of businessmen, to coordinate these economic aspects of the war effort (McConnell,

1966, p. 260). Without such councils—and the cooperation of business which their existence implied—no wars could be effectively fought.

Even when the direct investment of corporate resources is not involved, every important government activity requires the continuous and voluntary cooperation of major businesses. Consider government finance, which derives from five major sources: loans, income taxes, tariffs, sales taxes, and property taxes. Loans are invariably obtained from major banks, personal income taxes are collected through payrolls, corporate income taxes and tariffs are collected directly from business, and sales taxes are collected by retailers; only property taxes are collected directly by government. Business refusal to cooperate in government revenue collection could therefore have catastrophic effects on government viability, as was demonstrated by the New York City financial crisis in the early 1970s, in which lenders refused to renew city bonds (McCue, 1977). Government's reliance on the cooperation of business gives business significant leverage.

Business also derives leverage indirectly from its discretion in directing capital flows. This power, in and of itself, is frequently sufficient to influence policy formation.[1] Consider, for example, Governor Nelson Rockefeller's announcement that he had reduced the 1971 New York budget by $300 million, in order to avoid tax increases, because "employers controlling thousands of jobs within the state have informed me that they will feel compelled to remove to other states under the combined total impact of the proposed increases in state and local taxes" (*New York Times,* March 16, 1971). In the 1980s, the exodus of corporations from the Northeast and Midwest, which occurred despite such government accommodation, was to become a major issue—in large part, precisely because it illustrated the political impotence of local, state, and even the federal government in the face of business power (Bluestone and Harrison, 1982; Barnet and Mueller, 1974; Wu and Korman, 1985; Schwartz et al., 1985; Wu, 1986).

Effective business leverage usually requires that corporations act in unison. Their ability to do so has been documented in Part I. Most other groups in society, even if able to act in unison, nonetheless lack leverage because they do not occupy critical positions in the structure of the economy. Aside from the business elite, only workers occupy a strategic position vis-à-vis the basic operation of society. By simply withdrawing their labor power, certain workers can bring the economy to a halt. In a sense, then, two powerful groups face each other. But the form of power they wield is not really identical. Although labor can engage in disruptive action, it cannot, say, make production decisions or determine investment. Morever in contrast to the unity of business, labor is largely unorganized and is fragmented along many dimensions, including race and sex. Unified action, even for labor within a given industry, is difficult. Nonetheless, labor is potentially powerful, and it is this potential power that renders government so essential to business prosperity.

This reason for the importance of government to business finds a parallel on a more general level. Just as there is often a conflict between the needs of business and those of labor, so, too, the needs of business and those of the general population may conflict. For example, the public's need for a clean environment, well-made products, and affordable public transportation conflicts with business's drive for maximum profits. When, as often occurs, corporate interest prevails over popular needs, a social control problem arises: support or acquiescence must be created for policies that do not serve the people. Hence government is important to business because it performs a social control function.

Social control is a complex and varied task, and it is accomplished through a wide range of mechanisms. Rarely in the United States is social control achieved through overt repression. One reason for this is that violence and other means of repression (e.g., court cases, public denunciation, and executive orders) may prove counterproductive, dampening the enthusiasm of, or even alienating, those who would otherwise support a particular policy. In the late 1960s, for example, opposition to the war in Vietnam was undoubtedly strengthened by police violence toward demonstrators. Such alienation can become an important negative factor if government policies require the active support of the American people. In order to fight the war, material had to be obtained consistently and reliably; it had to be transported efficiently and expeditiously; and soldiers had to be recruited, trained, and motivated to fight. Without even beginning to consider the effects of the mutinies and absolute disobedience to orders which sabotaged the army's effort in Vietnam in the late 1960s and early 1970s, simple lack of soldier enthusiasm and low morale limited government's ability to pursue its war aims.[2] When General Electric workers struck in 1969, and then refused to heed President Nixon's plea to return to work, their action hampered the production of jet engines for Vietnam (*New York Times,* October 19, 1969, p. 50). Although their strike was for higher wages and not against the war, the failure of GE workers to enthusiastically identify their own personal interest with those of our government hampered American policy. Similarly, a 1971 West Coast longshore strike could have paralyzed war supplies, had the union not agreed to load war material. (This action aided the war effort, at the expense of the union, since owners successfully resisted the strike because of the income from war shipments.) Had the longshoremen been a little less patriotic, placing the needs of their strike above the demands of the war, military effectiveness would have been threatened (*New York Times,* July 18, 1971, part 5, p. 24). Though these social control problems connected to the Vietnam War did not involve open government support of business activity, they reveal clearly the same range of problems which arise in such circumstances. Thus, in the 1970s, government attempts to control protests against nuclear power publicized the protestors' concerns, and, in the early 1980s, arrests of antiapartheid demonstrators in Washington, D.C., and New York gave impetus to boycotts against companies that invested in South Africa.

Social control, therefore, necessarily extends far beyond forced acquiescence. For the most part, the government achieves social control by legitimating public and business policies. Thus, the Nuclear Regulatory Commission carried the burden—much more than the private companies that construct and operate nuclear plants—of trying to convince the public of their safety, and President Reagan's policy of "constructive engagement" was designed to justify continued corporate investment in South Africa. The political system is structured so as to produce, along with business-oriented policies, a sense of popular control. Political parties are especially important in this respect. As stated by R. W. Apple, a leading political reporter for the *New York Times,* "The goal of the American political system is to contain protest and rage within the electoral process, thus keeping it from bursting into the streets as revolution. The goal of the parties is to provide a vehicle for such protest" (May 15, 1972, p. 26).

We can see how parties function in this way if we consider the seemingly very different presidential candidacies of Eugene McCarthy and Ronald Reagan. In 1968, when anti-Vietnam protest was growing rapidly, Senator Eugene McCarthy openly described his presidential candidacy as an attempt to move protesting students from the streets to the electoral process, to prove to the youth of America that they had a place within the political system.

> I am hopeful that this challenge which I am making may alleviate at least to some degree this sense of political hopelessness and restore to many people a belief in the process of American [electoral] politics and of American government . . . that it may counter the growing sense of alienation from politics which I think is reflected in a tendency to withdraw from political action, to talk of non-participation, to become cynical, and to make threats of support for third parties or fourth parties or other irregular political movements. (*New York Times,* December 1, 1967, p. 40)

However sincere his opposition to the war, McCarthy adopted a moderate electoral posture. He did not call for immediate removal of American troops from Vietnam, or even for an immediate end to offensive military action. Instead, he recommended peace talks aimed at "phased withdrawal," which would not, he insisted, be injurious to American interests in Southeast Asia. He never advocated any policy more drastic than the one ultimately adopted by Richard Nixon: gradual withdrawal contingent upon favorable negotiations (*New York Times,* August 12, 1968, p. 17; August 18, 1968, pp. 1, 66). Moreover, although McCarthy, like most senators, had access to information about American atrocities in Vietnam (Sheehan et al., 1971), he did not seek to publicize them and thus draw new people into the antiwar movement. He did not, in short, attempt to convince the American public that U.S. goals in Vietnam were unjustified or misguided; he argued that they could be fully accomplished by less belligerent means.

McCarthy's candidacy was nevertheless enormously successful, both in involving antiwar activists in electoral politics and in attracting a large proportion of votes in a number of important primaries. This success rested on the fact that McCarthy's political posture, no matter how moderate, appeared to offer a real departure from the policy that was then being pursued in Vietnam. In this way, McCarthy's campaign helped both channel dissent into the electoral process and moderate demands for immediate withdrawal.

Ironically, the Reagan election in 1980 was in some ways a mirror image of McCarthy's 1968 campaign. Under Carter, a conservative drift in policy had already begun, exemplified by the arms buildup, an increasingly militant stance toward the Soviet Union, major cutbacks in social services, and declining commitment to social reform (Shoup, 1980). Thus the policies advocated in Reagan's conservative platform were much less distinct from Carter's ongoing programs than they appeared to be (Chapter 13; Cockburn and Ridgeway, 1981; Ferguson and Rogers, 1981). But by advocating these policies in a more strident and ideological way, Reagan was able to channel dissent, this time from the right. And, significantly, many of Reagan's more militant positions were quietly modulated during the campaign and/or after his election.

As is evident from the above examples, the two-party system can be effective in containing protest and limiting debate because it offers the possibility of apparent (and sometimes real) change without unpleasant disruptive action. The Republican party is the party of business autonomy, of order, of the status quo; the Democratic party is the party of labor, of liberal reform, of ethnic and social minorities. Each election therefore apparently has important implications. Beyond this, the individual candidates are either conservatives, liberals, or moderates, and candidates' contrasting positions on specific issues imply further policy choices.

The policies pursued by the winners, however, are rarely as ideologically consistent as candidates would have their constituencies believe. While he was in the House of Representatives, Everett Dirkson's views on agricultural supports switched some 70 times. On foreign affairs he was equally dependable: he changed his position on isolationism 62 times, on military preparedness 30 times (Pearson and Anderson, 1968, p. 100).

Nor do presidential administrations consistently reflect their party affiliation or the incumbent's image, though the publicity surrounding policy and policy-makers often does. John F. Kennedy, popularly considered to be the most liberal president since Franklin Delano Roosevelt, organized the unsuccessful Bay of Pigs invasion and the successful blockade of Cuba, initiated substantial American commitment to the defense of the corrupt Diem regime in Vietnam, created the Green Berets, and developed counterinsurgency as a diplomatic strategy.[3] While he signed a nuclear test ban treaty with the Soviet Union, he did so only after the Soviets had submitted to the conditions laid down by the United States in the late 1950s, thus maintaining the image of the United States as a forceful and uncompromising bargainer in the world.[4] Domestically, despite Kennedy's public endorsement of the civil rights, the Justice Department failed to vigorously prosecute civil rights violations in the South and introduced legislation so moderate that many black leaders failed to support it. Of thirteen federal southern judges appointed during Kennedy's administration, all but one were staunch segregationists (Carson, 1981, pp. 83–87; Zinn, 1965; Forman, 1972).[5]

On the other hand, the arch-conservative Richard M. Nixon began a major overhaul of the armed forces, from the relaxation of dress codes to the establishment of a volunteer army (*New York Times,* April 24, 1970, p. 1; December 9, 1970, p. 1). Whereas President Kennedy had maintained a militant posture toward the Soviet Union, Nixon initiated a process of détente, despite differences over Vietnam and Pakistan.[6] Whereas Kennedy refused to consider China's admission to the United Nations and continued the policy of unremitting hostility toward that country, Nixon reversed this hostile stance, made a historic trip to Peking, and placed the full force of his office behind the concept of peaceful coexistence. Domestically, President Nixon was unable to push through his dramatic reform of the welfare system, which would have guaranteed a minimum income, but he succeeded in imposing a wage-price freeze; his Justice Department desegregated more southern schools than all previous administrations combined.[7]

One should not conclude from this recitation that Kennedy was a secret conservative and Nixon a secret liberal; it would also have been possible to list Kennedy's liberal acts and Nixon's conservative ones. Rather, we must realize that the "liberal" and "conservative" labels usually applied to administrations are largely a consequence of the electoral rhetoric and of the manner in which policies are advertised. Nor should one conclude that all administrations in fact adopt the same policies. The circumstances change, and so do the actions of the government. Very often these changing circumstances are intimately connected to the desires of the corporate elite. In the early 1960s, for example, the corporate elite did not want détente with China, but in the later 1960s it was deemed feasible and useful (Shoup and Minter, 1977). Just because Kennedy, a liberal, was president in 1960 did not mean that relations could be opened with China. And simply because Nixon, a conservative, was president in 1971 did not mean that the policy of détente could not be initiated.[8] Instead, the advertising put out by the administrations was adjusted. Kennedy offset his conservative foreign policy with liberal rhetoric supporting black equality, while Nixon sustained his conservative reputation by focusing attention on his "hardline" attitude toward the black and student movements. The political complexion of the incumbent is not a major factor in policy formation.

The electoral system, because it offers a choice between two or more candidates with different platforms, provides a perfect mechanism for the selection of officeholders best equipped to convince the general population to accept and support the outcome of the policy formation process. The conservative-liberal debate, the constant stream of new officials, and the public presentation of political careers as ideologically coherent are all functional parts of this political process. The political history or public platforms of an incumbent has a great deal to do with his or her possibilities for reelection, but it does not determine the policies he or she will pursue in office. A choice among two or three such candidates does not imply popular rule.

Many political analysts insist, despite arguments like those made in this book, that elections provide a mechanism by which the population can control the policies of government. Their theory, simply stated, holds that if an officeholder does not do what people desire, they can elect someone else in the next election. Even the politician who is unconcerned with serving his or her constituency's interests is therefore forced to raise a popular issue to win reelection and must then act on that issue to remain in office. In short, the politician must please the voting public, and the system is therefore structured in such a way that the self-interest of the politician coincides with the needs of his district (Rose, 1967; Dahl, 1961a, 1966).

From this central theme flows a whole theory of American democracy which views all policies through the prism of public opinion. Government officials tirelessly attempt, but frequently fail, to please the public. This constant search for the action that will please the maximum number is inefficient, but it generally results in the ultimate adoption of policies the voting population favors.

Contrary to this image of government, we argue that the government—and more generally the political system as a whole—acts as an agency of social control. Behind a veil of neutrality and the rhetoric of public interest, the government operates to legitimate and protect the interests of the business elite. For the most part, it operates to shape the contours of debate and limit the range of alternatives on public policy issues to those that do not challenge the hegemony of corporate interest. Rather than defending people's interests, it acts to channel discontent into a political process that limits change. Thus, Kennedy's public advocacy of civil rights, at that time immensely popular with voters, which concealed a policy of nonenforcement, controlled public protest for a period of time, just as President Johnson's reputation as a dove enabled him to forestall resistance to the Vietnam War (Sheehan et al., 1969).

Some would argue against our interpretation by pointing to the enormous complexity of American government. There is an intricate web of federal, state, and local governments, each divided into executive, legislative, and judicial branches. Regulatory agencies are sprinkled throughout the system. There are all manner of individuals, groups, and commissions, myriad bureaucrats, the White House staff, blue ribbon commissions, and quasi-governmental bodies. The enforcement apparatus is equally complex: the armed forces, the attorney general, the district attorneys, the FBI, the CIA, and the tactical force of local police. This apparently endless elaboration of government activity is taken as prima facie proof that no one group runs American government and that any analysis which sees consistency in governmental behavior must be incorrect (Rose, 1967).

In our view, the complexity is real, and it does represent a melange of competing interests, but the melange includes only a small part of the spectrum of interests in America. More significantly, this complexity reflects the multitude of tasks government has come to perform. In performing these functions and responding to changing conditions, government has established and reestablished contact with varying business leaders and those who represent them. This results in the embedding of the interests of business, or of a sector of business, into the very structure of government. In some cases, the coordination of business and government is explicit; in others it is invisible yet powerful; in others it is problematic. Despite this variety, we can pinpoint certain basic types of structural links through which the ties between business and government are effected.

STRUCTURAL LINKS BETWEEN BUSINESS AND GOVERNMENT

The structural links between business and government can be divided into four broad types.

1. Personnel transfers. Corporate leaders or representatives are appointed or elected to regular government jobs, either because of their special expertise or because of the particular political importance or sensitivity of those positions.

2. Policy-planning groups. Established and financed by major businesses, these groups develop and refine major policy proposals and then seek to implement them in government.

3. Advisory commissions. These are appointed by government officials to formalize and finalize major policies, or to oversee the ongoing operation and modification of such policies. These advisory boards generally are made up of business people, experts, and politicians, each of whom brings special skills to the task.

4. Boards of directors. Many public institutions are governed by these boards. They are consistently dominated by businesspeople, who set guidelines for policy and monitor the performance of top administrators.

None of these particular forms of structural linkage are essential in and of themselves. As we argued above, corporate power ultimately derives from control of the economy; the particular forms that activate it can and do change.

Personnel Transfers

The attention of many recent analysts of American government has focused on the widespread presence of business representatives in government, and particularly in certain top government positions. Thus, for example, Domhoff (1967, pp. 99–110) found that 8 of the 13 individuals who served as secretary of defense between 1932 and 1967 were businessmen who were also listed in the social register and that the remaining 5 were bankers or corporate executives. Between 1932 and 1964, every U.S. ambassador to a key post derived from the social elite or from major business leadership. Similar patterns have been demonstrated for a wide variety of offices in the administrations of all presidents, Republican and Democrats, liberals and conservatives.[9]

Though these studies are impressive, they are not conclusive. The problem is that some government posts are not dominated by elites. Only 7 percent of congresspeople in Domhoff's study had elite ties, and while this percentage certainly indicates considerable overrepresentation, it hardly signals dominance of Congress. If the argument that personnel transfers constitute a key structural link depended solely on such statistics—despite the dramatic figures for Cabinet officers and ambassadors—the evidence would be less than convincing.

We must consider, therefore, another form of personnel transfer, one that may not come immediately to mind. Specifically, we must take into account the fact that personnel transfers may also occur in the opposite direction. As a politician rises in the political structure, his or her career options greatly increase. After even a short time in elective office, defeat in reelection may be cushioned by appointment to another public office or to a lucrative and important job outside of government. Even moderately successful politicians can rely on a bright future inside or outside government (Mintz, 1975). These career possibilities are foreclosed only if the politician alienates the political and business communities that control the jobs.

An officeholder therefore may face a curious dilemma if a proposal favored by his or her business backers is not popular with his or her constituency. He or she can support the policy and risk not being selected if it generates public outrage, alternatively, or refuse to support it and risk both not being elected and losing the possibility of secure employment outside electoral government. Not surprisingly, many politicians risk popular disfavor to retain corporate support. This form of actual and potential personnel transfer creates a sympathetic posture among many politicians toward business interests.

Let us return again to the first form of personnel transfer. As already implied, the business elite is concentrated in some government posts and not others. Whereas virtually all the ambassadors to major foreign countries derive from business origins, only half of all ambassadors do (Domhoff, 1967, p. 105). While the secretary of defense seems an exclusive province of the corporate elite, generals rarely have elite origins (Domhoff, 1967, pp. 99–117). Consider the key subcabinet policy-making positions in the U.S. government. Of the 800 under and assistant secretaries appointed between 1933 and 1961, 32 percent were business executives, 25 percent were lawyers (most with important business affiliations), and 33 percent had been public servants for the major part of their working lives (Mann, 1965, pp. 29–32, 292). The business executives were by no means distributed evenly across departments. The following comments from *The Assistant Secretaries* (Mann, 1965)[10] offer some clues as to which areas of government are most likely to have subcabinet slots filled from the business community.

> Since Commerce is mainly a service department for the business community, emphasis on filling these positions with businessmen is understandable.
> Recruitment for the Department of the Treasury, has in recent years, been predominantly a search for men in the banking and legal fields who appear to have the specialized knowledge and experience to perform specific functions within the government. (pp. 55, 37)

The point is clear: the personnel transfers occur primarily in sectors of government in which businesses have a special interest. Businesspeople in government typically connect a government agency with segments of the business community whose interests are directly affected by that agency's operations. While the foregoing comments imply that the motive for such recruitment derives from the search for expertise available only from business, this does not alter the consequences—these sectors of government are led by individuals who are sympathetic and loyal to major corporations.

In summary, personnel transfers accomplish two interrelated tasks. First, transfers from government to business create incentives for political incumbents to favor business interest, even when it conflicts with popular needs. Second, transfers from business to government mean that newly minted government officials are familiar with analyses and programs favored by the inner circle of the business elite.

Policy-Planning Groups

Many people's image of government decision making centers on a lonely chief executive working late at night, developing the guidelines he will present to a hostile Congress. This image has little to do with reality: every important political policy is the result of careful research, multiple authorship, collective judgment, and in most cases, a long period of incubation. And usually, the policy-planning process will begin outside of government in groups that are established and financed by major business interests.[11]

Such groups constitute a corporate policy-making superstructure, which is based ultimately on the intercorporate and interpersonal links analyzed in Part I and which has grown and evolved ever since the founding of the National Civic Federation at the beginning of this century.[12] Most people have heard of the Chamber of Commerce or National Association of Manufacturers and are aware of their roles as representatives of business. But these are by no means the principal forums in which collective corporate policy is determined. Three less publicized institutions, which first achieved prominence during the Roosevelt period, have been far more important in recent decades: the Council on Foreign Relations (CFR), the Committee for Economic Development (CED), and the Business Council.

The CFR and CED are tax exempt research organizations that sponsor discussion groups involving prominent individuals from the corporate, government, and academic worlds. Both groups are funded by leading corporations and major foundations, and their membership lists read like a *Who's Who* of American business (Domhoff, 1970a, 1979, 1983; NACLA, 1971; Shoup and Minter, 1977). Through the discussion groups and the position papers that emerge from them, the business elite develops program proposals, one example being the electoral reforms advocated in the CED report discussed in Chapter 6. These proposals are often translated into public policy. Thus, CED reports have often become "guidelines for American economic policy in the postwar era," setting forth, for example, many of the provisions of the Employment Act of 1946, as well as the stabilized budget concept (Domhoff, 1970a, p. 121). The CFR's impact in the realm of foreign affairs has been at least as great. The United Nations charter was largely shaped by the CFR. The Marshall Plan, the U.S. program for reconstruction after World War II, was planned by a CFR policy seminar which began in 1939 (Shoup and Minter, 1977). The U.S. strategy in Vietnam was developed and modified by a series of CFR study groups (Shoup and Minter, 1977). President Jimmy Carter's foreign policy was developed by the Trilateral Commission, a multinational offshoot of the CFR, and implemented by commission members who became officials in Carter's administration (Shoup, 1980).

The Business Council was founded in 1933 as an advisory agency to the Department of Commerce. In its early years, it was consistently consulted in the development of President Franklin Delano Roosevelt's legislative program and it actively solicited support for the program among corporate leaders. During that period, the group could claim membership of such inner circle leaders as Henry I. Harriman, president of the United States Chamber of Commerce; Winthrop Aldridge of Chase National Bank; James Rand of Remington Rand; W. A. Harriman of Brown Brothers, Harriman; E. T. Stannard of Kennecott Copper Company; Gerald Swoop of General Electric; Walter Teagle of Standard Oil; F. B. Davis of United States Rubber; and R. M. Deupress of Proctor and Gamble (Domhoff, 1970a, p. 214).

After World War II, the group abandoned its official link to the Commerce Department but continued to meet as a policy-planning forum for inner circle business leaders. In 1955, for example, its membership included representatives from 2 of the 4 largest rubber manufacturers, 3 of the 5 largest automobile manufacturers, 3 of the 10 largest steel producers, 4 of the 10 largest chemical companies, 2 of the 3 largest textile manufacturers, and 4 of the 16 largest oil companies (McConnell, 1966, p. 276).

The Business Council meets about six times a year with high governmental officials, in order to present its views on a range of important public policy issues. Its advice and recommendations, like those of the CFR and the CED, "reach into the farthest confines of Washington's bureaucratic structure" (McConnell, 1966, p. 299). The influence of the Business Council on elected officials is reflected in comments made by President Jimmy Carter at its December 1977 meeting. Carter told the assembled business representatives that if they encountered government action "that unnecessarily encroaches on your own effectiveness, I hope you'll let either my Cabinet officers or me know, and I'll do the best I can to correct it. . . . If you let me have those recommendations, I'll do the best I can to comply with your request" (Carter, 1977, p. 1866, quoted in Shoup, 1980, pp. 169–170).

Though these are the most important groups active in formulating policy on the federal level, they are not the only ones. The Business Roundtable, the National Association of Manufacturers, and the myriad chambers of commerce are complemented by numerous associations, representing particular industries. In the 1970s, the Trilateral Commission achieved temporary prominence, and in the early 1980s, the American Enterprise Institute and other groups with a more conservative cast increased their influence (see Chapter 13; Sklar, 1980; Shoup, 1980).

It is worth noting that these policy-planning groups often concern themselves with issues far beyond our intuitive sense of business's narrow economic interests (see Useem, 1984). An example is the Carnegie Foundation for Advancement of Teaching, which in 1967 established the Carnegie Commission on Higher Education "to examine and make recommendations regarding the vital issues in higher education in the United States" (Carnegie Commission on Higher Education, 1971, p. iii). In any event, once tentative policies have been suggested, the policy-planning organizations finance research and experiments to assess implementation strategies. Government may become involved in this process at any stage of level; but even without direct government participation, this process of domestic and foreign policy development continues within these networks of private planning organizations. Sometimes only after many years of research and development are policies brought to the government for consideration. At this point, the leverage these groups have as representatives of business becomes the chief tool for attempting to translate proposals into action.

Advisory Committees

The appointment of advisory committees is a routine part of government. Most of these committees are not concerned with the strategic formulations undertaken by policy-planning bodies; they are created only when specific policies have been adopted by the government. While they do not create policy, advisory committees do play an important role in refining and implementing it.

Advisory committees normally consist of business representatives, politicians, and experts. The business members often provide broad guidance for the program because they are frequently directly involved in (and experienced with) the subject of the policy; politicians provide understanding of administrative problems, enforcement procedure, publicity strategies, and the dynamics of popular approval and dissent; and experts offer knowledge of the technical aspects of the program. Often, however, as we shall see, business is—either overtly or covertly—overrepresented on advisory committees.

There are basically three types of advisory groups: blue ribbon commissions, which assess newly introduced policy proposals; formal advisory committees, which oversee operations once policies have been fully formulated; and ad hoc advisory groups, which meet for a short time to advise government on critical decisions concerning ongoing programs. We will look at a typical example of each in turn to document the overrepresentation of business.

In October 1971, Governor Nelson Rockefeller of New York appointed a blue ribbon commission, the Fleishmann Commission—with a budget of $1.5 million—to develop broad proposals for changes in New York's educational system.[13] The commission included politicians (mainly from New York state), experts (recruited from as far away as Stanford University), and businesspeople (including the former board chairman of First National City Bank). Many members fell into more than one of these categories. Among the politicians, for example, was Assemblymember Constance Cook, an expert on education. The experts included H. Thomas James, a dean at Stanford University who was also a member of the Board of Directors of AV Electronics Corporation and a consultant to other electronics companies. The businesspeople included Francis Keppel, onetime U.S. commissioner of education. Three members of the CED and two members of the Carnegie Commission on Higher Education were among the appointees, and other business planning groups were also well represented.[14] The Fleishmann Commission was well qualified for judging the technical aspects of educational policy while guaranteeing that the adopted measures would be in keeping with the views and interests of business.

As an example of formal advisory commissions consider the Citizens Advisory Council to the Peace Corps, appointed with great fanfare by President John F. Kennedy in 1961 to give the Corps "guidance and counsel in the development of its activities" (*New York Times,* March 31, 1961, p. 7). If we looked only at their listed affiliations, the council members would seem to be a balanced group, representing most constituencies interested in or affected by the new program (see Table 12). Besides six present or former government officials, there were nine educators, many of them prominent in the development of overseas programs. Balancing the five business executives were six philanthropists, including the head of the American Friends Service Committee and directors of at least three groups active in international aid. Also included were three union representatives, two students, Harry Belafonte—a popular entertainer with liberal politics—and Eleanor Roosevelt. The council included three blacks, three women, numerous Republicans, two famous liberals, at least two pacifists, and a farmer.

But the listed affiliations tell only part of the story. Many of the "nonbusiness" council members had quite clear business connections. Although only 5 members were officially designated by President Kennedy as representing business, fully 19 of the 33 members were officials (past or present) of giant corporations.

Two of the policy-planning organizations discussed earlier—the CED and the CFR—had a presence in the form of members listed as having government affiliations. Oveta Culp Hobby, a director of the CED, was described as a former government official, while David Lilienthal a member of the CFR, was described as the former chairman of the Tennessee Valley Authority. Similarly, health corporations, which would be involved in the health delivery aspects of the Peace Corps, were represented by two council members billed only as educators. Two other educators in fact had strong ties to the major media.

Nor did the links to business end there. One of the two students on the council was John D. Rockefeller IV, heir to one of the greatest business fortunes ever accumulated. (The other student, James Scott, was not just a student but also a CIA operative.) Mrs. Robert Kintner was selected because of her experience with the International Children's Fund of the United Nations, but the fact that her husband was president of NBC indicates a second set of loyalties. Even Sargent Shriver, who was the new director of

Table 12
MEMBERSHIP OF CITIZENS
ADVISORY COUNCIL TO THE PEACE CORPS

Name	Listed Affiliation[a]	Other Affiliation[b]
Lyndon B. Johnson (Chairman)	Vice president of the United States	Major holdings in broadcasting industry
William O. Douglas (Honorary chair)	Supreme court justice	
Leona Baumgartner	New York City commissioner of health	Many connections with overseas public health organizations, director of many health corporations
Oveta Culp Hobby	Former secretary of agriculture	Director of Committee for Economic Development, on board of directors of many corporations, including General Foods, Mutual Insurance Company
David E. Lilienthal	Former chairman of Tennessee Valley Authority and Securities and Exchange Commission	Member of Council on Foreign Relations and on board of many business sponsored economic development corporations
Frederick R. Mass	Philadelphia director of commerce	Business executive
Listed as educators		
Dr. Mary Bunting	President of Radcliffe College	Director of health businesses, including Kaiser Foundation
Dr. Albert Dent	President of Dillard University	Former vice president of Safety Construction Company Served on many health agencies
Listed as citizen philanthropists		
Rev. William Sloan Coffin	Chaplain of Yale University	Central Intelligence Agency (1950–1953) Director of Operations Crossroads (Peace Corps)
Rev. John J. Considine	Director of the Latin American Bureau of the National Catholic Welfare Conference	
Mrs. Robert Kintner	Active in International Children's Fund of the United Nations	Wife of the president of the National Broadcasting Corporation
Mrs. E. Lee Ozbirn	International president of General Organization of Women's Clubs	Many health groups, including several with foreign connections

Table 12 (continued)

MEMBERSHIP OF CITIZENS
ADVISORY COUNCIL TO THE PEACE CORPS

Clarence E. Pickett	Executive secretary of American Friends Service Committee	Experience in Peace Corps type of programs
Rev. James Robinson	Director of Interracial Morningside Center (Chicago)	
Listed as representing other groups		
Joseph Beirne	President of Communications Workers of America	
Harry Belafonte	Singer and actor	Member of Council on Racial Equality
Leroy Collins	President of National Association of Radio and TV Broadcasters	Many public offices, including governor of Florida Important corporate lawyer and business representative
Cornelius J. Haggerty	President of National Building Trades Council	Member of many international labor federations
James Scott	President of National Student Association	CIA agent
John D. Rockefeller IV	Student	
Eleanor Roosevelt	Former first lady	
Dr. Benjamin E. Mays	President of Morehouse College	Board of directors, Danforth Foundation and many YMCA and church groups
Dr. James A. McCain	President of Kansas State College	Director of several insurance companies including Manhattan Mutual Life
Franklin D. Murphy	Chancellor of University of California, Los Angeles	Consultant (and later director) to many corporations, including Ford Motor, Times-Mirror, Norton Simon
Dr. Eugene V. Rostow	Dean of Yale Law School	Frequent government official
Dr. George L. Sanchez	Chairman of Department of History, University of Texas	
Dr. John Fischer	Dean of Columbia Teachers College	Director of Cowles Communication Corporation Trustee of many business-financed research groups

TABLE 12 (CONTINUED)
MEMBERSHIP OF CITIZENS
ADVISORY COUNCIL TO THE PEACE CORPS

Roger Revelle	Director of Scripps Institute	Director, First National Bank of San Diego
Listed as Businessmen		
Thomas J. Watson	President of IBM	
Henry Crown	Vice president of Hilton Hotel Corporation	
Peter Grace	President of W. R. Grace Corporation	
E. Palmer Hoyt	Publisher of *Denver Post*	
Murray D. Lincoln	President of Nationwide Insurance Company	

[a] Listed affiliations were found in the *New York Times* (March 31, 1961, p. 7).
[b] Other affiliations were derived from a variety of sources, and they are by no means complete. Thus, committee members may have substantial business interests or connections that are not listed in the references. This occurs either because the individual is not prominent enough to be listed in these books (for example, George L. Sanchez) or because when filling out the questionnaires, the person does not give complete information (for example, Lyndon Johnson does not list his media holdings in *Who's Who* for political reasons).
The references particularly useful in this research were:
Leaders in Education: A Biographical Dictionary (4th edition), Jacques Cattell Press, 1971.
Who's Who in America, 1970–1971, Marquis Who's Who, 1970 (also previous edition).
Who's Who in American Politics, 1970–1971 (3d edition), R. R. Bowker, 1971.
Who's Who in Consulting (1st ed.), ed. Paul Wasserman,
Who's Who in the South and Southwest, 1970–1971, Marquis Who's Who, 1970.

the Peace Corps and a Kennedy relative, had been a Chicago businessman before joining Kennedy's political team.

The Citizens Advisory Council to the Peace Corps had a public and a private face. Its public face exhibited a profile that included most of the groups with a significant interest in the Peace Corps. The private face revealed a significant imbalance; business affiliations were infused into its core, assuring that its deliberations and conclusions would not challenge the interest of large corporations.

The third type of advisory committee, the ad hoc group, has no formal role or official existence. There is no fanfare. Its meetings are not reported, nor is its existence mentioned with any regularity by the press. Such a committee can arise, function, and die without any public notice. The basic role of the ad hoc advisory group is to provide government leadership with a constant and direct link to the outside world and to help make critical decisions that cannot wait for elaborate policy development. That such groups can serve as an important mechanism for the transmission of business influence can be illustrated by the U.S. decision to deescalate the war in Vietnam after the Tet offensive in early 1968.

The Tet offensive of the National Liberation Front substantially disrupted the American war effort. As a result, the U.S. government began preparing a new escalation of the war, which was to include an 200,000 man rise in troop strength, additional draft calls, activation of army reserves, the mining of Haiphong Harbor, and increased bombing of Hanoi and Haiphong.[15] These actions were planned and about to be executed when, on March 31, 1968, President Johnson appeared on television and announced not only deescalation of the bombing, but also his withdrawal from presidential contention.

According to the *Pentagon Papers,* Johnson's announcement was as stunning to high-level officials in Washington as it was to ordinary American citizens. Within the planning regions of government, the debate had been "devoted to various kinds of escalation. . . . The proposal that was eventually to be adopted, namely cutting back the bombing to the panhandle only, was not even mentioned" (Sheehan et al., 1971, p. 603).[16] What caused the change? The *Pentagon Papers* analyst "inclines to view that, if [President Johnson] was still waivering at this time, the decisive advice was given by the Wise Men, who assembled in Washington on March 25 and 26" (p. 609).

These "Wise Men" were the Senior Informal Advisory Group (SIAG), men who had "served in high Government post or had been presidential advisors during the last 20 years" (Sheehan et al., 1971, p. 609). They were not just connected to major American business: almost all were members of the corporate inner circle (see Table 13). Beyond this, SIAG exhibited the same structure as other advisory groups: experts, politicians, and businessmen. In this case, the experts were military men—three of the most famous American generals in the post–World War II period, each of them with substantial business connections. The politicians were Abe Fortas, McGeorge Bundy, Dean Acheson, and Henry Cabot Lodge, each with long involvement in Southeast Asia policy and the last three longtime activists in the corporate inner circle. The businessmen were all former government officials currently affiliated with important and central firms in the American economy: Morgan Guaranty Trust, Chase Manhattan Bank, IBM, and American Telephone and Telegraph among others. Most of the Wise Men were also affiliated with the Council for Foreign Relations where they had participated in a spirited debate on Vietnam policy in the months preceding this decision (Shoup and Minter, 1977).[17]

Thus, the most significant policy change in the American Vietnam war effort was made without any elaborate official policy planning. The government bureaucracy was not involved. The cabinet was not even involved. The decision was made by representatives of business—by an informal group that combined experience in government with inner circle affiliations. It appears, in fact, that the Wise Men met at every critical juncture in the war and that its opinion consistently prevailed (Sheehan et al., 1971, p. 610).

As this example graphically illustrates, advisory groups of various sorts may play a central role in the functioning of American government. Their huge number alone attests to the ongoing need for coordination of government and business activities. Although these groups possess no formal

Table 13

THE WISE MEN:

MEMBERSHIP OF THE SENIOR INFORMAL ADVISORY GROUP[a]

Name, government position	Major business affiliations
Military Experts	
Gen. Omar N. Bradley	Director and chairman of the board of Bulova Watch Company
Gen. Matthew B. Ridgway	Director of Colt Industries
Gen. Maxwell Taylor	Chairman of the board of Mexican Light and Power
Politicians	
Dean Acheson Former secretary of state, many other government posts	Head of corporate law firm bearing his name with important connections to Southern Railway, Alabama Great Southern Railway, and other large companies
McGeorge Bundy Former presidential advisor	President of Ford Foundation
Abe Fortas Associate justice, Supreme Court	Head of corporate law firm bearing his name
	Director of Federated Department Stores
Henry Cabot Lodge Former ambassador to South Vietnam, many other government posts	General counsel for Time, Life, and Fortune
	Member of major Boston aristocratic family
Businessmen	
George W. Ball Former undersecretary of state	Chairman, Lehman Brothers International, one of the most important American banking investment concerns
Arthur H. Dean Negotiator of Korean Armistice	Director of at least nine major corporations including Bank of New York and Campbell Soup Company
Douglas Dillon Former secretary of treasury	Director, Chase Manhattan Bank, Dillon Read and Company (another major investment banking firm), and American Telephone and Telegraph
John J. McCloy High commissioner in Germany	Director, Allied Chemical, Dreyfus Corporation, and others
	Former chairman of the board of Chase Manhattan Bank
Robert D. Murphy Former career diplomat	Directors of Morgan Guaranty Trust and others
Cyrus R. Vance Former deputy secretary of defense	Director of Aetna Life Insurance, IBM, Pan American World Airways, and others

[a] Sources for this table include: Neil Sheehan et al., *The Pentagon Papers* (New York: Bantam Books, 1971), p. 609; *Martindale-Hubbell Law Directory in Five Volumes*, 104th Annual Edition, 1972 (New Jersey: Martindale-Hubbell, 1972); *Standard and Poor's Register of Corporations, Directors and Executives, 1971* (New York, Standard and Poors, 1971); *Who's Who in American Politics*, (3d ed.) 1971–1972, ed. Paul A. Theis and Edmund L. Henshaw (New York: Jaques Cattell Press, 1971).

power, they are an important means by which major governmental policies are referred to businesspeople for suggestions, criticisms, advice, and consent. In the day-to-day life of government, constant attention is paid to the opinions of the business leaders. This attention is both a symptom and a cause of the hegemony of business.

Boards of Directors

Authority over many public programs and activities is delegated to agencies that are insulated from elected government officials. A city hospital, for example, is not administered by an official accountable to the mayor. Rather, control is vested in an independent board of trustees which hires the necessary professional administrators and then oversees general policy.

There are a great many such public boards of directors performing a wide variety of tasks. It is useful to divide them into three categories.

1. Boards of trustees administering independent government services such as schools and hospitals

2. Special administrative committees with short- or long-term investigatory, regulatory, or enforcement functions

3. Regulatory commissions, which are created to regulate business activity and prevent abuses by large enterprises

As indicated, these functionally different bodies share an important characteristic: their structural independence from normal political influence or domination. Since these commissions regulate or administer institutions that affect the daily lives of individual citizens or companies, they must be insulated from partisanship, which might produce favoritism or other biases. Louis Kohlmeier, concluded, for example, that the Federal Aviation Administration operated as "government protection for the biggest airlines" and that other regulatory agencies served the largest corporations contained within their respective jurisdictions (1969, p. 69). The Antitrust Division of the Department of Justice arrived at a similar conclusion: "The history of every regulatory agency in the government is that it comes to represent the industry groups it is supposed to control" (Harris, 1964, p. 145). Regulatory agencies do not regulate the giants in an industry; rather, they assist these corporations in coordinating their activities and help them defend against competitors.

Peter Freitag's comprehensive analysis (1979) of federal regulation investigated why this loyalty to industry develops even when the industry is not well represented on the regulatory panel. He concluded that the answer lies in the myriad structural relationships that are created between a government agency and its business counterparts and that the contraints created by these ties condition the agencies' actions even without direct personnel transfers.

These constraints fit well with the structuralist portrait of business-government relations. Regulatory agencies are constructed in such a way that even those commissioners who hold no particular loyalty to the regulated industry find themselves bound by the law, by the established rules, and by the realities of politics as the "art of the practical" to undertake actions and make rulings that support the largest firms in their sectors.

Consider, for example, the fate of the Securities and Exchange Commission (SEC) rule that no major trader on the New York Stock Exchange could own a stock brokerage.[18] This rule had for many years been supported by the largest brokers, who were guaranteed a commission on every sale; but it hurt the large insurance companies and mutual funds, who wanted to save themselves brokerage fees on their massive stock purchases and sales. The rule was enforced by the brokers themselves, and it was therefore effective until the large investors took matters into their own hands, moving their business to small exchanges, like the Philadelphia Stock Exchange, which permitted them to own brokerages. The loss of these sales cost the New York Exchange brokers a great deal of money. Furthermore, because the large quantity of business going elsewhere inhibited their efforts to predict trends in the stock market, this development undermined their general effectiveness as investment advisors.

Finally, the New York Exchange capitulated. Using the SEC as the mediator, the large insurance companies and investment funds negotiated an agreement with the brokerage houses whereby an investor could own a brokerage if the predominant business of that brokerage was not with the owner. In effect, this meant that only the very largest investors were able to save themselves brokerage fees, while all the smaller ones, without the resources to purchase brokerage houses large enough to do most business with other customers, were forced back to the New York Exchange because their trading partners were there. The two giant sectors—the large insurance companies and the large New York brokerages—made an agreement that was mutually beneficial, while the smaller investors and the Philadelphia Exchange were left to bitterly complain. The SEC, which had tried to prevent this development, acknowledged its failure and announced the new rules, but, in effect, the enforcement had already begun: the New York Exchange simply declared the compromise, and the large investors returned to New York.

The role played by the SEC was that of a mediator between two antagonists.[19] As go-between it informed each group of the other's actions, but had no effective power in the situation. Significantly, although federal regulatory commissions handle over 100,000 pieces of business each year, all but a handful of these are resolved by "informal adjudication," the process just described (Kohlmeier, 1969, p. 69).

A key purpose of boards of trustees is supervision of professional administrators to insure that the institutions fulfill their ultimate goals and social purposes. This kind of oversight should not be performed by professionals who share the worldview of the executives they supervise. Responsible private citizens, properly selected, have the time, interest, and perspective for this work. For this reason, most state university systems are governed by boards of regents, most public hospitals are administered by boards of trustees, schools have boards of education (often elected), parks are run by parks commissions, and so on. These groups do not usually consist of technical experts: the members are concerned private citizens for whom the board membership is not a full-time occupation. They do not administer the program; they oversee it. They function in almost identical fashion to the board of directors of a corporation.

The appointees to boards of trustees are usually corporate leaders, with the most important public institutions attracting the leadership of larger and more important firms.

Consider the board of trustees of the State University of New York. Of the 15 board members in 1972, 13 were corporate leaders (or wives of corporate leaders), and 7 of these 13 were connected to Fortune 500 corporations (see Table 14). Only two trustees had no clear corporate connections: Dr. John Holloman and Morris Iushewitz. The former was a black doctor and the latter a union leader. Their presence illustrates the small degree to which this board was drawn from constituencies other than business.

Special administrative committees, unlike boards of trustees, are temporary. They are established to oversee the implementation of a controversial policy which might be subject to biased or partisan enforcement. President Richard Nixon, for example, appointed two such commissions to administer his 1971 wage-price freeze, one to regulate prices and the other to regulate wage increases. As Nixon emphasized when he announced the freeze, the success of the program depended in large part on public approval of the policy, since dissatisfaction could lead to disruptive strikes, refusals to comply, or even outright rebellion (*New York Times,* August 16, 1971, p. 1; May 4, 1972, p. 33). If the committees had been dominated by political partisans, dissatisfaction might have become unmanageable, since, even before Watergate, large numbers of Americans were already distrustful of Nixon's actions on controversial issues. An insulated structure was needed, and independent commissions were therefore established. To further reassure the public of the impartiality of his administrators, Nixon divided the wage board into one-third labor, business, and public representation, while the price board was to consist of seven public representatives, "with no special interests" (*New York Times,* August 16, 1971, p. 1; October 13, 1971, p. 14).

An examination of the connections and loyalties of the commissions' membership reveals that the price board combined technical expertise with extensive ties to the business community (Table 15). Certainly its members had the necessary skills to judge the fairness of proposed price increases: it included a certified public accountant, capable of professionally examining companies' books; the former president of Dun and Bradstreet with extensive experience in assessing the financial condition of companies; two business consultants with expertise in calculating the profitability of enterprises; a lawyer well versed in corporate law; and several trained economists with a variety of technical specialties. But, with one exception, the members also had intimate ties to corporate America. One member was a director of four major companies including Chemical Bank; another was the director of five major companies including IBM. Two were leading members of the Chamber of Commerce; another was a bank consultant, one was a partner in a major

Table 14

THE BOARD OF TRUSTEES OF THE STATE UNIVERSITY OF NEW YORK, 1972

Name	Affiliations[a]
Mrs. Maurice T. Moore (Chairperson)	Wife of partner of Cravath, Swaine and Moore, (major corporate law firm)
	Director, Time, Inc.
	Director, Chemical Bank of New York
	Director, General Dynamics
James J. Warren (Vice chairperson)	President, James D. Warren and Son (contractors)
Warren W. Clute, Jr.	President, Watkins Salt Company
	Chairman, Glen National Bank and Trust
	Director, Columbia Gas of New York
Charles R. Diebold	Partner, Diebold and Millonzi (corporate law firm)
	Trustee, Western Savings Bank
	Director, Dickenson Mines, Ltd.
	President, First Empire Corporation
Manly Fleischman	Partner, Jaeckle, Fleischman, Keely, Swart and Augsburger (corporate law firm)
	Director, Equitable Life Insurance Company
	Director, American Airlines
	Director, Sierra Research
George L. Hinman	Partner, Hinman, Howard and Dattell
	Director, IBM
	Director, New York Telephone
	Director, Lincoln First Banks, Inc.
	Director, Security Mutual Life, Insurance
	Director, First National City Bank (Binghamton)
Dr. John Holloman, Jr.	
Morris Iushewitz	Secretary of NYC Central Labor Council, AFL-CIO
Hugh R. Jones	Partner, Evan, Pirnie and Burdick
Clifton W. Phalen	Director, New York Telephone
	Chairman, Marine Midland Bank
	Former vice president, American Telephone and Telegraph
	Director, Kennecott Copper Corporation
	Director, Eastern Airlines
Mrs. Bronson Quackenbush	Wife of president, H. M. Quackenbush
John A. Roosevelt (son of FDR)	Vice president, Bache and Company, (New York investment firm)
Oren Root	President, Irving Trust Company
	President, Charter New York Company, (bank holding company)
Roger J. Sinnot	President, Bank of Utica
	Director, Utica Fire Insurance Company
Don J. Wickham	Owner, fruit farm in Hector, N.Y.
	Former Director, New York Telephone

[a] Sources for this table include: *New York Red Book, Who's Who in America,* and *Martindale-Hubbell Law Directory.*

Table 15

PRESIDENT NIXON'S PRICE CONTROL COMMISSION[a]

Name	Listed Affiliation	Other Affiliations
C. Jackson Grayson (Chairman)	Dean, Business School, Southern Methodist University	Consultant to Texas oil firms Director, Dallas Chamber of Commerce, Director, Petro Fund and Computrol Owner, C. J. Grayson (Plantation)
William T. Coleman	Black Lawyer	Partner, corporate law firm Director, Lincoln National Bank Director, Western Savings Fund
Robert F. Lanzillotti	Dean, College of Business University of Florida	Consultant: Michigan banks
J. Wilson Newman	Former chief executive, Dun and Bradstreet	Director, Chemical Bank Director, Fidelity Union Trust Trustee, Consolidated Edison Trustee, Mutual Life Insurance Trustee, Council of Economic Development
John W. Queenan	Former partner, Haskins and Sells accounting firm	Director, International Chamber of Commerce Director, Commerce and Industry Association of New York
William W. Scranton	Former Republican governor of Pennsylvania	Director, IBM Director, A & P Director, Fidelity Bank Director, Scott Paper Corporation Director, Liberty Life Assurance Many other directorships
Dr. Marina Whitman	Professor of Economics, University of Pittsburgh	

[a] Sources for this table include:

Leaders in Education 4th ed., New York: Jacques Cattell Press, 1971.

Martindale-Hubbell Law Directory in Five Volumes. New York: Martindale Hubbell, 1971.

New York Times, October 23, 1971, pp. 1, 14, 15.

Who's Who in Consulting. 1st ed., Paul Wasserman. Philadelphia: Graduate School of Business and Public Administration, 1968.

Who's Who in the East, 1970–1971. Chicago: Marquis Who's Who, 1969.

World Who's Who in Commerce and Industry: 1966–1967. 11th ed., Chicago: Marquis Who's Who, 1965.

corporate law firm; and the seventh was a member of the CED. Despite Nixon's claim that it represented the general public, the price board had impeccable business credentials.

In contrast to boards of trustees and special administrative commissions, regulatory commissions are not always dominated by members of the business elite. Nonetheless, studies have consistently found that regulatory agencies represent, rather than regulate, the industries to which they are assigned (see Freitag, 1979, 1983).

CONCLUSION

Our central point throughout this chapter has been that there are complex interlocking relationships between business and government. We have argued that while government often appears to be independent and autonomous, it is actually subject to a broad form of business hegemony. Because of its leverage, the business class is able to both influence the structure of government and obtain access to decision-making positions within government. This is the essence of class rule.

Over time, the structure of government has been permeated at all levels by the needs and the logic of capital. Business's domination of government takes many different forms. Frequently, business dominance has been assured before an agency begins to operate, as we shall see in Chapter 8. In other circumstances the interpenetration of government by business is so extensive that government becomes a junior partner in a joint venture. But, even where business dominance is much more subtle, government cannot function effectively unless it consistently takes into account the concerns and interests of business. Ultimately, the very organization of government has developed in such a manner that the interests of the business elite have been incorporated into its institutional structure.

NOTES

1. Sometimes the impact of corporate decision-making overwhelms government policy. East Saint Louis, Illinois, provides an agonizing example. In the 1960s (ironically, just after East Saint Louis was named an All-American city by *Look* magazine), over 300 businesses left the city because they found more profitable sites elsewhere. As a result, city taxes rose dramatically, driving out everyone who could leave. Thus, the city was ultimately left a slum, lacking funds to supply even minimal services to its now largely lower-class residents. (see *New York Times*, May 14, 1972, section 3, pp. 1, 7.)

2. By 1972, previously suppressed information about the difficulties the army was facing in mobilizing draftees began to get widespread publicity after the exposure of the My Lai incident and the actions of the Vietnam Veterans Against the War. See Eugene Linden, "Fragging and Other Withdrawal Symptoms: The Demoralization of the Army," *Saturday Review,* January 8, 1972, pp. 12–17, 55, for a typical discussion of deep discontent among soldiers.

3. Detailed accounts of the Cuban blockade and the missile crisis can be found in Schlesinger (1965, pp. 233–297, 795–830). Schlesinger (1965, pp. 340–342) and Sheehan et al. (1971, pp. 79–158) document the Kennedy administration's belligerent posture in Vietnam.

4. Arthur Schlesinger wrote, "America and Britain had offered the Soviet Union the same limited test ban four times in four years; now [1963] it was accepted the fifth time around" (1965, p. 909). For a complete chronology, see pp. 448–477, and 889–923.

5. The *New York Times* (September 29, 1961, p. 26) reported that Kennedy was following the routine procedure of allowing southern senators control of these appointments.

6. As an example of Kennedy's militancy consider the following quote, made in the context of America's posture toward Cuba: "But let the record show that our restraint is not inexhaustible. Should it ever appear that the inter-American doctrine of non-interference merely conceals or excuses a policy of non-action—if the nations of this Hemisphere should fail to meet their commitments against outside Communist penetration—then I want it clearly understood that this government will not hesitate in meeting its primary obligations which are to the security of our Nation!" (Schlesinger, 1965, pp. 287–288).

On the other hand, during the major escalation of the Vietnam war in April–May 1972, Nixon traveled to the Soviet Union. The main thrust of this visit was continued détente, even though the Soviet Union was the main supplier of the offensive mounted by the National Liberation Front and the North Vietnamese. (See *New York Times,* April–May 1972, passim.)

7. *New York Times,* (May 19, 1968, p. 41, August 9, 1969, p. 10, and August 16, 1971, p. 1).

8. Nixon thus became an articulate public spokesperson for a policy that was previously associated with radical leftism.

There can be no stable peace and enduring peace without the participation of the People's Republic of China. . . . It is in this spirit that I will undertake what I deeply hope will become a journey for peace, peace not just for our generation but for future generations on this earth we share together. (*New York Times,* July 16, 1971, p. 3)

9. See, for example, Mills (1956), Domhoff (1967, 1970a, 1970b, 1979, 1983), Shoup and Minter (1977), Ferguson and Rogers (1981), Freitag (1975), Mintz (1975). See also Lieberson (1971), NACLA (1971), Fellmuth (1970), Mintz (1975), Freitag (1975, 1979, 1984), Shoup (1975, 1977, 1980).

10. Mann (1965, pp. 297 and 299), and Freitag (1975). President Nixon instituted a formal policy of recruiting businessmen on loan (and sending government officials into business) to foster "mutual education and understanding of problems and activities of business and government." See Ralph Nader, "Cozy Corner in Washington," *Newsday* (May 8, 1972, p. 23).

11. The best accounts of this process can be found in Domhoff (1970a, 1970b, 1979), Shoup (1975, 1977, 1980), and Shoup and Minter (1977).

12. The best sources for this history are Weinstein (1968), Kolko (1963), Domhoff (1970a, 1979, 1983), and Shoup and Minter (1977).

13. This account of the Fleischmann Commission is taken from *Newsday* (January 29, 1972, p. 7).

14. Material on affiliations of the Fleischmann commissioners was taken from *Who's Who in America* (1970–1971) and *Leaders in Education, 4th Edition* (1970).

15. The chronology presented here is taken from the *Pentagon Papers* (Sheehan et al., 1971, pp. 510–623). See also Shoup and Minter (1977).

16. These are the words of the Pentagon historian and not the *New York Times* reporters.

17. See Shoup and Minter (1977, Chapter 6) for a description of the debates within the Council for Foreign Relations and the logic that led to deescalation.

18. Documentation for this chronology can be found in the following sources: *New York Times* (February 6, 1972, section 3, pp. 1 and 9, February 10, 1972, p. 1, February 26, 1972, pp. 37–43, March 3, 1972, p. 55); *Newsweek* (February 14, 1972); *Newsday* (February 11, 1972, p. 68A).

19. To see how these incidents are turned into proof of the viability of these commissions, one can consult the coverage of this episode in *Newsweek*, which treated the settlement as though it had been a unilateral pronouncement of the SEC that was stuffed down the throats of the large investors and New York Brokers. (February 14, 1972, p. 72).

8

Means of Movement: The Political Economy of Mass Transportation

J. Allen Whitt

The transportation systems that exist in our cities—the cars, buses, trolleys, and subways—have been generally thought of as rather straightforward results of technological advancement and civic will. New scientific discoveries and engineering innovations provide ever-better ways to move goods and people and these ways are then implemented, as long as out city fathers are farsighted enough or are sufficiently prodded by public opinion. In this manner, the horse gave way to the trolley, the trolley was supplanted by the bus and then the automobile, and the automobile may someday be replaced by swift "people movers" of the space age. Progress in transit comes with progress in technological capabilities.

Since the mid 1960s, however, our confidence in our transportation systems and in progress in transit has greatly diminished. Quite clearly, the goal of cheap, safe, and efficient transportation has not been met. Transportation has come to depend on the automobile, and public transportation has declined.

Our present system is a costly one, in terms of both personal and public costs. In the last seventy years, such costs have more than tripled and the energy crisis insures that these trends will continue. The increased personal costs are apparent in all areas—in the purchase, operation, maintenance, and insurance of automobiles.

The public costs stem, in large part, from an overemphasis on building highways. Direct federal expenditures between 1956 and 1981 for the National Highway Program totaled between $200 and $300 billion. Highway lobbyist Peter Koltnow, who has served as president of the Highway Users for Safety and Mobility and the National Transportation Research Board, has concluded that it will take even more than that amount (in new funds beyond those already allocated) to repair and maintain those same roads. Moreover, federal highway expenditures have not lessened the fiscal burden on cities and states: since World War II, state and local highway debts rose from $3.6 to $24 billion.

Overemphasis on highways has created many other fiscal burdens as well, including high levels of expenditure on police and safety services, local road construction, and snow removal. In 1973, the Federal Highway Administration estimated that these services cost well over $20 billion annually. In addition, of course, overdependence on highways, and on the automobile in general, has brought numerous indirect costs including auto accidents, energy waste, environmental damage, urban sprawl, and crises in many of the nation's inner cities.

Our transportation system is also very wasteful of time. Although motorization was supposed to overcome the barriers of space by decreasing travel time, it has instead led to land use patterns that actually increase travel time. Thus, in those urban centers that are more dependent on the automobile than public transportation, the average travel time to work has increased. Moreover, projections show this average travel time increasing 15 to 20 percent further by the year 2000.

Another cost is the depletion of resources. The motor vehicle industry consumes a substantial proportion of the total U.S. steel, aluminum, lead, iron, rubber, and zinc production. Since auto production and profits are based largely upon obsolescence (annual style changes and lower annual years of use), resource depletion will continue. Environmental Protection Agency projections indicate that the resource reserves necessary for current levels of auto production will dissipate by the year 2000. This will necessitate costlier extraction processes and new technologies, which will boost the direct costs of transportation even further.

Similarly, transportation's share of petroleum consumption has increased over 50 percent since World War II. In 1975, cars, trucks, and buses consumed 80 percent of the petroleum in the United States as compared to only 25–30 percent in European countries (Office of Technology Assessment, 1975; pp.17–24). Europe's greater emphasis on public transportation, transit-coordinated land use planning, conservation, and alternative fuel uses accounts for this immense discrepancy, which was reduced only slightly by fuel efficiency measures of the late 1970s and early 1980s.

Nor can the safety costs of our transportation system be expected to decline significantly, as long as the system itself is not altered. Since World War II, deaths from traffic accidents catapulted from insignificance to the third major cause of mortality. For people aged 15–34, traffic accidents are now the major cause of death. Disabilities from motor vehicle accidents have increased for all age groups. Although there has been strong consumer support for seatbelts, safer construction, and airbags, the future of automobile safety looks grim. Since mortality increases with decreased auto weight, the reduction of car weight and increased fuel efficiency ("downsizing") will likely produce even more highway deaths in the absence of new safety measures. Yet, in the rush to dominate the new small car market, producers have actually cut corners on safety.

In short, transportation has become expensive, wasteful, and dangerous. The crisis that exists today in American transportation cannot be blamed on technological development. If technology does not automatically lead to progress, neither does it automatically produce problems. Rather, this crisis is the result of a set of transportation policies—policies developed by large corporations and translated into government action through the processes outlined in Chapters 6 and 7.

In this chapter we look at the development of, and changes in, mass transportation in our nation's cities. We show how both can largely be accounted for in terms of the short-range interests of large corporations (though the specific industrial groups whose interests were honored has changed with the shifting composition and concentration of corporate capital). We are concerned with policy changes, corporate intervention in policy formation, and the influence of corporate power, both through direct investment, which nurtured certain types of transit development at the expense of others, and through political intervention, which influenced public decision making. We are therefore concerned with both the structural constraints on public policy and the instrumental interventions of corporate representatives in the policy formation process.

THE GROWTH OF PUBLIC TRANSPORTATION AND THE BEGINNING OF ITS DECLINE

The rapid urban growth after the Civil War taxed the horse-drawn trolley systems beyond their capacity (Ward, 1971, pp. 131–134), as the limitation of horsepower made these trolleys unsuitable for even medium-sized cities. This problem gave impetus to the creation of electrified trolley lines and dovetailed nicely with the development of the electrical manufacturing industry, the most important industry of that early growth period (Passer, 1953; McKay, 1976).

Electrification created boom years for public transportation. For most of the period between 1890 and 1918, ridership grew faster than the urban population. The streetcar network allowed cities to expand spatially and spurred industrial growth as well. Not surprisingly, land speculators and transit owners nearly always spoke with one voice in support of expansion (Wilcox, 1921, pp. 67–100). They portrayed public transportation as a "moral influence" which removed people from unhealthy environments in inner cities and relocated them in "better" areas (Tarr, 1973; MacShane, 1975; Warner, 1976).

Because of the increased cost of investment, the opportunity for high profits, and the possibility for lucrative real estate investment, electrification within each city encouraged the consolidation and concentration of transit ownership and the integration of this industry into the logic of capital flows. Ralph S. Bauer, president of the Lynn, Massachusetts, board of trade noted in 1920:

> I found that a little later on in the nineties, banking interests in the Northeast became interested in the street railway problem, and believed that by consolidating these competing companies there could be evolved from such consolidation a unit system which would pay tremendous profits. . . . I further found that the ground hogs in different communities—the land speculators—had brought certain influences to bear on the local governments which compelled the street railway to build extensions into property for the sake of adding rental and sales values to pasture land, and the politicians in charge of the localities in those times brought sufficient influence to bear on the railway to compel them to build the kind of extensions *which would never profit producing lines*. (Federal Electrical Railroad Commission; p. 1622)

The resulting tendency toward the control of street railways by land speculators, public utility interests, and steam railroads set the stage for electrical transportation's decline. The street railway building booms of 1890–1908 had been lavishly financed. Many transit executives had pocketed investment capital or earnings and/or constructed unnecessary lines that were profitable only for those involved in land speculation and investment. The combination of corruption and poor management resulted in a credit collapse between 1916 to 1923, when over a third of the transit companies in the United States went bankrupt (Smerk, 1975, p. 135). As one major transportation financier testified before the Federal Electrical Railroad Commission (FERRC) in 1919, "We insiders are selling out just as fast as we can, and when ten years are up, you won't find your Uncle Dudley or any one of us that will own a share of stock or bond in electrical transit" (FERRC, 1920, p. 1058). Several factors contributed to the decline in investment in public transportation.

The first was the militant reaction of public transport workers to more restrictive supervision and to the poor working conditions stemming from the financial crisis. Between 1916 and 1920, the transit industry experienced the highest level of strike activity in its history (Kuhn, 1952, pp. 26–27), and as a consequence, wages in the transit industry increased faster than average industrial wages (without, however, any resolution of the disputes regarding working conditions) (Schmidt, 1935). These higher labor costs, along with wartime inflation, which increased material costs, drove the ratio of operating expenses to gross income of transit firms from 50 to 77 percent.

The second factor was the equally vociferous reaction of transit riders to problems of deteriorating service, which included fewer, more crowded trolleys, more delays, and inadequate service in newly urbanized areas.

During this early period, the right to operate public transportation was typically franchised by local government to private companies. This franchising power of local government became the political lever by which consumer groups demanded municipal control of the overcrowded, poorly maintained, or abandoned lines. Between 1898 and 1920, virtually every major U.S. city was the scene of legal battles, referenda over rate hikes, public ownership campaigns, and investigation of transit corruption.[1]

In this politically volatile climate the National Civic Federation—the first major corporate policy-planning organization—decided to investigate the transit problem. A report by Auguste Belmont, owner of New York's transit properties and president of the federation, argued that public ownership would be less efficient than adequate regulation (Jensen, 1959). The NCF then went on to successfully push for this policy in many major cities and states (Yago, 1984).

Regulation moved the political struggle over transportation from the public sphere of city politics to the forums of appointed, business-oriented, public utility and public service commissions at the state level. Transportation decisions were thus in effect insulated from public pressure. Indeed, transportation planning by appointed state-level organizations was substantially less responsive to public opinion than had been the case when decisions were made in local city councils and by popular referenda. These commissions, like those discussed in Chapter 7, were usually captured by industry.

Typically, students of urban transportation have attempted to isolate a single cause for the origin of public transit's decline, variously focusing on corruption, poor business practices, the lack of technological innovation, overcrowded service, land use dispersion, and the rise of the automobile. Though all of these factors are significant, it is necessary to analyze their relationship to one another. The central factor, which linked all these apparently distinct forces, was the shift of investment capital from public to private transportation and from rail to rubber-wheeled vehicles. This shift was made possible by the promising expansion in auto production in the first two decades of this century, but this was only one factor in the redirection of capital flows. Another was that the shift allowed business to avoid the rising costs in public transit, as unionized workers in this sector would decline through attrition, while automobile production was already established as a nonunionized industry.[2] Moreover, the ongoing protests over corruption and poor business practices would be muted by withdrawing from the semipublic arenas of franchised mass transportation. Consumer movements over rate hikes, overcrowding, and abandoned lines would also be avoided by privatization. Finally, the locus of political action would be transferred from the volatile local level to the more tractable national level, where lobbying would usually take place without the glare of continuous controversy that had characterized the local level. Though regulatory commissions had for the moment resolved at least some of these problems, there was no confidence that they would not return.

The redirection of investment capital into automobiles and other rubber-wheeled vehicles thus became the lynchpin of the transformation of

American transit policy. This private decision, made by the business elite in the context of the search for maximum profit, constrained and conditioned all later policies—public and private—relating to transportation.

CORPORATE STRATEGY AND STATE POLICY: THE FALL OF MASS TRANSPORTATION

The fall of public mass transportation did not immediately follow the redirection of investment capital. Indeed, after the initial rash of bank-ruptcies following World War I, conditions within the transit industry sta-bilized. The idea that more autos meant less public transit, an idea prominent in Federal Railway Commission testimonials and among modern historians, seems a gross oversimplification. Between 1918 and 1927 the ridership increased for a substantial proportion of major U.S. cities: a moderate 3 percent in St. Louis, a substantial 10 percent in Chicago, and a whopping 37 percent in New York (Barrett, 1976, pp. 418–419; memo of the effect of the automobile on patronage, APTA File No. 075.441). Decreases in public transportation usage occurred mostly in cities with less than 500,000 popula-tion (Dewees, 1970, p. 569). In cities where modernization was undertaken, public transit trips increased at a higher rate than automobile trips (25 percent compared to 17 percent) (*Transportation Journal*, 1970, pp. 4–5).

The crisis in public transportation had been arrested. In spite of finan-cial disasters, rising fares, and the first wave of disinvestment, rail transit was surviving and was cheaper than the operation of private automobiles (St. Clair, 1980).

This stabilization in ridership and operating costs did not, however, save the rail equipment manufacturers from financial catastrophe (Hilton and Due, 1960). The transfer of investment capital into rubber-wheeled vehicles (i.e., cars and buses) crippled technological innovation and product development in the street railway industry. The steel industry reoriented its production toward the growing auto and construction (highway and factory) sectors, further undermining the economic viability of public transport. Reflecting the lack of flat demand in trolley equipment, electrical manufac-turing shifted its emphasis—both in terms of production and innovation—from machinery to consumer goods production (Duncan and Lieberson, 1970). As a result of these processes street railways had become econom-ically peripheral by 1930.

Meanwhile, economic centralization and concentration in new growth sectors—auto, oil, and rubber—proceeded. The first successful commercial automobile in the United States had been introduced in 1893, and by 1908 there were 253 companies manufacturing automobiles in the United States (Flink, 1970; p. 302). As centralization took place, this number shrunk rapidly. As early as 1912, 7 companies accounted for over half of the U.S. production. There were only 108 companies by the early 1920s and only 44 in 1929.

The new car market was saturated and this saturation produced nu-merous crises and corporate reorganizations (Chandler, 1968; Weiss, 1961;

Kennedy, 1941; Seltzer, 1928).[3] Despite attempts to produce more rapid turnover through frequent style changes, extensive advertising, franchise distribution, and cheap financing, the market did not expand sufficiently to absorb the production of the major companies (Flink, 1970; pp.145, 152). Henry Ford was wrong: the United States could not be motorized simply by producing cheap automobiles. By 1927, Chevrolet had overtaken Ford, not because it had produced a cheaper product but because of Alfred Sloan's innovations in product diversification, marketing, and auto purchase financing (Flink, 1975; Chandler, 1968). But Sloan was also wrong: refinements in automobile production and distribution did not accomplish full motorization either.

The competition from public carriers simply would not disappear. The resiliency of mass transportation in the 1920s exacerbated the automobile industry crisis by drawing off potential customers. The stagnation of automobile demand, overproduction, and general indicators of economic crisis all pointed toward the necessity of a new corporate strategy: the destruction of urban rail transit. This destruction was in effect accomplished by ripping up rails and replacing streetcars with buses and by simultaneously displacing thousands of transit passengers into automobiles.[4] The replacement of trolleys with buses guaranteed that public transportation routes could be used by private autos, that levels of service could be changed quickly and that the auto industry would be in control of product development and manufacture of mass transit.

The auto industry complex (i.e., the auto, oil, rubber, and associated industries) used various methods to promote conversion from rail transit to buses: direct acquisition of electrical mass transit companies, which allowed them to unilaterally convert to rubber-wheeled vehicles, the establishment of noncompetitive supply contracts, which required transit firms that bought some buses to buy only buses thereafter, partial ownership in transit lines by corporate officers or managers, which allowed them to pressure mass transit into conversion, financial leverage through lenders who refused loans for rail transit, and various trade association activities. The long and complicated history of this transformation of urban transportation is detailed elsewhere (Snell, 1974; Yago, 1980).

The consequences of the conversion were disastrous for mass transportation. The bus systems abandoned previously established routes, either because they were unprofitable or because the companies sought to encourage automobile usage. Thus the area served by public transportation shrank significantly and many riders were left with no alternative to the automobile. Generally, buses were also less appealing to passengers than streetcars (St. Clair, 1980).

Public transportation equipment manufacturers and their representatives (e.g., Dr. Thomas Conway, the Brill Company, and Westinghouse) opposed these conversions. Throughout the thirties, Conway called meetings of industry groups and the concerned public to defend rail lines and to popularize the use of modernized streetcars that would reduce operating costs. These efforts were not successful, since the resources—both political and economic—available to General Motors and its allied companies were far greater than those of the rail transit sector. The industrial groups that might have opposed this corporate strategy either had become dependent upon this growth coalition or had little remaining power.

STATE POLICY: THE COMMITMENT TO MOTORIZATION

Extensive federal involvement in transportation did not occur until the New Deal, when, in 1934, the federal government began its first highway-building programs. Although these programs involved relatively modest levels of funding, they firmly established the principles that the federal government rather than states, would be primarily responsible for the construction of the highway infrastructure and that this would be the major focus of federal involvement in mass transportation. The National Resources Planning Board and the Reconstruction Finance Corporation, two of the key New Deal agencies, as well as the Bureau of Public Roads, developed policies that ultimately facilitated motorization after World War II.[5] Local and regional planning authorities were encouraged to draft proposals for highway projects with federal assistance.

Business was a major force in all these early developments. The records of the National Resources Planning Board show that chambers of commerce, manufacturers associations, and other business organizations had been critical of the road-building programs of individual states and local communities and these same groups also formulated the recommendations that ultimately emerged from federal planning agencies. Industry-backed planners and engineers argued that new roads should be built parallel to railroad rights-of-way—thus competing with, rather than complementing, rail transport. As transportation planning came under the direction of the National Resources Planning Board, during the 1930s, automobile, oil, and rubber company representatives typically were overrepresented on both the state and federal level (Yago, 1984).

On the local level measures were initiated to reduce the expense and inconvenience of private auto ownership. Parking regulations were adapted to the needs of auto usage (Barrett, 1976, pp. 400–401; *Motor Age*, December 1923). Accommodation to the automobile, through new taxes, improved roads, expanded parking facilities, extensive surveys, and systems of regulation, became the goal of local planning policy. In the process, the neglect of public transportation development and maintenance became institutionalized—systems were neglected, no funds were allocated for rail transit feasibility studies or for product development, and right-of-way was not established or preserved.

The impetus for local regulation came from the emerging profession of urban and traffic planners as well as automobile interests, motor clubs, and central city business interests worried about adverse effects of congestion on central city shopping. Planning was most reactive, that is, it sought to respond to problems created by the new emphasis on rubber-wheeled transportation, rather than to anticipate needs and attempt to meet them. This limited, problem-solving conception of planning left urban development particulary vulnerable to the corporate strategy of opposing mass transportation, since only a systematic overall plan could have countered the impact of disinvestment from public transport. Without such a plan, local and state government could only work with, and ameliorate, the motorized reality presented to them by the automobile industry and its allies.

What developed was a largely unsystematic, almost accidental, relationship between cities and transportation systems. Instead of comprehensive, long-range, publicly determined goals for city and regional development (with plans for transportation systems that complemented and facilitated overall urban development), cities have grown in a haphazard way, while transportation systems have been incomplete and/or inadequate (Meyer, Kain, and Wohl, 1972; Ornati, 1968; Davies and Albaum, 1976). Thus, for example, urban areas were structured without any concern for minimizing the need for unnecessary travel. To the extent that there has been urban planning, that planning has involved a surrender to the automobile. As Flink (1975) observed, "Thus, instead of attempting to discourage the use of private passenger cars in cities, politicians and city planners adopted the expensive and ultimately unworkable policy of unlimited accommodation to the motor car. That American life would conform to the needs of automobility rather than vice versa was obvious by the early 1920s (p. 164)." In this way, the choices made by the corporate elite—to shift investment from street railways to rubber-wheeled vehicles—became a political given, a structural constraint, which directed and delineated the shape of local policy.

At the same time, the automobile industry and its allies operated in a more instrumental way at the federal level. The industrial coalition that promoted bus conversions and motorization also organized the highway lobby, which informally developed national transportation policy. As the Automobile Manufacturers Association itself admitted:

> From the beginning of the automobile industry in the U.S., vehicle manufacturers have recognized their direct stake in highway development and financing policies. Both through industry-wide programs and through leadership by industry executives, continuous activities have been carried out through the years. (Memo of AMA Committee on Highway Economics, November 1, 1959, GM files R-89)

The automobile complex has determined and designed the American highway system. As early as 1913, the National Automobile Chamber of Commerce joined with tire, parts, oil, and cement companies to map and promote the first transcontinental highway. These corporations contributed money to build "seedling miles" of the highway to demonstrate its utility. They also contributed to the highway promotion work of the American Automobile Association. The first federal aid program for the highways was begun "after an industry delegation met with President Woodrow Wilson and won his support for proposed federal highway legislation" (Memo to AMA Committee).

In 1932, General Motors president Alfred P. Sloan, Jr., established the

National Highway Users Conference as the main highway lobbying organization, with support from trucking groups and bus associations, as well as from the rubber, petroleum, and automobile industries. The 2,800 lobbying groups associated with the conference were decisive in creating the highway trusts, which freed highway funds from competing with other state budgetary items and insulated highway building (both fiscally and politically) from effective opposition.

The composition of the National Advisory Commission for Highway Policy, which officially designed the Federal Highway Act of 1956, illustrates the degree of transportation industry control of the policy-formation process. Its members were W. A. Roberts, president of Allis Chalmers Manufacturing Company, a major construction equipment manufacturer; Stephen D. Bechtel, president of Bechtel Corporation, a major construction company; S. Sloan Colt, president of Bankers Trust Company, a New York money market bank; former General Lucius D. Clay, chairman of Continental Can, which was not directly involved in transportation; and David Beck, president of the International Brotherhood of Teamsters, the nonbusiness member who nevertheless shared the motorized transport perspective of the other members.

A series of conferences in the 1950s and 1960s sponsored by the Automotive Safety Foundation (which was founded by the Automobile Manufacturers Association) and the National Committee on Urban Transportation outlined issues to be considered by state and local officials, traffic engineers, and city planners in the process of transportation planning. The recommendations that emerged were virtually the only coherent policy available to localities, and this fact reinforced and expanded the established pattern of auto domination (Holmes, 1973, pp. 381–383). Moreover, because the federal government financed up to 90 percent of the costs of local highway building if such construction conformed to its guidelines, local highway agencies had little fiscal, legislative, or administrative discretion in the implementation of freeway, primary, secondary, and feeder route construction. Highway engineers could therefore counter any coalition of municipalities or civic groups committed to policy alternatives such as combined rail and motor systems, by invoking the constraints of federal law.

Highway planning thus moved the locus of transportation policy to the federal level, and it insulated the commitment to the automobile from the sphere of public decision making. The 1962 and 1965 Highway Acts called for "comprehensive, cooperative, and continuous planning," at the federal level, and this phrasing reflected the lack of input of the localities affected. Although public hearings were, of course, held, they served primarily to test local opposition, develop grass roots support, and construct a viable political strategy for completing already-planned highways (Morehouse, 1965).[5]

The developments just discussed definitively removed highway policy from the political arena. A recent study by the U.S. Department of Transportation found that, in 24 of the 30 communities examined, the initiative for route selection, project staffing, and planning was taken by state (rather than local) agencies, working through appointive (not elected) metropolitan planning bodies (U.S. Department of Transportation, 1976). And public opposition to highway construction in the 1960s resulted in several court rulings, which confirmed highway location as a strictly technical decision, not subject to the preferences of local residents.

THE PATTERN OF POLICY FORMATION

The history of urban transportation policy vividly illustrates the dual aspects of policy formation discussed in Chapter 6. Partly, public policy has been determined by the structural constraints placed on it by the investment decisions of private mass transport and motorized vehicle industries, and partly it has reflected the direct influence of these industries on government. The crisis of mass transportation in the early part of this century resulted from overexpansion and dysfunctional route selection by private companies (often seeking speculative profit in construction and real estate). These developments were sanctioned by local governments because they were, for long periods, politically dominated by the transportation industry. This was an instance of direct intervention.

In the 1920s, the flood of investment in rubber-wheeled transport undermined the industrial base of rail transit. This, together with the auto industry acquisition and transformation of street railways into bus companies, left local and state government with little choice but to acquiesce in the motorization processes, since the cost of preserving rail transit was beyond their means. To prevent such an attempt, however, the auto industry mounted a major lobbying effort, which successfully pressed for enactment of industry-sponsored legislation favoring automobiles. Here structural constraint and direct business intervention combined to determine public policy.

Finally, national highway building also reflected both forms of policy formation. The government had few viable ways to support the atrophied mass transit systems. At the same time, the automobile complex sponsored highway building legislation, lobbied effectively for it, placed its representatives on planning bodies, and oversaw final enforcement. This combination of structural constraint and political intervention was so successful that a deep institutional bias was created for government construction, insulated from the normal political process.

THE RESURGENCE OF MASS RAIL TRANSIT

As discussed in the beginning of this chapter, the domination of the automobile has had a devastating effect on America's cities. Each day traffic comes to a standstill as hoards of private, mostly single-passenger, vehicles fight for a space during rush hours. Noise and exhaust fumes fill the air. The suburbs have receded even further, as more and more land has been covered with concrete. The fiscal status of central cities has become chronically problematic.

These and related problems have profoundly affected major corporations as well. For example, financial firms whose portfolios have come to include major commercial real estate investment have faced the possibility of huge losses from the decline of central business district property values; corporations have had difficulty recruiting employees to headquarters located in congested downtown areas, and poor public transportation has undermined the viability of downtown merchants.

Some farsighted corporate planners, in trying to respond to these adverse consequences for business, have concluded that the auto-highway system has reached its practical limits in many urban areas. What was once useful for corporate capitalism has become dysfunctional. As a consequence they have begun supporting a variety of schemes for both urban redevelopment and new urban mass transportation systems. In the 1960s and 1970s, ambitious high-tech rail systems such as the Bay Area Rapid Transit (BART) system in San Francisco and the Metro in Washington, D.C., were built—not in response to popular pressure or public opinion, but at the initiative of major corporations (Whitt, 1982).

Despite claims that these new systems would ease air pollution, reduce traffic congestion, benefit low-income groups, and, in general, make it easier to get around the city, their actual effects were minimal (Whitt, 1982). Thus, ironically, battles have developed in city politics (including San Francisco, Los Angeles, and Washington) in which corporate leaders press for mass transit, while many voters do not see the need for an expensive new system.

Conflicts have also arisen between the remaining elements of the highway lobby and the new forces for street railways, both over methods of financing costly transit development and over where routes will be laid. A particularly significant contradiction has arisen over the issue of tapping highway funds for mass transportation. The structural constraints built into the highway acts have become fetters on the process of policy change and have limited access to the capital needed for a shift in transit policy.

By the early 1980s, political paralysis had occurred: after two decades of agitation, and the development of model systems in San Francisco and Washington, construction of urban transit had virtually halted. The urban crisis, precipitated to a considerable degree by automobilization, left local governments without capital, while the larger recession made federal support equally impractical.

The cycle of contradictions had been perpetuated. The pursuit of short-term profit, which had determined both private investment and, ultimately, public policy, had also undermined the long-term profitability of the automobile complex. New plans and investment strategies had arisen to restore profits, but this corporate scramble failed to meet the needs of commuters and cities for rational, coordinated, efficient public transportation.

NOTES

1. Contrary to some current interpretations, the movement at the turn of the century for public ownership of transit, utilities, ice manufacturing, and so forth was not simply a middle class movement of the Progressive Era. Yago's (1984) archival research concerning the "Traction Question" in Chicago demonstrates extensive working class mobilization (including com-

munity groups, socialist and people's parties, and religious groups) in alliance with many small business interests in the community against what was called "the exploitation of people's needs" including food, transportation, and electricity (Vickers, 1934; Goodwyn, 1976). For information on popular oppositional movements regarding transit during this period see, for San Francisco, Bean (1968); New Orleans, Jackson (1969); Baltimore, Crooks (1968); Detroit, Holli (1969); Cincinnati, Miller (1960); Philadelphia, Warner (1976); and Milwaukee, MacShane (1975). Cheape (1980) presents additional analyses of these referenda and mass protests in Boston, New York, and Philadelphia, demonstrating that their demands were ultimately transformed into regulatory management procedures.

2. The auto industry remained nonunion until 1937 (Guerin, 1979).

3. For descriptions of the market saturation problems of the major growth industries of this period (auto, oil, rubber, etc.) see Weiss (1961), Flink (1975; pp. 148–150), and Sloan (1962; p. 208).

4. The most important insights regarding the decline of public transit have come from the investigation by Bradford Snell, *American Ground Transport* (Hearing before the Subcommittee of Antitrust and Monopoly, U.S. Senate, Washington, D.C., 1974). Much of the present discussion is based on Snell's thorough study.

Despite Snell's works, unsubstantiated claims about highway transportation's technological superiority persist in both popular and scientific works. Dunn (1981), for example, stated: "But the economics of the declining transit industry would have dictated much of this switch [from streetcars to buses] in any case, since buses were cheaper to purchase and operate (in the short run) than trolleys" (p. 75). Concerning automobiles, Altschuler (1980) argued: "In the course of achieving this overwhelming dominance, the automobile appears to have become [the least] expensive mode for most purposes, as well as the more rapid, convenient, and flexible" (p. 21). Neither Dunn nor Altschuler provides any evidence for these claims. In fact, the evidence from Germany as well as the United States, detailed by Yago (1980, 1983), supports just the opposite case. David St. Clair (1980; pp.579–600) examined aggregate data from trade sources to compare costs and profits of motor buses, electric buses, and electric streetcars for the years 1935–1950. He concluded that "motor buses were consistently the least economical transit vehicle during the period 1935–1950." (p. 600). St. Clair's study, which includes consideration of both capital and operating costs, is the most definitive look at comparative modal costs.

5. The Reconstruction Finance Corporation was quite active in supporting bus conversion programs during the 1930s (APTA Files, No. 900.01, 308.01, various city files). These subsidized loans aided the corporate strategy of bus conversions. See also U.S. National Resources Committee, 1940.

6. Top officials recognized that this bureaucratic control of highway planning helped to de-democratize, as numerous policy memoranda demonstrate (BPR Policy and Procedure Memo, 20-8, August 10, 1956; see also Morehouse, 1965). This is part of a broader trend analyzed by urban political scholars, who have demonstrated the loss of administrative power by large urban populations due to organizational changes within the state and local bureaucracies.

PART III
The Business Elite as a Policy-Making Class

Introduction

Most of the literature concerned with policy formation in the North American and Western European societies assumes, without offering evidence, that governments are capable of imposing their institutional will on all other sectors of society. This assumption of governmental preeminence, which is made not only by standard accounts but also by the most critical Marxist analyses, has diverted attention away from a careful exploration of the actual policy-making capabilities of modern states. In Part II of this volume, we have reassessed the role of the state to define its more limited place in the nexus of policy formation. In Part III, we extend this logic to explore the ways in which policy formation takes place outside of government structure.

The underlying theme of this part rests on the sometimes conflicting needs of corporate leaders to advance the interests of their particular business and attend to the interests of the corporate community as a whole. The corporate leaders who become enmeshed in this dilemma tend ultimately to rise above their particular interests to form a class which (episodically) acts in a unified and cohesive way.

The construction of the business elite as a class implies both the seeking out of collective self-interest and the use of the business and other institutions as tools of this interest. Ultimately, the business class must forge ties with government; it does so both through the application of institutional constraints and through personnel transfers which place members of the business class in positions of decision-making authority in government. This personal involvement of members of the business elite in nonbusiness institutions is not limited to government. Most realms of American society are dominated by a handful of significant institutions in which the business elite is actively involved. In higher education, for example, a small group of universities (led by the Ivy League Schools) pioneer curriculum, dominate research, and train those who will staff and lead the other colleges. The boards of trustees of these colleges are populated by business leaders. A few foundations (notably the Ford Foundation) dominate the nonpublic funding of research in most disciplinary areas. These foundations are guided by boards of directors drawn largely from the business elite. A small number of important charities (led by the United Way) determine the main foci of social altruism. The local and national governing boards of these groups are led by corporate executives. The American Medical Association acts as a coordinating body for medical care in America, aided and sometimes dominated by the drug and medical equipment industries. The leadership of the AMA has intimate ties to the largest medical companies. Public information is divided into separate realms such as books, newspapers, and television, but each sector is dominated by a small number of major companies whose leaders are integrated into the corporate elite.

It is tempting, in the managerialist tradition, to see each of these sectors as governed by an independent elite which enters into negotiations and relationships with other elites on an equal or unequal basis. In this conception, the domination particular elites exercise over their own realms does not lead to coordination among them and centralization of power. But the mechanisms we reviewed in exploring the relationship of business to government are more general, and they imply a further set of coordinating mechanisms which tie these apparently independent institutions into the coordinative apparatus—however loosely bound—of the business elite.

These mechanisms are easily summarized but difficult to analyze. Essentially, the constraints resulting from centralized decision making over capital flows create relationships between business institutions and the institutions of education, philanthropy, information, and so on. Further ties are constructed which bring personnel from the inner circle of the business elite into contact with, and authority over, decision makers in these other institutions, while transferring leaders from these sectors into the center of the business world. This set of interinstitutional exchanges and interlocks allows the business elite to episodically coordinate the broadest range of societal sectors and hence to implement societywide social policy.

In this sense, the business elite, and the inner circle, constitutes a ruling class. It is a ruling class because it sits in the leadership of the main institutions of society, and because it alone has access to the broad range of institutional leadership necessary to coordinate full-scale, societywide policy. In Part III, we introduce and explore some of the mechanisms that allow for at least occasional orchestration of many institutions that are apparently segregated from one another.

Chapter 9 describes the two ingredients that are crucial for this coordinated structure. First, as discussed earlier, the interchange and interlocking among corporations places certain executives in leadership roles of several large corporations simultaneously. This process promotes classwide rationality—the sense of the broadest interest of the business class as a whole. Thus, the members of the corporate inner circle pursue this class interest, over and above the interest of the specific corporations to which they are connected.

Second, inner circle members, in addition to embracing a particular viewpoint, actually become links that ultimately permit coordination of policy. They involve themselves in a broad range of societal institutions, precisely because they understand the impact of these institutions on the health and welfare of business. Not only are they key members of policy-forming institutions and frequent travelers on the government-business shuttlebus, they also serve on the boards of trustees of major universities, hospitals, philanthropies, foundations, and other nonprofit, nongovernment institutions. As a consequence, they become a structural link between these institutions and are able to orchestrate their activities.

Chapter 10 explores the consequences of classwide rationality and interinstitutional interlocks for policy-making within the business community of Saint Louis in the 1960s and 1970s, when businesses invested capital and savings from Saint Louis in out-of-state locales. This process of disinvestment was mediated by Saint Louis based inner circle members who participated in the creation of investment policy at major banks, and it reflected their understanding that the interest of the national and local business elite was not consonant with the continued growth of the Saint Louis metropolitan area. This case study, though it is located strictly within the realm of business decision-making, illustrates the impact of classwide rationality on our society as a whole, since disinvestment in the older industrial cities of America has become a major social problem and a major social controversy.

Chapter 11 illustrates the consequences of the same set of processes in the realm of educational policy. It begins by discussing the structural arrangements that gave institutional life to the eugenics movement in the early part of this century. The eugenics movement combined with the flow of capital from the inner circle into the educational sector to facilitate the development of measurement devices such as the IQ test. The subsequent introduction and proliferation of IQ testing in the public school system as the foundation for educational tracking was, like the initial development of such tests, made possible by inner circle funding and through the coordination of many disparate institutions, both within and outside government. In this case, corporate interest became congealed into educational structures as diverse as Columbia Teachers College and the New York public schools, and became expressed in a fundamental premise of modern education.

Chapter 12 analyzes how changes in an academic field—and, ultimately in the perceptions of the American public—are traceable to the hegemony of the corporate elite. Specifically, it looks at the Ford Foundation's efforts, beginning in the late 1940s, to restructure political science to meet inner circle needs. The perception of public apathy and the fear that such apathy would nurture unrest resulted in the creation of an ambitious new program to study problems and propose solutions. This required a behavioralist approach to political science, and largely as a result of Ford's institution-building efforts, this approach, which had previously been unimportant within the field, soon came to dominate it.

The institutional organization of American society is constrained by the dynamics of capitalism, by the presence in leadership positions of members of the business elite who constitute a ruling class, and by the congealed interest of the business elite in the ways in which structures are created and perpetuated. At the same time, this institutional structure never completely constrains the desires and actions of ordinary citizens, and the friction and alienation which has always characterized American society reflects the misfit between the structure of institutions and the needs of the country as a whole. The tension created by this contradiction of interest is the juice from which reforms flow and change occurs. The changes become integrated into the institutional structure, but they then reconstitute themselves as further frictions and further upheavals. The essays in this section illustrate both the institution building that congeals business interest and the tensions that force a constant process of change.

9

The Inner Circle and the Political Voice of Business

Michael Useem

The political concerns of members of the corporate elite are affected by three competing principles. These principles have fundamentally different implications for the ways in which business managers participate in policy formation.

The *upper class principle* asserts that the corporate elite is drawn from a social network of established wealthy families, which share a distinct culture, occupy a preeminent social status, and are unified through inter-marriage and common experience in exclusive settings ranging from board-ing schools to private clubs. This principle is the point of departure for Baltzell's (1958, 1964, 1966, 1979) studies of metropolitan and national business aristocracies, for Domhoff's (1967, 1970a, 1970b, 1974, 1979, 1983) inquiries into America's social upper class, and for Collins' (1971, 1979) treatment of upper class cultural dominance. Although many mem-bers of the upper class also occupy positions in large companies, these corporate locations do not critically define their political action. Rather, the main political objectives of such individuals are to preserve the social bound-aries of their class, maintain the intergenerational transmission of privileged position, and protect the wealth on which privileged station is based. Control of the corporation is only one means to these ends, though it has emerged as the singularly most important means. Illustrative of this line of argument,

Baltzell, for example, states that one "of the functions of upper class solidarity, is the retention, within a primary group of families, of the final-decision-making positions within the social structure. As of the first half of the twentieth century in America, the final decisions affecting the goals of the social structure have been made primarily by members of the financial and business community" (1966, p. 273).

The *corporate principle* suggests that a senior manager's primary political concern is not with the interests of his or her family, but with the welfare of the corporation. Upper class allegiances are largely incidental, since any family loyalties have long since become faint by comparison with the executives' single-minded drive to advance the interests of their respective firms. By implication, corporate leaders enter politics primarily to promote conditions favorable to the profitability of their own corporations.

The *classwide principle* asserts that top corporate managers are more influenced in their political thinking by their position in a set of interrelated networks transecting large corporations. Acquaintanceship circles, interlocking directorates, webs of interfirm ownership, and major business associations are among the central strands of these networks (see Chapter 5). Entry into the transcorporate networks is contingent on successfully reaching the executive suite of some large company, and it may be facilitated by old school ties and the other trappings of old wealth. But both corporate credentials and upper class upbringing become subordinated to a new political logic of classwide organization. The central participants in this overarching network are prone to favor policies that coincide with the interests of the largest corporations as a collectivity. Some of these classwide policies will inevitably be opposed by corporate managers whose companies they might adversely affect. Nevertheless, there is at least a group of senior corporate managers with some awareness of, and capacity to promote, the broader needs of large companies.

These three principles thus have significantly different implications for, and make significantly different predictions regarding, the role of business in American policy formation. If the upper class principle prevails, top company managers fight against confiscatory inheritance taxes and state-mandated invasions of its club sanctuaries, even if their actions work against the political interests of their corporations. If the corporate principle prevails—that is, if corporate managers lobby primarily for policies most favorable to their own enterprises—the business elite would often be divided and the resulting programs would not necessarily serve business as a whole. The broader political interests of business would not be well served; in the succinct phrasing of Vogel (1978): what is "rational from the perspective of the individual firm [is often] irrational from the perspective of the economic interests of business as a whole" (p. 68).

If classwide rationality prevails, however, social policies far more coincident with the overarching interests of big business should arise. This chapter will suggest that the classwide principle is increasingly important in shaping the relations of business with government. Supportive evidence is drawn from a range of primary and secondary information sources. Systematic data were taken from three large-scale national samples of senior executives and directors of large companies, and qualitative data were derived from personal interviews conducted with 57 executives and directors of large American companies.[1] Additional background information was obtained from open-ended interviews conducted with several dozen well-placed and well-informed observers including, e.g., an executive with the London office of an American petroleum company, a financial journalist, and staff members of the Business Committee for the Arts, the Business Roundtable, and of several organizations devoted to research on business.

This interview data was complemented by a wide range of written materials. Useful sources included documents, many unpublished, obtained from organizations such as the Business Roundtable; annual reports and other company publications; studies produced by organizations that service business, such as the Conference Board, or that service antibusiness movements, such as the Corporate Data Exchange; and, of course, the business press, especially *Business Week* and the *Wall Street Journal*. Finally, the discussion has drawn on other studies of corporations and corporate management.

The present chapter focuses on a critical strand of the classwide business organization that facilitates collective political action by business. That strand is an overarching and diffusely structured network of shared directorships among large companies. The network has helped define a group of senior company executives who are in a position to aggregate and promote general business political concerns. The creation of this circle of top corporate managers has been the critical ingredient in facilitating the emergence of classwide political behavior.

SHARED CORPORATE DIRECTORSHIPS AND THE CREATION OF THE INNER CIRCLE

Interviews with the executives confirm that specific economic relations among large corporations are of little moment in the forging of shared directorships. The logic of the interlocking directorate is not reducible to particularistic ties; it is an expression of what can be termed a company's "external scan." The scale of large companies makes their effective management dependent on a continuous monitoring of new developments in government, labor relations, markets, technology, and business practices. An external scan includes a search for profitable investment opportunities, better stock-option plans, new charitable contribution schemes, and a wide range of other potential activities. Companies rely on many procedures for enhancing their external scan, including the maintenance of public affairs offices and special staffs responsible for producing systematic assessments of the political environment (Korbin, 1979a, 1979b). Perhaps the most important means by which senior managers keep themselves informed, however, are personal contacts and experience. In a study of American companies operating abroad, for instance, Bauer et al. (1972) concluded that "knowledge of foreign economic affairs came either from the most general news sources, or more vividly, from correspondence and personal experience" (p. 470).

Few experiences, according to corporate executives, are more useful for current intelligence on the business environment than service on the board of directors of another major corporation. Learning about the practices and experiences of another large company, and hearing about policies of still other companies from the other outside directors, was a major concern of virtually all the executives interviewed who sat on several boards. The president and chief executive of a large American manufacturing firm, who also served on the board of two other industrial companies among the nation's top 500, commented:

> I think the most significant benefits of serving on the board [of another company] are input you get from the board and from the other board members as well as the CEO of the board you serve on. And the manner in which that corporation addresses similar policy-making areas versus the way you address them in your own company—such things as strategic planning, personnel development, budgeting, internal controls, managing pension funds under ERISA [Employee Retirement Income Security Act]—you are getting a significant, valuable, diverse opinion on very timely subject matter which can help you make better judgments in your own business. That's really the most significant thing . . . [it's] the exposure of being on a board of directors and being in the company of those who are your equal or betters in many areas of expertise.

Summing up an evaluation universally expressed, this executive offered one final judgment: "If you want to just bottom-line it, it's a hell of a tool for top management education." Said another American executive: "You're damn right it's helpful to be on several boards. It extends the range of your network and acquaintances, and your experience. That's why you go on a board, to get something as well as give. . . . [You get] a more cosmopolitan view—on economic matters, regional differences, international [questions] these days. It just broadens your experience, the memory bank that you have to test things against."

Recognition of the importance of this external scan is reflected in company policy in several ways. First, executives who are being groomed for ascent into the most senior company positions are encouraged to take on outside directorships as a means of enhancing their awareness of the company's environment. Several chief executive officers, for instance, reported that when they were offered outside directorships that they could not accept, they recommended the appointment of another executive in their company who showed considerable promise for eventual promotion to chief executive or chairman.

A second indication of the importance accorded to external scan is the fact that outside directorships are maintained despite the considerable internal costs such service places on a corporation. Senior managers experience extremely heavy demands on their time, and any absence from the day-to-day operations of a firm obviously requires compelling justification. Effective service on another board may consume as much as a day per month or even more: the typical outside director of a large corporation attends eight board meetings per year for each company on whose board he or she serves, requiring approximately two work weeks annually. Since outside directors of large American firms typically hold between three and four positions, two working months on average are taken by the outside service (Harris, 1977, p. 5). This level of "released time" must obviously have some recognized compensations for the individual's company. Few of the interviewed executives could point to specific gains in terms of enhanced relations with the interlocked companies, but virtually all asserted that their company deemed it a worthwhile investment in terms of enhanced business awareness of the directors involved.

As might be expected, then, it was also reported that a decision by a manager to join another board was not his or hers alone. Rather, a manager discussed such offers with colleagues, and the final decisions were made by the company. The response of one chief executive to a question of why he felt obliged to ask permission before joining another manufacturing board was typical: "Since it will involve some time away from the business . . . I think the board ought to make the judgment as to whether that particular company and industry and that amount of time would be beneficial to the corporation."

SOCIAL COHESION AND POLITICAL ACTION

The interlocking directorate thus maximizes the flow of information throughout the network. As we have seen, it largely originates in the need of individual corporations to have better information about the general environment. Yet, an unplanned and critical consequence is the formation of a communication network that helps a segment of the senior corporate management to overcome its atomization and to facilitate identification of its members' shared interest. The actual political role of this segment depends, however, on two related factors. The first is the degree of social cohesion among constituent members, and the second is the set of interests to which the segment is most strongly attached.

Some segments make little explicit contribution to the political process because they are internally atomized. Smaller firms facing highly competitive markets are a case in point; their managers rarely act in unison. Other segments are more unified but their immediate concerns are little related to the broadest concerns of business and at times are even contrary to them. Concentrated industrial sectors, such as petroleum or chemicals, can be viewed as a segment, and member firms are sufficiently united to have created trade associations that vigorously represent their positions in the political arena. Yet the limited foundation on which industrial-sector politics are based leads to circumscribed agendas that contribute little to classwide aggregation of business interests.

By contrast, those senior executives of the nation's largest firms who are also involved in the affairs of other large corporations possess both the cohesion and broader concerns necessary to promote the corporate community's general political interests. This inner circle of top managers has economic and social networks transcending major companies, insuring that its members comprehend the competing (and at times contradictory) problems faced by large enterprises. It is rooted in interests that go far beyond the parochial concerns of individual firms and sectors; and it possesses the organization necessary for it to act, albeit in a very imperfect fashion, as a politicized leading edge for large business as a whole.

However shortsighted or skewed its politics may be relative to some ideally defined standard, the inner circle comes far closer to expressing classwide political interests than any other group of business leaders. Disputes often arise over which strategies are the preferred solutions to a given problem (see, e.g., Chapter 13), but there is a decided tendency for the underlying interests to find some expression, however approximate, in the policy preferences that emerge.

Detailed consideration of the inner circle's internal cohesion is beyond the scope of the present chapter, but indicators point toward far greater social cohesion among its members than is present within the corporate elite as a whole. Consider, for instance, the participation of business leaders in the preeminent clubs of the great metropolitan business centers, such as the Century Association and Links in New York, and Pacific Union and the Bohemian Club in San Francisco. Though they have long been favored haunts of the upper class, in recent years most of the major clubs have come to be favored by (and to favor) business circles as well (Baltzell, 1964, pp. 362–374; Domhoff, 1974). If we divide our 3,105 American executives and directors (see note 1) according to the number of large corporations on whose boards they serve, those who have three or more directorships—and who may thus be considered to belong to the inner circle—are two to three times more likely to be drawn into club life than business leaders attached to a single company. Similarly, those with three or more directorships are more likely to be upper class descendants, according to such measures as attendance at an elite boarding school (e.g., St. Paul's or Groton), possession of great personal wealth, and appearance in the *Social Register*, the unrivaled roster of America's first families (also see Soref, 1976; Useem, 1978).

Through analogous procedures, it is established that the inner circle is more active politically than the remainder of the business elite. Political participation takes several forms: service on the numerous commissions and boards that provide formal counsel to the federal government (see Part II); leadership in the major business associations most directly oriented toward the promotion of public policies on behalf of all large business (Chapter 7 and 13); and financial support for political candidates (Chapter 6 and 13). Again, comparing members of the inner circle to other business leaders, the former appear three to five times more often on advisory committees of U.S. federal agencies (such as the National Industrial Energy Council of the U.S. Department of Commerce). In 1976, for instance, only 3 percent of the American managers outside the dominant segment served on a federal advisory committee, whereas 11 percent of those in the inner circle held such appointments. Similar participation disparities are also obtained in the case of leadership in the preeminent general business associations, notably the Business Roundtable, Business Council, Committee for Economic Development, and Council on Foreign Relations. Members of the inner circle thus take a leading role in shaping the associations' policies and lobbying with government on their behalf (Useem, 1978, 1979a, 1980b, 1984).

In addition to its greater personal political participation, the inner circle is also more active in soliciting and contributing financial backing for political candidates, parties, and institutions it supports. Koenig (1979) reports that multiple directors of large U.S. corporations were more likely than single directors to contribute to the presidential campaign in the 1972 election. Ratcliff and his associates found in a study of nearly 900 directors of 77 banks in the Saint Louis area that the level of their financial contributions to local, state, and national candidates in 1976–1979 varied according to the bankers' centrality to the local inner circle. Bankers holding multiple directorships with area corporations gave substantially more money to political candidates than did other bankers, and they tended to concentrate it more on Republican office seekers (Ratcliff et al., 1980, p. 19).

A study of corporate executives serving on university boards of trustees reveals that inner circle activism extends to nonprofit institutions as well (see also Chapter 11). In a survey of 341 colleges and universities, inner circle managers were found to be several times as likely as other business leaders to receive and accept invitations to serve on university governing boards. Moreover, while half of the inner circle had contributed $30,000 or raised $100,000 for their school, fewer than one in ten of the other corporate trustees had reached these goals (Useem, 1981).

This inner circle activism is, of course, time consuming for the leading participants. Senior business executives, laboring under staggering time demands from their own company, often must somehow attend government advisory committee meetings in Washington, participate in the committee deliberations of various business associations, and meet periodically with the governing board of their favorite hospital, university, or charity—in addition to, as we have seen, overseeing the operation of several other large corporations. Not surprisingly, in many instances, "civic duties become a more beastly burden for chief executives," as the *Wall Street Journal* (June 11, 1980) lamented. Statistics support the *Journal*'s impressions. A survey of 380 large corporation chairmen and presidents in 1975 found that better than 90 percent were associated with at least one philanthropic organization, and more than half served on the boards of five or more (Harris and Klepper, 1977, p. 1749). The weekly demand was, on average, 3 hours of company time and 3 hours of personal time, a total approaching 10 percent or more of the entire workweek (56 hours is the median workweek for chief executives of large corporations; Burck, 1976). Added to this is the Washington activity: two-thirds of the chief executives in another survey visited the capital at least every other week.

BUSINESS CONTACT WITH GOVERNMENT

These time demands are not balanced by tangible compensation; much of the advisory work with government, for instance, is unpaid and of little apparent immediate benefit to the firm whose managerial talents are being lent to the process. Shaping government policies in a fashion favorable to business is, of course, the ultimate return to a corporation. But a favorable outcome, at least in the case of formulating more general policies, benefits hundreds of other companies as well. What, then, are the corporate incentives for involving company directors in the production of a general "business good" which is not directly in the interest of the executives' firms?

One possible incentive may be the opportunity to secure a "company good" as a by-product of an executive's involvement in the activities. Some business leaders reported that they had accepted invitations to join certain government advisory boards because these invitations provided an opportunity for direct contact with federal agencies whose favor their companies desired. Thus, in some instances the benefits are tangible, if not immediate.

If this were the main consideration, however, those who occupy the interface between business and government could not be expected to represent classwide business interests to government. The network of contacts would be structured according to the specific concerns of individual firms, and the directors involved would emphasize company, not general business, political interests.

Another reason was offered, however, by many executives for their affiliations with government: most large corporations find value in a general assessment of the government environment. When asked if it was important for senior managers to have had government experience, a high-ranking executive of one of America's largest corporations offered this appraisal:

> We would not consider somebody [without such experience]; our belief is that to operate a modern business enterprise, you need some familiarity with the processes of government. . . . It is not so much the contacts that he might have made, but rather he can understand what the lobbyist is telling him, he can visualize in his mind's eye the intricate processes that have to take place [in Washington]. . . . The whole apparatus of government and how it works—it's of great benefit to the senior manager to understand that.

In this logic the specific government board that an executive joins is of less importance than its strategic location for contact with high government circles. As in the case of outside corporate directorships, then, government service is not primarily structured around the parochial concerns of individual companies. It is more diffusely spread across a range of positions so as to maximize a company's awareness of all major government trends. The resulting network is formed in a way that downplays expression of specific company concerns to government and encourages communication of their aggregated concerns. And this pattern of communication indeed prevails, at least according to the corporate executives' own reports. Special pleading, even circuitously expressed, is discouraged by informal norms. "A frank exchange of views" on broad economic policies of the moment, on the other hand, is expected.

Parochial concerns are further screened by an informal selection procedure related to the social foundation of the inner circle. Inner circle executives who have ongoing relations with government officials are often consulted about the composition of new government advisory panels, and occasionally even about the composition of new cabinets. This consultation may take the form of a request for evaluation of business names on a "short-list" or a solicitation of names to include on such a list. One executive described it this way:

> An incoming president has got to name a secretary of commerce, who, all other things being equal, should come out of the business world. The transition staff calls up Mr. CEO and says, "you got any ideas on who ought to be the Secretary of Commerce," and so you build a list. Then . . . you start testing it with [an] array of phone calls. A third party calls up and says that "we have on our list some potential secretaries of commerce, there's Bill Simon, I know he was a director of your company at one time, and I know you serve on a board with him. . . ."

When executives were asked to identify the criteria they applied in evaluating such candidates, they typically emphasized "character and integrity." When pressed to specify what they meant, they generally alluded to the capacity to transcend the immediate imperatives of one's own company and express a broader vision. The ability to bring forward information about the common concerns of a range of large corporations was deemed essential. Thus, one industrialist who had a long and distinguished record of service to the government, including several years as a top-ranking civilian appointee in the Department of Defense, and who sat on the boards of four major manufacturing firms at the time of an interview, named half a dozen prominent executives who typified the role of the business ambassador to the government as it ought to be played. These individuals were exemplary, in his view, because they "are down in Washington undertaking responsibilities beyond the requirements of their own operation. [They are] heading the [Business] Roundtable or the Business Council, and you see them willing to step out and accept public responsibility even while they will carry out their private responsibility."

Criteria utilized in determining whether a businessperson is capable of transcending parochial concerns and thus be worthy of nomination are both positional and behavioral. That is, judgments are based both on the person's service as a senior executive of a large company and as a director of other large corporations, and on his or her behavior in such settings as the Business Council or Business Roundtable. An executive who passes such scrutiny typically might first receive a minor governmental appointment and if effective in expressing a broader vision in that capacity, establish a reputation and eventually be brought into the front lines.

A reputation for objectivity is also valued by government officials. In describing the political role of three well-known chief executives, a senior manager of a major American utility firm suggested that these individuals, all current or former members of the Business Roundtable and Business Council, are typical of the executives to which government officials often turn: "If you follow guys who get around the network and who are authority figures in the network and have some currency in it—when you call them, first of all you get a straight answer, and secondly you get a pretty good piece of litmus paper."

The major business associations provide a forum for determining which corporate executives possess the breadth of wisdom that is needed to represent business as a whole; they also insure that those who move to the top will have continuing exposure to a full range of business opinion. Thus, when we consider the screening process, it is not surprising that the corporate executives in our large sample of managers located in the inner circle were two to five times more likely to be invited onto government advisory bodies if they also assumed active leadership roles in one of the major business associations (Useem, 1980b, 1984).

We have seen that the individual corporation's concern with monitoring its political environment leads senior executives to seek regularized contact with government. And the nature of the political scan generates a set of links favorable to the expression of generic viewpoints and unfavorable to special pleading. Government officials need not sort through a cacophony of competing demands from a thousand large companies, for much of the sorting has already been achieved before the demands are even presented. While the final product may not necessarily be a set of strategies that maximize business growth in the long run, it does represent an integrated approach to what a big business needs. Moreover, there is evidence that this vision, this generic viewpoint that is presented, is more accepting of government intervention and less rejecting of union power than would be a simple aggregation of business opinion, which suggests that the inner circle is sufficiently autonomous to draw its own conclusions about appropriate public policies. In short, the economic and social foundation of the inner circle shapes contact between business and government in a way that overcomes much of the atomization of business that would otherwise be the product of purely corporate principles of organization.

CONCLUSION

Classwide principles of organization are the product of inclusive and diffusely structured networks of intercorporate ownership and directorship linking concentrated units of business. These networks define a group of senior managers whose strategic location and internal coherence propel it into a political leadership role on behalf of all large business. Porter's (1965) description of the Canadian dominant segment could equally well have been developed for its American counterpart. He concludes that multiple directors linking large corporations "are the ultimate decision-makers and coordinators within the private sector of the economy. It is they who at the frontiers of the economic and political systems represent the interests of corporate power. They are the real planners of the economy" (p. 255).

Business leadership, then, is something far more than unorchestrated expression of opinion by the leaders of a thousand large corporations; business leadership is organized in a specific and complex fashion that has crucial implications for the kinds of policies it presents to government. As a result, more overall planning initiative is assumed by business, less by government. Government officials are presented with an integrated vision already developed by that section of the corporate elite best positioned to reconcile the competing demands. Of course, government and other decision makers are subjected to numerous other constraints and pressures, and there is no certainty that the business position will prevail. Nonetheless, the inner circle has an authoritativeness to its voice that cannot be easily ignored.

NOTES

1. The three samples are (*a*) 2,003 directors of America's 797 largest corporations in 1969 (sampling detail is reported in Useem, 1979a), (*b*) 3,105 senior executives and directors of 212 of the largest American corporations in 1977 (sampling detail on a slightly truncated set of these data is described in Useem, 1980b), and (*c*) 1,037 executives and directors of large American corporations who also served as university or college trustees in 1968 (Useem, 1978, 1981). Some points in the present discussion are based on unpublished analysis of the second data set prepared specifically for this chapter; other findings are drawn from analyses of all three data sets already reported in the above-cited articles.

The interviews required approximately one hour on average to complete, though they ranged in length from 45 minutes to well over two hours. All were undertaken in Boston and New York City during May, June, and August 1980. Interviews were requested with 162 American directors sampled from the second data set, which comprises the 60 largest manufacturing firms, the 50 manufacturing firms ranked 451st (by sales) and immediately below, and 102 of the largest companies in the financial, insurance, transportation, utility, and retail sectors. Half of the directors approached for an interview were on the board of at least two of the corporations included in the second sample above, and the other half were matched for company sector and size but only served on a single board. An additional geographic constraint was imposed to reduce the cost of personal interviewing: the directors were to have office locations in the metropolitan regions of Boston and New York City. Of those originally contacted for an interview, approximately two-thirds replied. Of these, 58 percent were interviewed, 31 percent turned down the request, and the remainder could not be interviewed for a variety of reasons (e.g., some agreed to the interview but were traveling abroad during the period of interviewing).

10

The Inner Circle and Bank Lending Policy
Richard Ratcliff

Part I of the book, and most of the major recent work on intercorporate networks, is intended to analyze the structure of economic power. Chapter 9 demonstrates that the inner circle of the elite is institutionally capable of promoting the general interests of the business community. The present chapter considers an example of the exercise of that power. In particular, it examines the ties that commercial banks in Saint Louis, Missouri, have networks of economic power and inner group social circles and documents how involvement in these networks substantially influences the bank's lending decisions. The chapter then looks at the repercussions of these decisions on Saint Louis.

The material in this chapter is critical to the perspective presented in the book, since our arguments about corporate networks and business-government relations, no matter how convincing, are unimportant unless we can demonstrate that these structures produce social policies which impact on the daily and yearly lives of individuals, communities, and the country as a whole. In focusing on the lending behavior of banks, this chapter is dealing with an area of economic behavior that clearly does have broad social implications, especially for contemporary urban problems.

As demonstrated in Part I, banks have a unique character as private enterprises: they have the function of accumulating funds from depositors throughout their communities and then making decisions on how this investment capital is to be allocated in the form of loans. Patterns of lending decisions can be assumed to represent policy priorities established by the officers of the bank and by its board of directors (Reed et al., 1976, p. 149). There is a broad range of demands for that capital and banks must determine which demands are met. As a result, they routinely influence "the allocation of real resources" in the society and, in effect, "what is produced, how it is produced, and to whom it is distributed" (Harvey, 1975, p. 125; see also Mintz and Schwartz, 1985).

Despite their official status as private, profit-seeking enterprises, banks therefore have a quasi-public character, which has long been recognized in this country. Louis Brandeis, writing over a half century ago, stated that because the "dependence of commerce and industry upon bank deposits as the common reservoirs of quick capital is so complete . . . deposit banking should be recognized as one of the businesses 'affected with a public interest'" (Brandeis, 1913, p. 15). Similarly, a modern textbook on banking states, "The major reason banks are chartered is to serve the credit needs of their communities. If this cannot be done, there is little justification for their existence" (Reed et al., 1976, p. 150). Government regulation of banking has also reflected the understood obligation of banks to meet community credit needs (U.S. Senate Committee on Banking, 1977).

Bank lending decisions are of particular importance in older urban areas such as Saint Louis, because bankers are repeatedly faced with choices between significant local investment opportunities, including both real estate and business finance, and other investment possibilities in more rapidly growing sections of the country (Ratcliff, 1980a, 1980b, 1980c). The resulting loan distributions of banks are thus related to issues of disinvestment within the metropolitan area (especially to such critical questions as the availability of capital for investments in local housing), and to the processes of stagnation and decline in older metropolitan areas (Bradford and Morino, 1977).

The research reported here is not based on any assumption that banks are inevitably the dominant forces in their relationships with other corporations. While the special character of banks as holders and distributors of capital makes them likely centers of class organization and coordination, both banks and corporations are decision-making nodes within larger networks of class interests. It is more useful, therefore, to focus on the inner circle, described by Useem in Chapter 9, which maintains ties to major public, quasi-public, and private nonprofit institutions as well as to the largest financial and industrial corporations. Members of the inner circle, because of their multiplex affiliations and consequent classwide mentality, are likely to maximize overall profits, rather than protect the welfare of particular companies. This view has been nicely expressed by Zeitlin:

> Neither "financiers" extracting interest at the expense of industrial profits nor "bankers" controlling corporations, but finance capitalists on the boards of the largest banks *and* corporations preside over banks' investments as creditors *and* shareholders organizing production,

sales, and financing, and appropriating the profits of their integrated activities. (1976, p. 900; emphasis in the original)

That is, both banks and corporations serve as vehicles for the classwide interests of the inner circle and, insofar as banks command capital flows and therefore constrain the behavior of industrial firms, they become instruments for its broad policy perspectives.

The general thesis guiding this research, therefore, is that the largest banks tend to operate, not only as profit-seeking enterprises in their own right, but also as the capital-accumulating appendages of the groups and interests within the class of which they are most closely connected. This dual character of banks is of course most relevant for those banks that are closely tied to the inner circle. Banks can therefore be expected to loan their funds in ways that reflect the structural position of their leaders (Ratcliff, 1980a, 1980b, 1980c).

The internal structure of the capitalist class can be analyzed along two dimensions of centrality: economic power and upper class social interaction. The dimension of economic power can be measured by the economic importance of the companies on whose boards an individual serves, while upper class social interaction is represented by his or her memberships in exclusive private upper class organizations (Ratcliff et al., 1979). While the association of the first dimension with greater capital demands is apparent, research has also shown how upper class social ties are important in integrating the sometimes divergent economic interests of leading capitalists (Domhoff, 1970a; Baltzell, 1958).

Our argument, then, is that banks whose directors are members of the inner circle (who are closely tied to centers of either economic power or upper class social interaction, and especially those tied to both) should concentrate their lending with capitalist borrowers similarly located in the class structure; that is, corporate loans should dominate their loan portfolios. In contrast, banks whose directors are not part of the inner circle can be expected to be subject to a different range of demands for capital, as well as a set of opportunities less concentrated in the corporate sphere; as a consequence, their loans will be less exclusively directed toward major capitalist borrowers. One very important implicaton of this pattern is that the more marginal banks should be substantially more involved in mortgage lending.

This thesis was strongly supported by my study of mortgage disinvestment by banks in the Saint Louis area (Ratcliff, 1980a, 1980b, 1980c). Looking at home mortgage loans during 1975 and 1976, I found considerable variation among banks (relative to their size), both in the extent to which they provided home mortgage loans and in the extent to which they provided such loans in older low and moderate income neighborhoods. Evidence of disinvestment and withdrawal of capital from home mortgage lending in such neighborhoods was shown to be characteristic of those banks most closely tied to the centers of economic power and upper class social integration within the capitalist class.

The study includes all 77 commercial banks that, in 1975, had their headquarters either in Saint Louis City or Saint Louis County, the two dominant counties in the Saint Louis metropolitan area.[1] In this analysis, three distinct types of loans are treated as outputs. The first type consists of loans where the borrowers were corporations or individual capitalists borrowing money for investment in profit-seeking activities outside of real estate and often outside of Saint Louis. The second type includes all conventional and government guaranteed mortgage loans on one to four unit residential properties (predominantly single family homes). The third type was all other loans, mainly mortgages on large apartment buildings, auto loans, and credit cards.

In order to determine the economic networks within which each bank was situated, all interlocks between bank directors and the 350 largest corporations in the Saint Louis area were identified. Two measures of economic interconnections were also calculated for each bank. The first measure, the total number of firms among the 350 to which the bank was directly linked through a shared director, indicated the centrality of the firm. The second measure, the total combined number of employees for all corporations with which each bank was linked, indicated the importance of a bank's interlock partners.

The bank directors were also studied to determine which of them had been involved in any of five organizations found to be the most exclusive in upper class social circles in Saint Louis: two men's clubs, one country club, the Saint Louis Social Register, and the Veiled Prophet Society, a secret organization of Saint Louis men which holds a highly exclusive debutante ball each year (Ratcliff et al., 1979). Membership lists or directories were obtained for the first four organizations. For the Veiled Prophet Society, a search through newspaper archives was conducted in order to determine all bankers who had either had a daughter as a debutante or a wife as a "Lady of Honor" in the ball during any of the previous 20 years. Involvement in these organizations was found to be highly intercorrelated and distinct from other clubs and social organizations for which membership information was collected. We computed the proportion of directors in each bank who were tied to at least one of these five exclusive social organizations.

The great advantage of these data on exclusive social organizations was that they made possible the incorporation of the dimension of upper class networks in a manner that is conceptually and empirically distinct from the data on corporate or economic networks.

The focal point of analysis was the determinants of lending patterns among Saint Louis banks. This chapter will first look at differences in loan distributions for banks in different size categories. Next, it will present a series of measurements comparing the importance of size of bank and inner circle leadership in determining lending patterns. Finally, the distribution of loans and other bank characteristics will be examined in relation to bank profitability.

The distribution of bank loan capital among lending categories is presented in Table 16 for banks of different sizes. For all banks taken together, loans to capitalists accounted for just under one-half (45.8 percent)

Table 16

THE DISTRIBUTION OF TOTAL BANK LOANS AMONG LENDING CATEGORIES BY
BANKS GROUPED ACCORDING TO SIZE, DECEMBER 31, 1975

Size rank of bank	N	Total amount for all types of loans[a]	Percentage of loans to capitalists[b]	Percentage of home mortgage loans[c]
Top 5 banks	5	$2,136,165	60.5	7.2
Banks ranked 6–15	10	522,323	30.2	27.3
Banks ranked 16–40	25	747,099	26.7	27.0
Banks ranked 41–77	37	467,052	26.9	24.3
Totals	77	$3,872,539	45.8	15.8

[a] In thousands of dollars.

[b] Percentage of total loans outstanding December 31, 1975, to commercial and industrial borrowers (except for real estate), to banks and other financial institutions, and to brokers and nonbrokers for the purchase of securities.

[c] Percentage of total loans secured by one to four family residences.

of the total, while about one-sixth (15.8 percent) of this total was invested in home mortgages. Over a third (38.4 percent) of the loan total was invested in multifamily residential loans, credit cards, auto loans, and several smaller categories.

Banks differ in their loan distributions according to their size. The top five banks concentrated their lending, allocating 61 percent to capitalists and much less than 10 percent to home mortgages. The three categories of smaller banks, which do not differ significantly from one another in their loan distributions, allocated much less to capitalists (less than 30 percent) and much more to mortgages (more than 25 percent).

Taken just by themselves, these findings seem to indicate that differences in bank lending practices are a function of the size of the bank. This fits with the thinking of many economists, who typically see size as a major determinant of bank performance. In particular, larger banks are seen as trying to emphasize wholesale banking operations with businesses rather than engaging in retail or consumer-oriented banking. These analysts argue that wholesale banking is both more efficient and more profitable (Starr, 1975, p. 86; Leinsdorf and Etra, 1973, p. 81).

Table 17 undermines this argument significantly, suggesting that the intensity of a bank's lending to capitalist borrowers was strongly related to the bank's ties into networks of economic power and to its directors' social interaction within the local capitalist class. The relevant correlations, which include those between loans to capitalists and (a) the range of corporation ties ($r = .573$), (b) the combined size of linked corporations measured by total employees ($r = .547$), (c) and upper class social ties ($r = .540$), are all strong. This means that those banks whose leadership was in the inner circle also gave the largest share of their loans to capitalist borrowers. On the other hand, those banks whose leadership was not in the inner circle were much more likely to give mortgage loans.

However, also as expected, a strong positive relationship existed between capitalist-oriented lending and bank size in deposits ($r = .402$). Holding company banks (those banks owned by a company simultaneously owning more than one bank) were also more likely to be involved in loans to capitalists ($r = .179$) and less likely to emphasize home mortgage loans ($r = -.255$).

Thus, since large banks were usually those whose directors were members of the inner circle, we cannot immediately tell whether it was the inner circle affiliation of their leadership which led to the commercial lending policies of large banks, or whether this investment profile was a consequence of size considerations, as many economists believe.

To determine which of these was the primary factor we need to compare a group of large banks whose leadership was in the inner circle with another group of large banks whose leadership was not in the inner circle. If all the banks were heavily invested in corporate lending, this would prove

Table 17

CORRELATIONS AMONG BANKS LENDING TO CAPITALIST BORROWERS AND TO HOME BORROWERS, THE CAPITALIST CLASS CONNECTIONS OF BANK BOARD MEMBERS, AND THE SIZE AND HOLDING COMPANY STATUS OF THE BANK[a]

	2	3	4	5	6	7
1. Combined loans to capitalist borrowers (%)	−.530	.573	.547	.540	.402	.179
2. Loans for home mortgages (%)		−.342	−.476	−.289	−.070	−.255
3. Number of top 350 corporations with which bank is interlocked			.589	.724	.687	.182
4. Total number of employees in top 350 local corporations with which bank is interlocked				.585.	.464	.247
5. Proportion of bank's directors who belong to top upper class organizations					.575	.184
6. Total deposits of banks						.198
7. Holding company status of the bank						
		(N = 77)				

[a] A correlation coefficient ranges from −1.0 to +1.0. A positive correlation means that when one variable is high or low, so is the other. A negative correlation means that when one variable is high, the other is low, and vice versa. A near zero correlation means that no pattern exists between the variation of the two variables

that size was the determining factor. If, on the other hand, only the well-connected banks had large corporate portfolios, this would demonstrate that inner circle leadership was the cause of heavy corporate investment and the relative avoidance of home loans.

While we did not have such a comparative sample, multiple regression techniques allow us to statistically disentangle the effects of size from those of inner circle leadership. When this is done we discover that it is, indeed, the network connections of the large banks which produced their lending profiles. Investment in corporations rather than home loans was not a consequence of bank size.[2]

This finding is strengthened by the results reported in Table 18. One might suspect that corporate loans were more profitable and that this was the reason large banks sought them out. Actually, however, those banks with more commercial loans were no more profitable than the mortgage-oriented companies. Moreover, the banks with inner circle leadership were no more profitable than the others. These directors were not using their influence to enhance the profits of the bank itself, but to pursue policies that would enhance their broader interests and those of the corporate elite as a whole.

The lending decisions of banks are important social consequences of the internal structure of the capitalist class. The findings presented here provide strong support for the thesis that bank lending practices are influenced by the linkages that banks have with the centers of economic power and by upper class social interaction within the capitalist class. Those banks which are most closely tied to these centers serve, in effect, as capital-accumulating appendages of the corporate elite and lend their money in ways that best meet the capital needs of the class as a whole. They concentrated their loans with capitalist borrowers and avoided loans in categories such as home mortgages that produce a broader distribution of loan capital within a community.

These patterns appear to be relatively independent of the size of the banks. The banks emphasizing lending to capitalists were those whose directors were tied to numerous local corporations which represent major concentrations of economic power and, to a less extent, exclusive upper class social circles. In contrast, banks that occupied more marginal positions within the structure of the class, even if they were relatively large, were much less engaged in lending to capitalists and much more engaged in mortgage lending.

This pattern, in itself is troubling and becomes more so when we note that the money in commercial banks comes from a wide range of deposits, including individual checking and savings accounts, government accounts, certificates of deposit held by pension funds and other similar nonbusiness institutions, accounts of churches and other private organizations, and small business accounts. This money would not necessarily be so heavily invested in corporate loans if banks tied to core corporate interests were not the major institutions in Saint Louis. Instead, such capital-starved sectors of the local economy as housing, urban development, and small business might be better

Table 18

CORRELATIONS BETWEEN BANK PROFITABILITY AND BANK'S LOAN
DISTRIBUTION, CAPITALIST CLASS CONNECTIONS, AND SIZE IN DEPOSITS

	Correlation with bank profitability[a]
1. Percentage of total loans that went to capitalists	−.016
2. Percentage of total loans that went for home mortgages	.010
3. Inner circle membership of leadership (number of top 300 corporations with which bank was interlocked)	.045
4. Total number of employees in top 300 local corporations with which bank is interlocked	.002
5. Proportion of bank's directors who belonged to top upper class organizations	.060
6. Total deposits of the bank	.201

[a] Profitability is defined as the net income of the bank before taxes and before security gains and losses in 1975 divided by the total assets of the bank as of December 31, 1975 (Reed et al., 1976, p. 434).

served. When certain favored borrowers gain sufficient capital through loans, other potential borrowers are denied such capital. In Saint Louis, which can be characterized as a declining industrial area, the concentration of loans found among capitalist borrowers—particularly the largest companies, which were least likely to utilize it in Saint Louis—represented a significant outflow of capital from the metropolitan area. Corporate investments are most likely to be made in higher growth areas, and since large corporations operate on a multistate and often multinational basis, they are in an advantaged position with respect to the transfer of capital investments.[3] There is considerable evidence that in the last several decades the largest Saint Louis based corporations have moved a major share of their investments and jobs out of the Saint Louis area (Defty, 1975; *Business Week*, November 1, 1976, pp. 47–48). The transfer of capital out of the Saint Louis area has also been clearly documented in regard to the sizable number of Saint Louis financial institutions that invested large shares of their mortgage loans outside of Missouri (Ratcliff, 1977).

The evidence thus suggests that Saint Louis, despite its image as a declining older industrial metropolis, was actually producing a net capital surplus that was deposited in the major banks and then exported for investment elsewhere, presumably to the Sunbelt and other high growth areas. This outflow of capital certainly was not an indication that there were no investment needs in the Saint Louis area. The mortgage loans made by Saint Louis banks were, for example, as profitable as the loans to (frequently not Saint Louis) business development. If Saint Louis were to reverse the long-term decline in the number of manufacturing jobs, and if the housing needs of the area's residents were to be met, sizable investments would have been an absolute necessity. The viability of Saint Louis, like that of other older industrial areas, was very much dependent on the success of locally oriented real estate investors in obtaining sufficient investment capital. Given these currents of investment and disinvestment within an older metropolitan area, the leading Saint Louis capitalists appear to have played a complex and even contradictory role. At the same time that they were closely tied to locally based structures of power and prominence, they were actively involved in the outward flow of investments from the metropolis. These tensions reflected the dual needs of the leading capitalists to protect both their local class bases and their long-term interests by taking advantage of national economic trends (Ratcliff, 1980a). Because the banks most centrally located in the capitalist class are also the ones that are steadily growing larger, it is likely that the share of funds deposited by Saint Louis residents and businesses in local banks that is loaned to corporations for investment outside the region will not only continue to be large but will actually increase.

NOTES

1. For a complete discussion of the methods used in the study, see Ratcliff (1980b).

2. For a more detailed description of this analysis, see Ratcliff (1980b).

3. It should be noted that all interpretations regarding the geographic transfer of capital must necessarily extend beyond the data presented in this analysis. It must be remembered that the data used here only identify the categories of borrowers and do not reveal the particular uses or the geographic locations of investments resulting from these loans.

11

The Corporate Elite and the Introduction of IQ Testing in American Public Schools
David Gersh

The introduction of IQ testing as a placement and tracking device in the public schools, perhaps the major educational innovation of the twentieth century, is an important episode in both the history of education and the development of inner circle influence in American public life. School testing, nonexistent before 1920, was common by 1930, standard by 1940, and virtually universal by 1950. No government educational policy-making body played a critical role in this transformation. Rather, it was developed by foundations, universities, and boards of education, coordinated by professional educators and psychologists, and funded by the business elite.

THE EUGENICS MOVEMENT

The history of IQ testing must begin with the eugenics movement, which sought to increase the "aristogenic" population—people with good heredity—and decrease the "cacogenic" population—those with bad traits. The movement arose from the contradictory consequences of rapid industrialization in America from the 1880s to the First World War, when, on the one hand, a new capitalist elite and a prosperous upper middle class arose, and on the other hand, the vast majority of the population, workers and farm laborers, was experiencing severe economic dislocation, oppressive working conditions, and extreme poverty (Weinstein, 1968; Boyer and Morais, 1972).

A number of explanations arose to account for the contrasting fates of different social classes. One, adopted by increasing numbers of people, beginning in the late nineteenth century, was that the upper classes were exploiting the lower classes. This analysis became the intellectual foundation of labor unions as well as socialist, populist, and other political groups advocating redistribution of money and resources from the rich to the poor. By the early 1900s, this ferment had become a major threat to the corporate elite's dominant position in American society.

A second explanation for the growing inequality was based on genetics; it asserted that those who did not prosper in America were biologically incapable of success. Many intellectuals, including biologists, psychologists, and anthropologists, believed this argument, and since it rationalized and justified existing social inequalities, the elite had a large stake in encouraging its development and acceptance. "It was not a conspiracy in the usual sense. There was no one powerful ruling class leader or group who laid out long-range plans [to help the eugenics movement]. But class interests are such that members of the class generally know what movements serve their vested interests and what movements pose a threat" (Allen, 1976, p. 8).

The major organizational expression of the eugenics movement was the Eugenics Section of the American Breeder's Association, founded in 1906 and headed by C. B. Davenport, a Harvard-trained biologist who worked at the Station for Experimental Evolution in Cold Spring Harbor, New York. (Davenport also headed the newly formed Department of Experimental Evolution of the Carnegie Institute.) The original members included David Starr Jordan, the section chairman and chancellor of Stanford University; Alexander Graham Bell, inventor and businessman; and Vernon Kellogg, a Stanford biologist (Haller, 1963, pp. 63–64). In 1910, Mrs. E. H. Harriman, the wife of the president of the Union Pacific Railroad, funded, as part of the Eugenics Section, the Eugenics Record Office (ERO), also in Cold Spring Harbor and also directed by Davenport. The office billed itself as "a clearing-house for data concerning the blood-lines and family traits in America" (Goddard, 1911), but it soon became the hub of the entire American eugenics movement (Haller, 1963, p. 65).

This wing of the movement was intimately tied to the corporate inner circle. From 1910 to 1917 Mrs. Harriman gave $246,833 to the ERO and John D. Rockefeller donated $21,432.[1] More broadly, the Eugenics Section was an early version of the later policy-making groups, in that it brought together the representatives of the inner circle of the corporate elite (Rockefeller and Harriman), policy-makers (David Starr Jordan of Stanford), and experts (C. B. Davenport and other researchers).

The second important eugenics group was the Race Betterment Foundation, of Battle Creek, Michigan, founded in 1913 by the Kellogg family, owners of the cereal company, which was, even then, a major corporation. David Starr Jordan was also a member of this group, as was Charles Eliot, the president of Harvard. The second conference of the foundation, held in 1915, included delegates from the Rockefeller Foundation, the Carnegie Institute, the Ford Motor Company, U.S. Steel Company, Aetna Life Insurance, Metropolitan Life Insurance, and National Cash Register (Progressive Labor, 1973a, pp. 84, 95; 1973b, p. 64). The elite credentials of the Race Betterment Foundation were as impeccable as those of the Eugenics Section.

In addition to these national organizations, there were myriad state and local groups. Moreover, charitable, scientific, and political groups formed internal eugenics committees, many of them sponsored by business contributions. There was, for example, the Eugenics Committee of the National Organization on Prisons and Prison Labor, whose activities included lectures to civic organizations and social work groups. One of its members was Robert Yerkes, a Harvard psychologist who was later instrumental in developing the IQ test. His presentation, entitled "Eugenics: Its Scientific Basis and Its Program," advocated both positive eugenics (superior people should marry one another and have lots of children) and negative eugenics (sterilization, segregation, marriage restriction, and immigrant restriction for those declared inferior).[3]

Although they were organizationally independent, most of these eugenics groups were tied to the corporate elite and all of them were related to the Eugenics Record Office at Cold Spring Harbor. The ERO employed many of the national leaders; it published a national newsletter, *Eugenical News;* and in 1913 it organized the Eugenics Research Association, which Haller (1963) described as "the most important organization to unite eugenists nationally" (p. 73). By the beginning of World War I, eugenics was a solidified movement. It was headquartered in specific locations; it published its own newsletter, monographs, bulletins, and books; it was widely publicized in the scientific and popular media; and it was well funded by sympathetic members of the corporate elite.

American psychology was immersed in the eugenics movement. Many early psychologists were movement leaders, including G. Stanley Hall and Edward L. Thorndike, both pioneering figures in scientific psychology. Many of the second generation psychologists received their training from eugenics activists, and as a consequence, many, if not most, were involved in the study of the origins of individual differences in achievement. They tended to combine Darwin's theory of evolution with an acceptance of the political assumption that expanding capitalism gave everyone an equal opportunity for success: the answer to Terman's (1922a) question "Were We Born That Way?" was "Yes." Therefore a change in the extreme inequality in American society was not only unrealistic, but against nature. "Men are born unequal in intellect, character and skill," declared Thorndike in 1927, "It is impossible and undesirable to make them equal by education" (p. 18).

The attempt to prove this unquestioned assumption of genetic differences determined the research agenda of early twentieth century psychology. Much of the pre–World War I work was devoted to demonstrating the superiority of northern European whites to nonwhites, especially blacks and Indians, and to non-Aryans, especially Jews, Italians, and other recent immigrants. (This led to some embarrassing results, since the early experiments showed, for example, that blacks did better than whites in such abilities as reaction time and memory [Gersh, 1981; Bache 1895; Stetson, 1897; Wissler, 1901]).

Eventually, researchers shifted their focus from group differences to individual differences, though they never abandoned their belief in the genetic superiority of Nordic whites.[4] This shift led to a focused concern on the measurement of individual intelligence.

THE EARLY TESTS: STANFORD BINET

"The first questions the author of a test must answer are these: Which abilities, aptitudes, proficiencies, or personality traits are to be measured?" (Freeman, 1962, p. 63). This specification amounts, in the case of an IQ test, to a definition of intelligence. The second step is to collect a large number of items which the psychologist hypothesizes will test these abilities (Freeman, 1962, p. 64). The items are then presented to a group of individuals—the standardization sample—that includes all ages for which the test claims to be accurate. Within this group are people who, in the tester's view, are clearly intelligent and those who are clearly not. "The author of a test . . . standardizes his test on a population sample that is *stratified* according to relevant factors" (Freeman, 1962, p. 64; emphasis in original). This stratification requires, therefore, a preliminary assumption of who is intelligent and who is not.

Once this is done, the answers of the two (or more) groups are analyzed. Those items on which the two did equally well, or on which the nonintelligent group did better than the intelligent, must be discarded. "Test items which do not help to differentiate subjects of known superiority from subjects of known inferiority are eliminated" (Terman, 1922a, p. 656). Those items on which the superior group excels are kept.

This process has two effects. The first is obvious: in the end the two groups will perform very differently on the test. The second is that the distribution of scores is molded by the test maker in a manner similar to that of a sculptor molding a piece of clay. For instance, if the examiner decided that too many intelligent individuals have failed the test, that is, they fall into the lower end of the curve, items can be eliminated, rearranged, or rewritten to shift these people into the higher end, just as clay can be pushed if a sculpture is lopsided. On some tests this molding process is facilitated by weighting certain items, that is, giving them more points than others.

The first successful IQ test, which differentiated a group of children identified as intelligent by their teachers from a group the teachers identified as less capable, was created by Alfred Binet in France in 1904 (Blum, 1978, p. 58; Eckberg, 1979, p. 139). A number of early American tests based on Binet's model, however, were rejected because they labeled well over three-quarters of the American population "feeble-minded."[5]

The Stanford-Binet, the adaptation of the Binet test developed by Lewis Terman of Stanford University just before World War I, gave testers and their backers what was needed: a "normal" distribution, which scored most people as average in intelligence and small minorities as brilliant and retarded. Terman's achievement, like other work in this period, was embedded in the eugenics movement. Stanford University was led by eugenics activist David Starr Jordan. Terman was financially tied to elite clubs and foundations, and was an active member of the Human Betterment Foundation, the key West Coast eugenics group.

Terman standardized the children's sections of this test on 982 students, all American-born, white, and of western European descent, 905 of whom were between the ages of 5 and 14. The adult sections were standardized on 30 businessmen and 50 high school students as the upper half of the scale, and 150 hobos ("migrating unemployed") and 150 juvenile delinquents as the lower half. The delinquents were inmates at the Whittier State School, and the hobos were found at a shelter for transients. The businessmen "had little or no formal education beyond the common school but had shown themselves ordinarily successful in the various lines of business represented in a small city" (Terman et al., 1917, pp. 9–10, 29–30).

The adult samples exhibit the bias of the test: Terman equated business success with intelligence. He did not include, for example, successful union leaders, resourceful immigrants who had escaped poverty and/or persecution in Europe, prominent members of the black community, or newly famous muckraking writers (many of whom had risen from working class origins) as members of his standardization group of intelligent adults. (Items would have appeared in the test which catered to their backgrounds and the groups which they represented. These groups would have, therefore, had higher scores on the resulting IQ test and business people would have had lower scores.)

In the first detailed presentation of the Stanford-Binet, Terman and his collaborators reproduced a table showing the IQ distribution of 492 children from different social statuses ranging from "very inferior" (lower class) to "very superior" (upper class). The table "gives a correlation of .40 between social status and intelligence quotient." The fact that the "very inferior" group had an average IQ of 85 and the medians ranged upward to 100 (the population mean) for the "average group" and 106 for the "very superior" group was taken as major evidence for the validity of the test, despite the fact that the test was designed to give this distribution (Terman et al., 1917, pp. 88–91). Terman (1916) expressed the class bias of the test clearly when he described "borderline" individuals (IQs between 70 and 80) in class terms: "Among laboring men and servant girls there are thousands like them. They are the world's 'hewers of wood and drawers of water.'" Most blacks, Hispanics, and Native Americans fell into this category, Terman added, and should be placed in segregated schools (pp. 91–92).

Already in 1916, Terman anticipated the use of IQ as a device for educational tracking. He claimed that his test would save the $40 million which was wasted each year "re-teaching children what they have already been taught but have failed to learn" by identifying those who were incapable of developing advanced skills (p. 3). And IQ testing would do more than merely save money. It could also be used, by targeting appropriate individuals for sterilization, to prevent "the reproduction of the feeble-minded," eliminate "an enormous amount of crime, pauperism, and industrial inefficiency" (p. 7), curtail prostitution ("That every feeble-minded woman is a potential prostitute would hardly be disputed by anyone" [p. 11]), and reduce political radicalism (p. 28).

Henry Goddard (1920), another prominent IQ tester, was very explicit on this last point. Strikes, socialism, and "Bolshevism" were all caused by employers not assigning workers to jobs based on IQ and workers not accepting that IQ, and therefore class status, is inborn. If IQ testing convinced people that their place in the economic hierarchy was fixed by heredity and that any attempt to change this "natural" order would be futile or even dangerous, much misplaced ambition would be reduced along with its consequent disruption (pp. 60, 96–103). In addition, there is great potential for mistrust among racial and ethnic groups that occupy different places in a competitive hierarchy; the results of IQ testing, by legitimizing such caste formation, would lend validity to these divisions and therefore reduce the potential for any cross-ethnic and interracial movements for change. That is, they would reinforce ethnic competition and undercut generalized political radicalism. Reich (1978) has shown that such racial or ethnic conflict can translate into tremendous profits for the elite in wage, benefit, and social service inequalities.

THE DEVELOPMENT OF GROUP TESTING; THE ARMY ALPHA

The Stanford-Binet had a major drawback as a device for educational placement; it was individually administered and therefore too expensive and time consuming to be used to evaluate large numbers of people. In 1917, therefore, Terman and Robert Yerkes began to seek funds from the Rockefeller-funded General Education Board (GEB) to develop a group test that was comparable to the Stanford-Binet.[6] Though this funding did not materialize until 1919, work on the group test proceeded rapidly under the auspices of the U.S. Army once World War I was declared.

Robert Yerkes, the Harvard psychologist, eugenics activist, and contributor to the Eugenics Record Office was made chairman of a War Department committee whose mandate was to develop a group IQ test for use in the Armed Forces (National Research Council, 1916, p. 509; Yerkes, 1918, 1921). This was the culmination of an elite funded-effort which had begun several years earlier (Camfield, 1970, p. 80; Gersh, 1981).

Within a month of the United States' entrance into the war, the committee submitted a finished proposal to Surgeon General Gorgas. Terman, who had joined the planning group, speeded test construction by introducing a group test developed by one of his graduate students, Arthur Otis.[7] With the Otis tests as a basis, a first draft was written by June 9, 1917, and over the next two months the tests were tried out on both military and nonmilitary personnel. The results of this pretesting were judged a success, as there was a very high correlation (about .5) between the scores of a sample of 313 enlisted men and their officers' ratings of their intelligence.

By August 1917, Surgeon General Gorgas appointed Yerkes major and charged him with the task of organizing a massive official testing program in the army. Yerkes was given a staff of 40 psychologists, who initially tested 85,000 men. On January 19, 1918, only six months after the test was created, testing of all recruits was authorized. Its objectives were "(a) To sift out those mental defectives who are not qualified for military service. (b) To discover men of superior ability for report to the commanding company officers. These men should be considered for non-commissioned officers or for tasks of special responsibility. (c) To discover men with marked special skills" (Yerkes, 1921, p. 123). The principle of tracking was thus the underlying logic of the Army Alpha test.

The use of these tests as tracking devices makes the item selection and standardization processes particularly significant. Insofar as the examinations discriminated against certain groups, these groups risked exclusion from attractive assignments or promotions.

Yerkes' main criterion for including items and scales was that officers scored better on them than did enlisted men (1921, pp. 328–37). This selection principle introduced a clear bias against members of the working class, immigrants, and racial minorities, since almost all officers were from prosperous families and were white, native born, and of northern or western European descent. The considerable number of items on which this group performed poorly or which did not distinguish between them and the enlisted men were eliminated from the test. Those items on which enlisted men did poorly were kept.

Why did researchers assume officers to be intelligent instead of establishing some criteria which was separate from military rank? This decision certainly reflected the beliefs of the researchers, but it also fit nicely with the practical realities of army structure. An examination that declared many enlisted men more intelligent than their commanding officers would imply the need for dramatic changes in officer recruitment, undermine respect for officers, and lend credibility to a broad range of soldiers' grievances. Such an examination would be a prima facie argument against the existing structure and could fuel efforts at reform. For both the IQ testers and the military leadership it would have been unthinkable (and probably preposterous) to adopt any test that did not assume and validate the qualifications of existing leadership.

This logic, variously expressed and assumed, can be found throughout the history of mental testing. The assumption that deserving people have risen to high positions, that American capitalism is a meritocracy, was built into the test construction process; it is deeply buried in—but nevertheless thoroughly infused into—the tests that emerged from it.

A total of 1,726,966 army recruits were tested using the Army Alpha and other IQ tests. Though the tests were widely publicized (see, e.g., Terman, 1918), their actual application in army decision making was apparently restricted to the selection of officers (Boring, 1957; Camfield, 1970; Kevles, 1968, p. 573). Evidently, among the enlisted men, those who scored below average on the tests were frequently good soldiers, and hence, many officers ignored the scores when making personnel decisions (Kevles, 1968).

The primary impact of these tests derived from the publicity surrounding their use, which laid the foundation for their application in the schools. (See Appendix A for a more detailed analysis of findings and interpretations.)

> [The] wide use of the examinations during the war had dramatized intelligence testing and made the practice respectable. Gone were the public's prewar wariness and ignorance of measuring intelligence. In 1920, Yerkes was inundated with "many hundreds of requests" for information about the Alpha and Beta examination. (Kevles, 1968, p. 581)

THE FOUNDATIONS OF SCHOOL TESTING

An indirect, and for our purposes important, consequence of the army testing program was the creation of strong ties among IQ psychologists throughout the United States. In 1961 Terman reminisced about

> the opportunity [the Army program] gave me to become acquainted with nearly all of the leading psychologists of America. . . . My intimate contacts with Yerkes, in particular, both in our daily work and during the long periods when I lived in his home, meant more to me than could easily be expressed. . . . One result of the war experiences was to confirm and strengthen my earlier belief regarding the importance of mental tests as an integral part of scientific psychology. Whereas I had thought that only a handful of psychologists were of this opinion, I now learned that many were. I no longer felt isolated. I could return to my work with more confidence than ever that, in the long run, contributions in the field of mental tests would receive the recognition they deserved. (pp. 325–326)

Thus, by the end of World War I, the process of creating a scientific basis for the defense of privilege and inequality was completed. The interaction of eugenics activists with elite funding produced a network of eugenics organizations, which, in turn, produced a growing interest in the creation of tests that would demonstrate the superior intellect of those in privileged positions. The interaction among elite-sponsored foundations, universities headed by eugenics activists, and psychologists trained in the perspective of hereditarian thought produced the first IQ test. This achievement, combined with the political exigencies of a wartime army, led to government sponsorship of the first massive testing program, in which the privately developed philosophy of tracking was imported into government.

The postwar period saw the consolidation of the gains of the army testing program. Four sets of interlocking institutions were instrumental in this consolidation: the eugenics movement, the National Research Council (NRC), the Psychological Corporation, and the philanthropic foundations.

National coordination of eugenics activities was now under the auspices of the Eugenics Committee of the United States of America, which was part of the International Commission on Eugenics. The movement achieved a number of long-sought legislative victories in this postwar period, including immigration restriction and sterilization laws. As in its early days, the eugenics movement benefited from the involvement of both the corporate elite and academic policy-makers. The Human Betterment Foundation, a California group, for example, included on its board of trustees E. S. Gosney, a banker, lawyer, and president of the Arizona Wool Growers Association, Harry Chandler, president of the *Los Angeles Times,* and Henry Robinson, a major banker, as well as David Starr Jordan, the president of Stanford University, and R. V. Klein Smid, president of the University of Southern California. The elite Commonwealth Club of San Francisco formed a eugenics section.

The various committees of the National Research Council had overlapping memberships with many eugenics groups. Yerkes, for example, was chairman of the Psychology and Anthropology Division of the NRC from 1917 to 1919, while maintaining his connections to a variety of eugenics groups. When he retired to head the NRC Research Information Service, eugenicist Carl Seashore took his place. Yerkes also chaired a number of other NRC committees, including the Committee on Scientific Problems of Human Migration, which researched "the scientific approach to selective migration," and the Committee on Intelligence Tests for Elementary Schools, which developed the National Intelligence Tests, to be discussed below (National Research Council, 1920a; 1923, p. 48).

Despite official connection with the federal government, the NRC relied mainly on foundations for funding (Joncich, 1968, p. 469). In its early years, for example, the NRC received $50,000 for its general use from both the Carnegie Corporation and Rockefeller Foundation (National Research Council, 1918, p. 69). It also received $25,000 from the General Education Board (a Rockefeller foundation) to develop the National Intelligence Tests and $60,000 from the Laura Spelman Rockefeller Memorial to support Yerkes' human migration committee (National Research Council, 1920a).

The Psychological Corporation was founded in 1921 to advance research in applied psychology, especially testing. The *New York Times* provided front-page coverage of its first public meeting. The article, "Psychology to Fit Job to the Man" (February 17, 1922), reported that by matching the proper person to the proper job, intelligence and aptitude tests could save the economy $70 billion each year.

The army testing had provided the impetus for the Psychological Corporation, which sought "to give psychologists the means of doing business with businessmen with more freedom and directness than a university professor usually feels that he can." The success of army testing had spawned the problem of "the charlatan who hides under the cloak of psychology" (*New York Times,* February 17, 1922). That is (in the view of the corporation's founders), tests were being misused, unscientific tests were being published, unsubstantiated claims were being made, and money was being made by psychologists other than those who had contributed to the widespread acceptance of IQ testing. The Psychological Corporation created an institutional liaison which could stabilize relationships with business and thus facilitate both the growth and regulation of applied IQ testing.

The Carnegie Corporation, the Rockefeller foundations, and the Commonwealth Fund were the major sources of support for the newly founded IQ establishment. Most obvious, perhaps, they provided funds to specific research projects. But in addition they helped guarantee favorable publicity, acted as a force for unity among competing researchers, and participated in the efforts to hammer out intellectual consistency among the contending academic perspectives.

Before the United States declared war in 1917 Terman and Yerkes had been in the process of applying to the Rockefeller-funded General Education Board for a grant to develop a group IQ test viable for use in the schools. After the war ended, Yerkes was quick to remind Abraham Flexner, the president of the GEB, of this proposal, since the army test was adult oriented and could not be used on children:

> Our duty, then, is to propose that the General Education Board finance the development and standardization of group procedure. . . . I wish to emphasize the word "group" for the principal point is to develop a procedure which can be satisfactorily applied to school children by rooms instead of individually [and] the results made available for use in connection with grading, promotion or vocational placement.[8]

> Already we are bombarded by requests from public school men for our Army mental tests.[9]

This grant was approved in 1919 and the money funneled through the NRC. The final product was the National Intelligence Tests, which were produced within a year and which by 1930 would be given to 7 million children, 1.5 million copies being sold in the first two years alone (Camfield, 1970, p. 285; Joncich, 1968, p. 389).

Terman was involved in two other major projects which also received massive foundation support: the revision of the Stanford-Binet and his longitudinal study of gifted children (those with IQs in the 99th percentile). The Stanford-Binet revision, eventually published in 1937, was funded largely by the Laura Spelman Rockefeller Memorial Fund, which provided $38,650 from 1927 to 1935.[10] The study of high IQ children was an attempt to trace the development of geniuses into adulthood. The predicted outcome was that these children would eventually become the leaders of business, the arts, politics, and science, but Terman's optimistic predictions were not fulfilled (Goleman, 1980). The major funding for this study came initially from the Commonwealth Fund, which had been founded by business activist Edward S. Harkness in 1918 to further the "scientific approach to education" (Joncich, 1968, p. 469). Between the years 1921 and 1928, the fund gave over $45,000 to this project. The Thomas Welton Stanford Fund gave $19,000 from 1922 through 1939, and after 1939 support was provided by the NRC, as well as the Carnegie, Ford, Columbia, Cushman, and Marsden foundations.[11]

The Commonwealth Fund was also active in supporting the development of tests for admission to, and tracking in, schools, giving an average of $100,000 annually during the 1920s for educational research (Joncich, 1968, p. 469).[12] In 1924, for example, it gave a $12,000 grant to Columbia University professor and army tester Ben Wood to develop college, law, and medical admissions tests (Downey, 1965, p. 15), $8,000 to the NRC, $10,000 to E. L. Thorndike of Columbia Teachers College, and $55,000 for a two-year study of subject matter in California schools.[13] Later, it funded the development of the New York State Regents exams, which became the major tracking and college admission instrument for New York State high school students (Downey, 1965, p. 16).

The Carnegie Corporation also provided lavish funding for testing projects. From 1915 to 1938, it supported 33 different studies of tests and measurements at a total cost of $3,081,000, including a $325,000 grant to E. L. Thorndike which facilitated his wide-ranging IQ-related activities, as discussed below (Marks, 1976–1977, p. 7; Karier, 1972, p. 166). Together with the Rockefeller Foundation, it gave several million dollars necessary to establish the Graduate Record Office which developed the Graduate Record Examination, the National Committee on Teachers Examinations, the Cooperative Test Services, the College Examination Board, and the American Council of Education (Marks, 1976–1977, p. 7).[14]

In the 1920s, the Laura Spelman Rockefeller Memorial Fund "initiated or assisted child-welfare research at six universities, Iowa, Columbia, Yale, Minnesota, Toronto, and Berkeley. [The fund] played a pivotal role in getting developmental research established in an institutional setting" (Lomax, 1977, pp. 283, 284). Much of this support "was administered for the Memorial by a committee on Child Development, established within the Division of Anthropology and Psychology of the National Research Council in 1925" (p. 285). Bird Baldwin and Robert Woodworth, both eugenicists, were members of this committee.

Ironically, several studies sponsored by this committee provided powerful evidence of the importance of environment in IQ performance. Helen T. Wooley, for example, director of the Columbia Teachers College Institute of Child Welfare Research, reported that after six weeks of enriched environment, the IQ scores of institutionalized orphans rose to superior levels (*New York Times,* January 5, 1929, p. 22). Despite such results, however, little follow-up research into the impact of smaller classes, preschool help, or other environmental adjustments was sponsored. Not until the civil rights movement in the 1960s were such programs seriously considered. The existence of significant evidence was insufficient to merit a change in educational philosophy. In the absence of political pressure, the Laura Spelman Rockefeller Memorial Fund, the other foundations, and the educational establishment explored and developed pedagogic theories and strategies congenial to their own interests and ideology.

This unity among the foundations was also evidenced by the significant extent of overlapping leadership. Psychologist James Angell, for example, who was appointed president of the Carnegie Corporation after Carnegie died in 1920, was also on the board of the Commonwealth Fund (Angell, 1961, p. 19). Beardsley Ruml, Angell's assistant at Carnegie, received his Ph.D. in psychology from the University of Chicago, where Angell had been his advisor. When Angell left Carnegie to become president of Yale in 1922, Ruml also left Carnegie to become director of the Laura Spelman Rockefeller

Memorial Fund, with recommendations from Angell and from Abraham Flexner of the GEB, who had funded Terman and Yerkes (Mulherin, 1979–1980; Seybold, 1978).

While there was certainly competition among the foundations, the common interest of the elite led them, as we have seen, to support the same research programs. The class logic underlying the foundations' involvement in the postwar testing movement has been succinctly expressed by Russell Marks (1976–1977):

> Like the psychological profession, philanthropic foundations had particular reasons for participating in defining individual differences and in promoting intelligence testing. While it was often argued that the two largest philanthropic foundations, the Rockefeller and the Carnegie, were not promoting industrial interests but the general welfare, the evidence indicates the contrary. . . . The system needed to preserve and educate a talented elite, to secure a means of selecting workers, to assure social control through fitting individuals into their places in society, and to provide a rationale for the unequal distribution of wealth. The psychological profession and philanthropic foundations aided industrial capitalism nicely in securing these ends.
>
> Philanthropic foundations supported psychologists in their efforts to increase the momentum of the testing movement after the war. Classifying children approached the importance of classifying recruits. (p. 6)

For a number of reasons, then, the 1920s was a period of increasing inequality and social instabililty, the culmination of a process begun in the late nineteenth century. There were massive population shifts from farms to cities, including the first great wave of black migration. Inequality of income—the top .10 percent of families received as much income as the bottom 42 percent—triggered protest against both poverty and privileged wealth. The continued entry of women into the low wage work force (by 1930 almost one-quarter of those employed were women) directed attention to both inadequate male wages (which forced unwilling women to work) and sex discrimination (Bernstein, 1960, pp. 48–60). The post-World War I wave of strikes, the growth of well-organized revolutionary groups including the Industrial Workers of the World and the Communist party, the resurgence of women's and black organizations were all alarming symptoms and causes for unease among the elite (Bernstein, 1960, p. 12).

In this context, the educational system became a focal point for containing discontent and for channeling the coming generation of adults into appropriate social niches. The proliferation of IQ tests was essential to completing this demanding task.

THE PROLIFERATION OF IQ TESTING IN THE PUBLIC SCHOOLS

The Army Alpha test had been based on a preliminary instrument designed by Arthur Otis. By 1918, Otis had produced a children's version of the Alpha, the Otis Group Intelligence Scale, which was then published by the World Book Company (World Books, known today as Harcourt Brace Jovanovich, was owned by a Stanford alumnus, and it employed both Terman and Otis as editors).

The Otis test was so popular that it sold 500,000 copies in three printings between March and September of 1918. A fourth printing was needed in December of that year to meet the demand for the spring semester (Sharp, 1972, p. 79). B. R. Buckingham, an educational psychologist and leader of the National Education Association, noted the significance of this commercial success:

> The test movement had reached maturity. . . . [Previously tests had to be ordered from the author himself but in] 1919 test materials first began to be issued by commercial publishers. Thus in 1919 test-making passed from an amateur to a professional basis. (1941, pp. 353–354; see also DuBois, 1970 p. 68)

The success of the Otis assured the viability of group testing in the schools. In 1919, the Alpha was declassified and began to be used as an entrance and/or placement exam at universities and high schools (Sharp, 1972, pp. 77–78).

In 1920, the much heralded National Intelligence Tests made their appearance. These tests had been standardized on 4,000 students at each grade level, third through eighth, in Washington, D. C., Pittsburgh, New York, and Cincinnati (Joncich, 1968, p. 389; National Research Council, 1921), and were also published by the World Book Company. They quickly established themselves as the best-selling group test, a position they retained until they were discontinued in 1942 (Sharp, 1972, p. 79). The National Intelligence Tests achieved their popularity partly because they appeared to have the government's stamp of approval (the test booklets contained the logo "Prepared under the auspices of the National Research Council") and partly because their creators—Terman, Yerkes, Thorndike, Haggerty, Whipple, and others—were the most respected names in the field (National Research Council, 1920b, p. 1; Freeman, 1926, pp. 165–66).

In addition to their collaborative work on the National Intelligence Tests, most of the leading army testers worked individually on other tests. Thus, Terman wrote the Terman Group Test of Mental Ability; Whipple, the Group Test for Grammar Grades; Thorndike, the Examination of Intelligence Independent of Language; and Haggerty, the Haggerty Intelligence Examination (Marks, 1976–1977, pp. 6–7; Joncich, 1968, p. 389). By 1926, there were at least 37 group tests, 11 of which were published by the World Book Company (Freeman, 1926, pp. 187–90).

By 1924, when Lewis Terman delivered his presidential address to the American Psychological Association (APA), IQ testing was an accepted feature of American life.

> [IQ testing in the Army] has transformed the "science of trivialities" into the "science of human engineering". The psychologist of the pre-test era was, to the average layman, just a harmless crank, but now that psychology has tested and classified nearly two million soldiers; has been appealed to in grading several million school children; is used

everywhere in our institutions for the feeble-minded, delinquent, criminal and insane; has become the beacon light of the eugenics movement; is appealed to by congressmen in the re-shaping of national policy on immigration; is furnishing high-powered explosives for the social reformers of one wing, while serving at the same time as the target drawing the hottest fire from the other wing,—no psychologist of today can complain that his science is not taken seriously enough. (p. 106)

In 1923, 60 percent of the approximately 450 members of the APA were involved in testing. By 1927, 23 percent of all American-written articles listed in the *Psychological Index* were on mental development (Marks, 1976–1977, p. 5).

The proliferation of testing depended on more than the test creation process we have just reviewed. While all factors and elements considered in the previous section provided the foundation of the testing movement, the practical use of tests in school depended ultimately on institutional bridges between their authors and locally run public school districts. This bridging role was played by universities, with Columbia Teachers College acting as the initiator and leader of the adoption process.

The Columbia Teachers College, founded in 1893, was the first teachers' college with intimate ties to the corporate inner circle. Grace and Cleveland Dodge, owners of Phelps Dodge Corporation and leading elite activists during the period, were the critical activists in the early years. Cleveland Dodge was an important member of the corporate inner circle. In addition to his Phelps Dodge and Columbia affiliations, he was, at various times, a director of New York Life Insurance, National City Bank, and other major corporations, treasurer of the Russell Sage Foundation, and trustee of the Carnegie Institute, and a charter member of the Eugenics Committee of the United States of America (Cremin, Shannon, and Townsend, 1954; *Eugenical News,* January 1924; Marquis, 1916).

In 1897, four years after the founding of Teachers College, George Vanderbuilt donated $100,000 "just in the nick of time" to secure a permanent building (Russell, 1937, p. 8). In 1902, John D. Rockefeller, Sr., offered a $250,000 donation and another $250,000 matching fund as soon as the institution eradicated its debts; the full $500,000 was collected by 1912 (Joncich, 1968, pp. 189–190).

The 1920s saw a continued growth in endowments to Teachers College. The GEB donated an additional $2.5 million by 1928. In addition, the GEB offered to match 50 cents for every dollar given to the Teachers College from other sources up to $1,000,000, and this pledge was also fulfilled. V. Everett Macy, chairman of the trustees, donated $500,000 in the form of 2,400 shares of Standard Oil stock. Edward Harkness donated $100,000, as did four other individuals. The Commonwealth Fund, the Laura Spelman Rockefeller Memorial Fund, and the Carnegie Corporation were also actively funding the college at this time. Individual trustees, all members of the corporate elite, contributed at least $1,000,000 in additional donations.[15] By the end of the decade Teachers College was by far the wealthiest institution concerned with primary and secondary education.

Edward L. Thorndike, who later became a prominent army tester, arrived at Teachers College in 1899 as an instructor in genetic psychology. By 1904 he was a full professor of educational psychology (Joncich, 1968, p. 192). As a leader of educational psychology in the United States and the most prestigious faculty member of Teachers College, he had great influence in American education. Terman, in 1926, commented, "In my opinion there is no other psychologist, living or dead, to whom education owes half so much as it owes to Thorndike. If there is anyone either, who has stimulated more psychological thinking in our present generation, I don't know who it is" (quoted in Joncich, 1968, p. 489). A firm advocate of eugenics, an admirer of Galton, and a believer in inherited intelligence, Thorndike helped shape the minds of both teachers and school administrators for more than 30 years. Even before intelligence tests were declared a success Thorndike wrote in his widely read textbook, *Educational Psychology:* "In the actual race of life, which is not to get ahead, but to get ahead of somebody, the chief determining factor is heredity" (1910, p. 140). This dogma was crucial to the spread of intelligence tests.

Columbia Teachers College produced thousands of teachers and school administrators, and Thorndike's view dominated its curriculum. In essence, this was like spreading fertilizer on the garden: long before their actual use, the ground had been prepared for the introduction of group tests. Joncich, quoting from contemporary reports, has documented the success of placing Teachers College in placing its alumni:

> Beyond training for leadership, there must be efforts to place the institution's graduates in positions of leadership. This is where Teachers College is successful far beyond words, establishing an effective system for providing advancements. With its alumni beginning to appear in important state and local administrative positions in the public schools, in the United States Bureau of Education, on the faculties of normal schools and colleges, openings for still more Teachers College graduates seems assured as long as the College can produce them. (1968, p. 189)

> The period immediately after 1906 represents something of a watershed, for enrollments in school administration more than doubled subsequently. And within another decade educational administration will possess the largest number of candidates for the Teachers College diploma and for advanced degrees in the entire College. . . . Professional placement of graduates between 1900 and 1916 total nearly 1,000 in public-school administration and supervision, and an additional 1,300 graduates are working as administrators in related fields. (p. 297)

But the rapid spread of Thorndike's ideology lay above all in the fact that Columbia Teachers College educated more graduate students in education than all other institutions combined. Teachers College thus trained the professors who then staffed other institutions that trained teachers and administrators.

> When E. P. Cubberley returns to his Stanford professorship in 1905, therefore, he is armed with a Ph.D. and the knowledge that at Columbia there are several men like Thorndike. . . . Other schoolmen can discover this elsewhere, for what Teachers College begins, popular interest in wartime testing completes: the three universities that offer courses in educational measurement before the war will grow to so many that by 1920 the new *Journal of Educational Research* can report that most public and private universities offer such work, as do about a quarter of the normal schools. This aspect of measurement is due for full bloom. (Joncich, 1968, pp. 293–294)

> And every teacher's college throughout the United States becomes a little Columbia. (Sinclair, 1924, p. 376)

The implications for elite control were not lost on social critics of the 1920s:

> Columbia's educational experts take charge of the school and college system of the country, and the production of plutocratic ideas becomes an industry as thoroughly established, as completely systematized and standardized as the production of automobiles or sausages. (Sinclair, 1922, p. 24)

When Yerkes wrote to Flexner in 1919 that he and other IQ testers were "bombarded by requests from public school men for our Army mental tests," he was probably not exaggerating. Thousands of educators, had been taught at Columbia and its satellites that hereditary differences in intelligence were a critical aspect of education and that tests would soon be available to measure intelligence. When publicity concerning the army testing program spread, the letters started pouring in. This spontaneous interest and the rapid national acceptance of the tests were an expression of 15 years of institution building.

A four stage process (similar to that outlined by Seybold in Chapter 12) had thus begun with the sponsorship of Teachers College as a center for innovation in education. The institutionalization of eugenics and intelligence differences as dominant ideologies was accomplished through the leadership of Thorndike. A generation of college administrators trained at Teachers College established a uniform curriculum in a broad range of the nation's teachers colleges. This resulted in a generation of primary and secondary school teachers committed to these ideas. Other Columbia graduates became public school administrators. When the tests arrived, school personnel at all levels were committed to them as a solution to the perceived problem of educational sorting.

The spread of testing in schools was accompanied by substantial efforts to win public support for their use. In 1919 Yerkes published an article in the widely read *National School Service* (put out by the U.S. Department of Interior) entitled "The Mental Ratings of School Children" recommending the use of IQ tests to place children in either professional, industrial, or manual tracks. The newspapers also provided testing advocates with a forum. For example, the *New York Sun* published an article headlined "Terman Reports Heredity and Race Play Part in Mental Leadership," in which Terman advocated tracking and observed that blacks, Mexicans, and southern Europeans produced few geniuses (April 23, 1924), and the *New York Times* published an article by Thorndike entitled "The New Psychology Sheds Light on Man" (August 21, 1927, p. 18). A. E. Wiggam published in a broad range of popular media, including *Cosmopolitan, American Magazine, World's Work, Pictorial Review,* and *Ladies Home Journal.* He also authored best-selling books on the subject. In this way, the popular media provided the finishing touches to the adoption process.

The use of IQ tests in American public schools consolidated the adaptation of the educational system to its twentieth-century function of sorting and tracking individuals and groups into occupational niches (Karier, 1972). When the U.S. Bureau of Education surveyed 215 cities in 1925, 67 percent of the school systems used individual IQ tests to place students in subnormal classes, and 64 percent used group tests to track elementary school pupils (Marks, 1976–1977, pp. 6–7; Joncich, 1968, p. 282). A year later, in a survey of 163 cities,

> 145 classified some or all of their elementary school students into ability groups, 119 similarly classified their junior high school students, and 81 classified their high school students. A variety of criteria were employed to classify students: 133 cities used teachers' judgements, 106 used intelligence quotients, 45 used educational ages, and 41 used mental ages. Testing was having definite impact on the school. (Marks, 1976–1977, p. 10)

Between 1920 and 1925, tracking became an accepted part of America's public school structure, and the critical instrument for tracking was the IQ test.

The Local Adoption Process

New York City provides an instructive example of the process and consequences of the introduction of educational tracking. Between 1913 and 1916 only two research projects relating to testing and pupil classification (tracking) had been conducted. In 1916, Eugene Nifenecker was appointed director of the New York school system's Bureau of Reference, Research and Statistics. Nifenecker, who would serve in this position until 1937, had received his Masters degree in political science at Columbia. His assistant, appointed in 1918, was John Stenquist, formerly an instructor at Teachers College, an officer in the testing group in the army, and an aide to the National Intelligence Tests committee. Nifenecker "hoped to . . . make New York's bureau a 'light house', acting as a beacon to light the way toward progress in education." In the next 10 years, 74 relevant studies were conducted, 49 aimed at investigating the practicalities of tracking and 25 related to pupil testing. This research represented as much as one-third of the bureau's work.[16]

In 1924 the superintendent of schools ordered that all students in elementary and junior high schools be placed in classrooms according to their ability to learn. Ideally, three tracks would be used, although if classes were too small, two tracks or individualized curricula within one class would suffice. While no specific guidelines for placement were laid down, IQ tests, achievement tests, and teachers' ratings were to be used (J. Chase, 1927, pp. 14–17).

"The following year, an attempt was made to classify the pupils of the entire school system on the basis of intelligence and group them homogeneously [according to IQ scores]. This was premature and failed, because the necessary groundwork for such a radical reorganization had not been laid."[17] Too many teachers and principals were unfamiliar with the tests, and the specific curricula for each track had not been fully developed.

The board of education sought to correct the problems that had led to the 1925 failure. Curriculum development committees were established, more experimental testing was done, and teachers were trained. In 1931, all the fifth-grade students in the city, over 100,000 in all, were given IQ tests. All first-grade pupils were tested the next year. In 1933, the state commissioner of education recommended the institution of a citywide three-track system. In 1935, a six-year testing and tracking experiment was put into effect in 70 schools. In 1939, citywide testing was initiated for both IQ and achievement tests.[18]

The official history of the research bureau summarized the years 1937 to 1949. "The city-wide testing program for the school system was developed during this period. . . . By 1949 it was developed almost to the point where it stands today [1964]. [IQ tests were given to students in the first, third, fifth, and sixth grades]." "[By 1960] over one million intelligence and achievement tests were given each year in the elementary and junior high schools."[19]

A crucial aspect of tracking is the vocational high school, introduced in the 1930s for students judged incapable of or uninterested in academic work. In 1931 there were 6,200 students in the vocational high schools; by 1940 this number had increased to 52,600, more than 20 percent of the high school enrollment.[20] The vocational high school became the educational terminus for many students. Those students who have been in the lower tracks throughout their educational careers and had not dropped out obtained training for a specific manual labor job. This was the denouement for Terman's "hewers of wood and drawers of water."

CONCLUSION

The institutionalization of IQ testing and tracking was accomplished without the direction of any government agency. Though the army played a crucial role in developing and popularizing the tests themselves, it did not coordinate or control the many institutions involved in the process. Its particular role, like those of the eugenics movement, the psychologists, Columbia Teachers College, and many other colleges and school districts, was part of a larger process which stood outside its sovereignty. Even the major funding agencies—the Laura Spelman Rockefeller Memorial Fund, the Carnegie Corporation, and the General Education Board—provided only limited coordination. They had little direct influence on the individual school district, and there is no evidence of the long-range planning generally associated with policy formation.

The adoption process is an example of collective and decentralized hegemony. The underlying coherence that connects all the elements of the process is the interest of the corporate elite. This interest was embedded in all the institutions that congealed into the testing movement, providing them with an unplanned, but extremely powerful, concordance of ideology and purpose. The outcome—testing and tracking—simultaneously served the implicit interest of the corporate elite while advancing the explicit individual and organizational interests of the professional psychologists and educators who actively sought it.

APPENDIX A: THE ARMY ALPHA—FINDINGS, INTERPRETATIONS, APPLICATIONS

The respectability of testing was further enhanced by widely publicized reports comparing the scores of different racial, national, regional, and occupational groups. The statistical analysis, which was directed by E. G. Boring, was used extensively by the eugenics movement in its various campaigns for immigration restriction, sterilization of low IQ individuals, and antimiscegenation laws (A. Chase, 1976). It was based on the scores of 162,526 men including 121,606 white enlisted men, 25,392 black enlisted men, and 15,528 white officers. (There were too few black officers for an analysis.) Of the total number of whites, 13,200 had been born outside the United States (Yerkes, 1921, p. 693). The major findings included:

1. Northern and western Europeans scored higher than southern and eastern (Yerkes, 1921, pp. 693ff). Although the original report did not interpret this result, Carl Brigham, in *A Study of American Intelligence* (1922), interpreted it to indicate the genetic inferiority of the Mediteranean and Alpine "races," which inhabited southern and eastern Europe, as compared to the Nordics of northern and western Europe. This analysis was endorsed in the book's forward by Robert Yerkes, who wrote, "The author presents not theories or opinions, but facts" (p. viii). This book became the mainstay of the eugenics movement's efforts to restrict immigration (Garis, 1927, pp. 229 ff.).

2. Earlier immigrants had higher scores (Yerkes, 1921, pp. 701 ff.). One might conclude that this was evidence that education, familiarity with the culture, and other environmental factors influenced scores on the army test, but Brigham and the army testers interpreted this finding differently: "The decline in intelligence [among later immigrants] is due to two factors, the change in the races migrating to this country, and to the additional factor of sending lower and lower representatives of each race" (Brigham, 1922, p. 178). This refers to the fact that most Slavic, Jewish, and Italian immigrants

came after the English and Scandinavians and that within each group the later arrivals were poorer (p. 197). "According to all evidence available, then, American intelligence is declining, and will proceed with an accelerating rate as the racial admixture becomes more and more extensive" (p. 210).

3. Whites scored higher than blacks (Yerkes, 1921, pp. 750 ff.). With no blacks in the standardization sample, this finding was an inevitable consequence of the construction process. In articles published after the war, however, army testers used it as proof of genetic inferiority of blacks (Terman, 1922a; Brigham, 1922; Yerkes, 1923). Arguments for bans on interracial marriage, reductions in allocations to black schools, and support for legal segregation would later be based on these findings.

4. The more schooling a soldier had, the higher his score (Yerkes, 1921, 747 ff.). Brigham gave the genetic interpretation of this result, which was actually an inevitable by-product of the higher educational attainment of the officers: "Very few people realize the severity of the elimination process that goes on from year to year in our schools and colleges" (1922, p. 63). In other words, those people with high levels of innate intelligence succeeded in school, while others did not.

5. Officers scored higher than enlisted men (Yerkes, 1921, pp. 763–766). It is almost unbelievable that this could be listed as a discovery, when the test was created to produce differences between these two groups. Brigham, among others, used this "result" to validate all test findings: "A very excellent criterion of the efficiency of a test is its value in differentiating between officers and men. . . . The Army tests uniformly show officers superior to enlisted men" (1922, pp. 15, 63).

6. The average mental age of the draftees was 13.08 years (Yerkes, 1921, p. 785). Some of the more extreme eugenicists, such as A. E. Wiggam and Lothrop Stoddard, would use this to say that the average mental age of the entire American population was 13.08 years—a sure sign of the dysgenic effects of immigration and feeblemindedness. Though Walter Lippmann (1922, p. 214) pointed out that the test was designed to produce this average mental age (and that an arbitrarily selected age could have been made the average), Terman nevertheless declared that this demonstrated "that the strictly average representative of the genus homo is not a particularly intellectual animal" (1922b, p. 116).

7. Individuals from higher status civilian occupations scored higher on the army tests (Yerkes, 1921, pp. 819 ff.). The Stanford-Binet, upon which the Alpha test was based, was standardized on businessmen and high school students as the superior adult group. Items on the tests were class—and education—biased, and the officers were from higher status occupations than the enlisted men. Once again the results were made inevitable by the test construction.

Though the entire array of findings can be traced to a standardization process that excluded certain groups and placed others at the bottom of the intelligence scale, that is not how they were interpreted. Hereditarian explanations abounded, and they were used to justify eugenics programs which sought to exclude individuals or groups from full participation in American life because of presumed genetic intellectual deficiencies. Immigration restriction was justified by army testing, and the 1924 law was supported by testimony taken from it (Garis, 1927; Kamin, 1974; A. Chase, 1976). Tracking in the public schools was also justified by the army program.

NOTES

1. Laughlin, H. H. *Official Records in the History of the Eugenics Record Office* (typewritten manuscript), December 1939, pp. 4–5. Cold Spring Harbor Laboratory Research Library Archives, Cold Spring Harbor, New York.

2. Davenport, C. B. *Carnegie Institute of Washington: Annual Report of the Director of the Department of Genetics,* 1912, p. 90. Cold Spring Harbor Laboratory Research Library Archives, Cold Spring Harbor, New York.

3. Yerkes, R. M. Robert M. Yerkes Papers. Yale University Library, Yale University, New Haven, Connecticut.

4. The work of these psychologists eventually became the foundation for Hitler's theories of Aryan superiority and the justification for genocide against Jews and other "untermenschen" (Chase, 1976).

5. See Gersh (1981), Eckberg (1979), Gould (1980), DuBois (1970), for analyses of these efforts. Henry Goddard (1917), the most famous of the early testers, declared that 83 percent of Jewish immigrants, 80 percent of Hungarian immigrants, and 79 percent of Italian immigrants were feebleminded; J. E. W. Wallin (1916), using Goddard's test, found it labeled many successful students and adults as retarded.

6. Yerkes, R. M. Letter to A. Flexner, January 16, 1917. Yerkes Papers, Yerkes, R. M. Letter to L. M. Terman, March 21, 1917. Yerkes Papers. Terman, L. M. Letter to R. M. Yerkes, March 29, 1917. Yerkes Papers. Terman, L. M. Letter to A. Flexner, undated (approximately March 1917). Terman Papers, Stanford University Archives, Stanford University, California.

7. Terman, L. M. Letter to B. D. Wood, May 4, 1937. Terman Papers.

8. Yerkes, R. M. Letter to A. Flexner, January 15, 1919, Yerkes Papers.

9. Yerkes, R. M. Letter to A. Flexner, January 17, 1919. Terman Papers.

10. Report of Progress of Research by Lewis M. Terman and Maud A. Merrill under Social Science Research Grants, September 1927 to March 1934 (undated). Letter, May 11, 1934. Terman Papers.

11. Terman, L. M. Letter to Kellogg Foundation, November 26, 1949. Terman Papers.

12. See also Cubberley, E. P. Telegram to L. M. Terman, May 22, 1922. Terman Papers.

13. Farrand, M. Letter to E. P. Cubberley, April 29, 1924. Terman Papers.

14. In 1918, the Harriman family donated the entire Eugenics Record Office, including buildings, land, books, lab equipment, and other assets (with total value in excess of $140,000) to the Carnegie Corporation. This gift was accompanied by a donation of $300,000 for future maintenance of the ERO. Carnegie combined the record office with its Department of Experimental Evolution and renamed the merged entity the Department of Genetics in 1921. It added $2,887,220 to Harriman's $300,000 endowment, thus ensuring its continued role as a center of eugenics research (Carnegie Institute of Washington, *The Carnegie Institute of Washington 1921* [illustrated pamphlet]; Laughlin, H. H., *Official Records,* pp. 4–5, Cold Spring Harbor Laboratory Research Library Archives). Between 1918 and 1939, when it was dismantled, the Eugenics Record Office pursued a broad and successful political program. It was instrumental in the passage of antiimmigration legislation, it promoted the extension of sterilization and anti-miscegination laws in some 25 states, and it publically defended the eugenics measures in Nazi Germany (Kevles, 1985; Kamin, 1974; Chase, 1976).

15. Teachers College. Minutes of the Board of Trustees, November 11, 1920; June 28, 1921; December 23, 1921. Minutes of the Executive Committee of the Board of Trustees, June 9, 1921; January 16, 1923; June 3, 1924; December 17, 1925; June 27, 1928. Teachers College Archives, Special Collections, Teachers College, Columbia University.

16. Shaw, F. (1964). *Fifty Years of Research in the New York City Board of Education* (Bureau of Reference and Research Publication No. 226). New York: New York City Board of Education, pp. 23–30. Records of the Board of Education of New York City, Special Collections, Teachers College, Columbia University.

17. McCormick H. W. (1948). *The First Fifty Years: A Brief Review of Progress,* Fiftieth Annual Report of the Superintendent of Schools, Board of Education, New York City, p. 91. Records of the Board of Education of New York City, Special Collections, Teachers College, Columbia University.

18. McCormick, H. W. (1948). *The First Fifty Years,* pp. 123–129. Report of the Superintendent of Schools, Board of Education, New York City, 1938–1939, p. 160. Report of the Superintendent of Schools, Board of Education, New York City, 1955–1956, Part III, Educational Research.

It should be noted that achievement tests, while still a tool of tracking, only claim to measure specific learning during a specific time period. They do not purport to measure innate mental abilities as do IQ tests.

19. Shaw, F. (1964). *Fifty Years of Research,* pp. 48–49, 88.

20. Shaw, F. (1964). *Fifty Years of Research,* pp. 135–137.

12

The Ford Foundation and the Transformation of Political Science
Peter Seybold

Before World War II, the field of political science had focused either on the formal operation of government institutions or on the moral and ethical issues of government policy. By 1960, its attention was riveted on voting patterns. The lone scholar sitting in the library, examining the details of a state constitution or philosophizing on the morality of legislature actions, was replaced by a team of survey researchers who sought to understand the electoral choices of American voters through the use of random samples and questionnaire surveys.

This transformation became known as the behavioral revolution. In a little more than ten years the whole foundation of political science was altered as behavioralists came to dominate the major journals and departments in the field. Traditional scholarship was brushed aside—labeled as too philosophical and abstract and therefore unable to meet the task of scientifically understanding modern political behavior. The victory was so complete that, in 1961, the *American Political Science Review* published what amounted to an official declaration of victory by Robert Dahl, a leading behavioralist, entitled "The Behavioral Approach to Political Science: Epitaph for a Movement to a Successful Protest."

It is the task of this chapter to develop an understanding of the social, political, and economic forces that contributed to the victory of behavioralism in political science. How was an academic field changed so fundamentally in such a short period of time? What factors contributed to this transformation? Why was the task of studying voting behavior so enthusiastically endorsed by political scientists and sociologists?

There are two possible approaches to analyzing this question. The first approach, called the internalist view, looks at the community of scholars within the field of political science in order to understand the transformation. This view is based on the idea that the internal dynamics of the discipline and the attitudes of scientists working within it are the principal factors in the fall of one perspective and the rise of another.

The second approach, called the externalist view, concentrates on the way in which social forces outside of political science affected its development. From this perspective, the influence of the larger society—and especially the availability of financial support from the federal government and private philanthropic foundations—is the principal determinant of what questions are considered important by the discipline and what methods are used to research these questions.

In order to understand the triumph of the behavioralists in the 1950s, we will borrow from both of these views. Our major thrust, however, will be externalist. We will argue that this great change was largely the product of the Ford Foundation's efforts to restructure political science to meet the needs of the economic elite. While the internal dynamics of the field were important, the basic structure of political science and, more crucially, the portrait of the American political system that social scientists presented to society were above all determined by forces operating outside the field.

From this perspective, the triumph of the behavioralists in political science was not principally the result of the mood of social scientists nor was it the result of the development by behavioralists of a more accurate portrait of how the system operates. Rather, it was a consequence of the operation of social forces in the larger political economy as mediated by the Ford Foundation.

A crucial factor that determined the intellectual complexion of post-World War II political analysis was the institutional leverage exercised by the foundation as a representative of the interests of the corporate elite. The rise to prominence of the political behavior approach did not signal the victory of a particular perspective in the marketplace of ideas; rather, it demonstrated the very significant influence that institutional support by major foundations can have on the production of ideas in our society.[1]

THE ROLE OF THE FORD FOUNDATION PROGRAM OF ACTION

The Ford Foundation was established in 1936 by the Ford family in Detroit, and until 1950 it remained a local entity, making grants largely to charitable and educational institutions in Michigan.[2] When Henry Ford and his son Edsel died within five years of each other in the 1940s, however, it was selected as the major repository for the family's stock in the Ford Motor Company, thus providing the Ford family with an alternative to selling control of the company in order to pay inheritance taxes. By the terms of the wills, the foundation acquired a 90 percent interest in the company—over 93 million shares of nonvoting stock. These shares made the Ford Foundation the richest of the great foundations and inspired the development of a national program. By the 1960s the foundation's net worth reached $4 billion, with grants exceeding $200 million per year. By the end of fiscal 1975, the foundation's grants and expenditures had totaled some $5 billion, with payments to over 7,000 institutions and organizations in the United States and in 83 foreign countries (Ford Foundation, 1976, p. 3).

In 1948, on the advice of Karl Compton, one of the leading nonfamily trustees and the president of the Massachusetts Institute of Technology, a study committee was appointed to develop plans and recommendations for the foundation's new national program (Nielson, 1972, p. 79). The committee was chaired by Rowan Gaither, who had been Compton's assistant at MIT's Radiation Laboratory during World War II. Gaither and other members of the committee traveled extensively to gather the views of prominent people on both methods of organization and fields of concentration. The study committee report was presented in 1949 (Ford Foundation, 1949) and was adopted virtually unchanged as the foundation's program.

The 1949 report provides the background for understanding Ford's support for the behavioral revolution in political science. It began with a discussion of the problems of human welfare in the United States. Of particular interest was the section on government in a democratic society, in which one of the major problems was identified as political apathy and ignorance among the masses of people:

> The Committee's attention was also directed to the widespread apathy, misunderstanding, and ignorance concerning political issues, personalities, and public needs. This poses a great danger to self-government. It is evidenced not only in the failure of many citizens to exercise their rights as voters with interest and intelligence, but also by their neglect of the many other opportunities for participation in public affairs—by taking part in organizations which are actively interested in public policy; by giving weight to the public interest in the conduct of private affairs, either as individuals or as members of trade associations, labor unions, or other organizations; or by assisting or serving part time with local or national governmental agencies. (Ford Foundation, 1949, p. 32)

This disaffection of special interest groups with basic political institutions was also troublesome for the study committee and trustees of the foundation because they felt that the very basis of American society was being challenged. It could lead to political instability and thus had to be met with a program that would restore the allegiance of these groups to the "greater good." The fear of unrest was made explicit in the section of the report that addressed racial prejudice:

> Democracy accepts the fact of conflicting interest and even encourages the positive expression of divergent views, aims, and

values. Democratic theory assumes, however, that conflicts can be resolved or accommodated by nonviolent means, and that discrimination and hostility between various groups on the basis of race, national origin, or religion can be kept below the point where the basic well-being of society is threatened. In a most realistic and practical manner, intergroup hostilities weaken our democratic strength by dissipating important resources of energy in internal conflicts, and by swelling the ranks of malcontents who constitute the seed bed for undemocratic ideologies. (Ford Foundation, 1949, p. 46)

Political alienation and apathy were not the only problems facing the United States during this period. The possibility of a return to the depressed economy of the 1930s, the still unsettled educational system, and what the committee saw as the problematic adjustment of many individuals to the rapid pace of social change in the United States, were all mentioned in this context. The committee found the prospect that problems in one area might affect the others particularly unsettling (pp. 46–50).

In response to these difficulties the study report recommended, and the trustees unanimously endorsed, the designation of five interrelated program areas in which the foundation should concentrate its efforts:

1. The problem of world peace—including the strengthening of the United Nations and its associated international agencies

2. The problem of democracy—including the elimination of restrictions on freedom of thought and other civil rights; the maintenance of democratic control over concentrations of public and private power; and the improvement of the political processes through which public officers are chosen and policies determined

3. Problems of the economy—including the achievement of high and stable employment levels; greater equality of economic opportunity for all citizens; more satisfactory labor-management relations; and the attainment of "that balance between friends and control in our economic life which will most effectively serve the well-being of our entire society"

4. Problems of education—including the clarification of educational goals and evaluation of current educational practices; the reduction of economic, religious, and racial barriers to equality of educational opportunity; and the more effective use of the mass media for nonacademic education of citizens of all ages

5. The scientific study of people—including the study of values, motivations, and maladjustments; and the application of the knowledge gained to every aspect of democratic life (Nelson, 1972, pp. 80–81).

Each of these areas became a separate division within the foundation. Area two, the promotion of democracy, and area five, the enrichment of social science knowledge, became the loci for foundation concern with the development of behavioral political science. We therefore turn to a closer examination of what the foundation viewed as the crucial problems and needs in these two areas.

The chapter in the report on strengthening democracy stressed the importance of clarifying the meaning of democracy and creating the conditions for maintaining democracy:

> The problems toward which the objectives of this program area point fall into two classes.
>
> The first covers those in which the meaning of democracy is not clear, for either of two reasons: the principles themselves may not be adequately defined or understood, or, although clearly expressed in general terms, the meaning or implications of the principles in particular situations may not be apparent or appreciated.
>
> The second class is one in which the democratic principle involved is clear and accepted but the means of solving the problem [of achieving democracy] are unknown or inadequately understood. (Ford Foundation, 1949, pp. 63–64)

In practice, the first issue called for the development of a definition of democracy that would help secure the continued loyalty of Americans at a time when apathy (if not dissent) threatened the country's internal strength.

> The value of democratic principles must be measured by the extent of adherence to them, and such adherence is adequate only if it pervades the total of our political, economic, and social actions. . . .
>
> As the Study progressed, the Committee and its advisors found that to a vast number of sincere and loyal Americans the principles of democracy are merely a collection of cliches, serving chiefly as reminders of historical events and social conditions of the past. At the same time the Committee was impressed with the struggle of thoughtful and informed persons to find a meaningful, contemporary, and usable definition of democracy. Without such a definition millions of Americans remain confused in their analyses of crucial problems. Consequently national policies may often be erratic and conflicting, and *many avoidable dangers to our internal strength can be the products of our own creation.* (p. 64; emphasis added)

This conclusion led to the second concern, the proper application of certain democratic principles. The report suggested a number of alternatives, including both basic research and structural reforms that would encourage citizen participation.

> For the most part these problems lie in the area of political processes—from public opinion and voting, through the selection of legislative and executive officials, to the formulation and administration of policy. . . . Processes of self-government, which are designed to keep political power responsive to the people and to express their will in action, are seriously affected by public apathy, by lack of citizen participation in government and civic affairs, and by defective government machinery. While these problems are widely recognized, knowledge of their causes and cure is inadequate. It is evident, however, that solutions will often require multiple approaches. Research, for example, will be required to analyze public apathy in order to understand its causes and the ways in which it may be lessened. In all such areas the use of special commissions of public inquiry may prove helpful in

achieving the public understanding necessary for sound action. (pp. 67–68)

One suggestion for combating public apathy involved demonstration projects in communities of manageable size, with scientists and educators stimulating and mobilizing an interest in public affairs. The particular programs would be based on systematic surveys and analyses of local problems and conditions. The report did not anticipate fundamental changes in the functioning of government. It did not entertain the possibility that nonparticipation represented a judgment (conscious or unconscious) that more active involvement would not redress the grievances that had produced the alienation. In a sense, this program proposed an advertising campaign to draw citizens into political participation.

While "area two" was concerned particularly with the practical problems of democracy, "area five" was concerned with research in human behavior, and it would soon become institutionalized as the Behavioral Sciences Division. The creation of this division was a clear expression of the foundation's belief that the behavioral sciences, if strengthened substantially, could make a key contribution to the solution of basic social problems in America. A major part of the program the Ford Foundation developed therefore required a more practical political science, one that would gather current data on the political behavior of the American electorate and develop the new, more serviceable, conception of democracy. Traditional political scientists were ill equipped to meet these mandates, as they were not empirically oriented. Confronted with an inappropriate and impractical status quo, the Ford Foundation threw its considerable weight behind the previously uninfluential behavioralist minority in the profession.

INSTITUTION BUILDING

The effort to nurture an empirical political science required a substantial financial investment in individual scholars, graduate departments, research institutes, and professional associations. Between 1951 and 1957, the Behavioral Science Division of the Ford Foundation granted over $23 million in support to researchers who shared its commitment to this endeavor (Ford Foundation, 1958, p. 10). This investment was made particularly significant by the fact that the federal government did not begin to support the social sciences until the 1960s. For a considerable period of time, therefore, grant money from the Ford Foundation was virtually the only source of funding for political science research.

The foundation's Foreign Area Fellowship Program illustrates its great influence on the field, since this program funded the graduate education of a substantial proportion of all researchers in comparative politics, which was largely concerned with defining and describing democratic processes:

Statistics will demonstrate just how successful this program has been in strengthening American higher education. Of the 984 former fellows, 550 hold faculty positions in 181 colleges and universities in 38 states. . . .

Some twenty-nine universities employed five or more fellows, and ten universities have employed ten or more. In addition to academic and teaching careers, eighty-two former fellows are now in government service, thirty-eight are now in philanthropic or non-profit organizations, and forty-five are in business or professions. Many former fellows have added to our knowledge of the non-Western world through the publication of results of research. Altogether they have published some 373 books and over 3,000 articles and short monographs; moreover, they have edited or contributed to another 516 volumes. (Beckmann, 1964, p. 18)

The training of foreign area specialists was just one part of the larger movement to develop a practical understanding of human behavior. Another aspect was, as already indicated, the transformation of political science into an empirical discipline. To accomplish this, Ford worked on building and institutional structure that would train a new generation of behavioralists committed to electoral studies and survey methodology (see Seybold, 1980, for a full discussion of this orientation). This required involvement at a number of different levels: support for individual scholars, the establishment and support of research institutes, the reorientation of professional journals, the recruitment of intermediary organizations, and the training of younger scholars in the methodology of behavioralism.

This prodigious effort began with an evaluation and definition of the field of political behavior:

> This topic refers not only to behavior involved in the operation of formal governments, domestic and international, but also to behavior in power relations generally. It includes such questions as the causes and consequences of political participation and apathy in democratic society, the distribution of political values and doctrines, and the characteristics and codes of political leaders. (Ford Foundation, 1953, p. 10)

It also defined a set of central research issues that the new discipline would address:

> How is public opinion formed on political issues? When and how is public opinion brought to bear on policy formation? How are political values and doctrines distributed throughout the community, what is their present status, and how do they change? (Ford Foundation, 1953, p. 18)

The definition of political behavior reflected an applied approach. The focus on the process by which political attitudes developed also fit neatly into the broader concerns expressed in the 1949 report. If the formation of political viewpoints was understood, apathy and political alienation could be reduced and even replaced by committed participation.

Two additional steps were also part of the general involvement of the foundation in the behavioral sciences. First, the foundation encouraged the creation of programs designed to develop behavioral political theory. At Columbia University, for example, a committee was set up to encourage behavioral research (particularly in political science) and to train new researchers in the most sophisticated available methodologies. At the University of Chicago, a year-long graduate seminar on research in political behavior was established. At the University of North Carolina, a political behavior committee was formed which impacted heavily on subsequent research there:

> The committee has fixed political behaviour research in the minds of students, faculty, and administration as an appropriate and continuing part of graduate training and faculty research programs of the university. Before the creation of the political behavior committee there were no voluntary applications from political science students for research assistantships in the Institute for Research in Social Science. The work of the committee led directly to the initiation of substantial research program in political behaviors. It was also instrumental in helping the department to recruit new faculty members who were interested in political behavior.[3]

At the University of Michigan, after discussions within the university's Committee on Individual Behavior and Human Relations, a Political Behavior Program was established in the spring of 1981. Like the other initiatives just discussed, the program was funded by a grant from the Ford Foundation for training and research in the behavioral sciences.

Second, Ford fellowships were made available to political science students showing promise as empirical researchers. This combination of faculty committees and graduate funding led to numerous graduate programs in political behavior, some of which built national reputations as major research centers.

In 1952, the foundation sponsored an inventory of the now changing field of political science, conducted by a group of Columbia University scholars that included Seymour Martin Lipset, David Truman, Richard Hofstadter, Herbert Hyman, and William McPhee. This effort was intended to review existing research, systematize recent findings, and designate those subareas which looked particularly promising for further work. Even at this early stage, the review openly excluded normative political science, historical studies, and political philosophy and the recommendations for further funding were restricted to the behavioral orientation. The inventory inspired a number of publications that were crucial in giving direction to the field.

In subsequent years the foundation became involved in three other forms of institution building. First a variety of grants was made to research institutes. For example, the Bureau of Applied Social Research at Columbia received a Ford grant establishing an international center of survey research materials and another that produced a casebook on applied social research. The National Opinion Research Center at the University of Chicago received $36,000 for behavioral research, and the Russell Sage Foundation received

$750,000 to develop a program on the practical utilization of the behavioral sciences. The grant to Russell Sage was especially significant, since it helped create two different sorts of institutional niches for behaviorally oriented researchers. It financed the appointment of postdoctoral scholars to residencies in operating agencies or professional schools, many of which had not previously been exposed to empirical political science. It also provided funds for the appointment of empirical political scientists to faculty positions, thus facilitating the addition of these scholars to the staffs of many universities.

Second, the foundation created and endowed the Center for Advanced Study in the Behavioral Sciences in Palo Alto, which opened in 1954. The founding of the center signaled the coming of age of the behavioral sciences as the center served as a gathering spot for social scientists who advocated the change to the behavioralist approach. The center was also crucial for the development of those younger scholars who would later consolidate the behavioralist domination of the field.

The significance of the center in promoting the behavioral revolution was assessed by Robert Dahl:

> The most durable offshoot of the Behavioral Sciences Program at Ford is the Center for Advanced Study in the Behavioral Sciences at Palo Alto. . . . In its early years the political scientists who were fellows there tended to be discontented with traditional approaches, inclined toward a more rigorously empirical and scientific study of politics, and deeply interested in learning whenever possible from the other social sciences. (1961b, pp. 765–766)

The center's symbolic importance cannot be underestimated. It represented a long-term commitment by the nation's largest foundation to the emerging behavioral approach.

The final institutional aspect of Ford's support for the behavioral revolution was its financial backing of the Social Science Research Council, and, in particular, the council's committees on political behavior and comparative politics. These committees became the foci for the successful campaign to reorient research in political sociology by funding the influential behavioralist studies of politics on the international, national, state, and local levels. The cumulative impact of these committees can hardly be overestimated. The publications that resulted from the research they supported make up a large part of the literature of the behavioral revolution, and the members of these committees form a roster of the key figures in the postwar behavioral movement.[5]

The Committee on Political Behavior was especially active during the formative period of the 1950s, when it distributed $340,000 in research funds to individual scholars for investigations of American governmental processes at the federal, state, and municipal levels. This support produced path-breaking work in a variety of areas including (*a*) descriptions of urban politics by Robert Dahl, Peter Rossi, Edward Banfield, Norton Long, and James Q. Wilson, (*b*) studies of state government by Avery Leiserson and

Heinz Eulau, (c) investigations of federal policy development by Lester Milbrath, Richard Fenno, Nelson Polsby, and Raymond Wolfinger, and (d) sophisticated voting analyses by Warren Miller and Phillip Converse.

The committee's impact was neatly demonstrated by Heinz Eulau's (1976) compilation of the 15 landmark books published in political science between 1952 and 1959. Of these, 12 were supported by Ford either directly or indirectly through the SSRC committee.

In 1964 the Committee on Political Behavior was disbanded because its pioneering mission was complete. It was replaced by the Committee on Government and Legal Processes. This new committee was very much a direct descendant of its predecessor:

> Four of the new committee's 6 members and 9 of the total of 13 who served on it at some time had received financial support from its predecessor. And all 13 members, as graduate students and young scholars in the late 1940's and 1950's, were the products of the "behavioral revolution" in political science that the Committee on Political Behavior had done so much to bring about. (Pye and Ryland, 1974; p. 4)

Not unexpectedly, the Committee on Government and Legal Processes concentrated its attention on political behavior, though it modified its focus to include two other kinds of research. First, it stimulated studies of the substance of public policies, a subject that was rarely a concern of the earlier SSRC committee. Second, it encouraged the development of "impact studies," which traced the consequences of particular policies for the life situations of the people affected by them. Subjects studied included, for example, the impact of urban renewal on a particular community and that of voter registration laws on political participation. The work of this committee therefore represented a firmer commitment to practical research, the next step in the process of contributing to the formation of public policy.

The SSRC's Committee on Comparative Politics was the second focal point of the early Ford effort. This committee reoriented the area of comparative government away from European studies and substituted a focused concern with the problems of political development of the new states that emerged after World War II (Pye and Ryland, 1971, p. 2). Even more than the Committee on Political Behavior, the work of the Committee on Comparative Politics reflected the need for up-to-date information and practical knowledge—in this case about emerging nations which adopt uncongenial policies and/or systems of government. Facts were therefore not the only needed resource: a body of scientific writing that demonstrated the superiority of American-oriented economic development and public policies was needed for the Cold War competition with the Soviet Union. In response to this need, the committee (along with other parts of the research apparatus) produced what has been called "an ideology of developmentalism," which argued that developing countries faced essentially the same problems as the United States had faced a century earlier and that they should and would follow the same pattern of growth. The United States was thus seen as the "First New Nation" (Lipset, 1963), which provided the model for modernization to emerging countries.[6]

The comparative politics committee, together with the institutes, programs, and individual scholars involved in the behavioralism network, effected profound changes in the structure of research in comparative government. The field was reformulated to include the entire contemporary world (rather than just Western Europe), the focus was riveted on economic development, and a generation of area specialists was trained who could provide valuable information to government officials and corporate leaders on previously underresearched regions and countries. The emerging body of literature brought another large area of political sociology under the purview of the behavioral revolution. The accomplishments of this committee, like those of its sister, were therefore crucial to the transformation of American political science.

The bulk of the Ford Foundation's efforts to construct a behavioral political sociology was channeled through intermediary organizations such as the SSRC because these institutions could access levels in the research hierarchy that Ford could not reach effectively. Thus the establishment of research institutes, the center, and the SSRC committees resulted in access to individual scholars who would otherwise have been invisible to the foundation.

But not all of Ford's influence was indirect. It also provided direct financial support for planning agencies and universities. As mentioned earlier, during this period the federal government was not involved in supporting social science research, and this enhanced Ford's influence considerably. Ford provided the seed money for the establishment of graduate training, undergraduate programs, and research institutes in behavioral studies. It organized and nurtured the development of this perspective at big universities, and relied on the prestige and graduates of these large institutions to influence the smaller and less prestigious colleges. The funds involved in these efforts were earmarked for behavioral research; they were not available to researchers or students with other interests or viewpoints. This channeling greatly influenced the career choices of students, as well as the research programs of both individual scholars and institutes. In some instances, the foundation took direct interest in the contents of particular programs.[7] This type of direct intervention was more typical in the early stages of the behavioral revolution, when the foundation was especially active and before a generation of committed behavioralists had been trained.

By 1965 Ford could claim credit for a vast transformation in political science, involving the upgrading of the technical competence of those in the field, the reorientation of research to emphasize empirical work, the creation of programs that produced well-trained researchers, the construction of centers for research on specific substantive problems in areas such as metropolitan government and international affairs, and the establishment of a highly flattering portrait of the American political and economic systems as accepted scientific wisdom.

CONCLUSIONS

The impact of the Ford Foundation's efforts to redirect the field of political science during the 1950s became evident in the early 1960s. Books and articles reflecting the "new behavioral political science" began to dominate the literature in the field. Institutions such as the Center for Advanced Study of the Behavioral Sciences, international affairs programs at major universities, and metropolitan government centers were staffed by behavioral political scientists. The specialists produced by this system would ultimately have a great impact on public policy (Henry Kissinger, for example, received SSRC support in the 1950s).

Skeptics might ask, What difference does it make that the field of political science came to be dominated by behavioral research? This is an important question, and the answer lies in noting that the Ford Foundation's actions were not motivated by a simple desire to further research in political science. The trustees sought to enlist political science and the social sciences in an effort to preserve the stability of the American institutional order. This ambition, which reflected the classwide view of the foundation's trustees, defined the agenda for social research within the field, but this was not the main goal of the foundation. The transformation of political science therefore did not occur in a social or political vacuum; it was part of a larger process, which linked developments and changes in an academic field to the broader issues of American life in the post-World War II period. Contrary to the view which suggests that perspectives which become popular in the social sciences are determined by competition within the academic marketplace, the restructuring of political science was an example of the subtle domination of the cultural sphere by elite interests.

The role of the Ford Foundation in this process was to identify actual and potential threats to the status quo and address them with a program of political research which could aid in the struggle to maintain political stability. This was not an easy task and it required involvement at a number of different levels in the knowledge-producing sector of society. The foundation acted as a coordinator: it aided universities in establishing a congenial atmosphere for behavioral political science, it created specific centers devoted to different aspects of the project (international affairs, metropolitan government, etc.), it founded the intermediary organizations and professional associations, and it supported the research of individual scholars. The foundation was the only institution capable of developing and guiding a network of institutions which had previously been either disorganized or nonexistent. The end product was a national movement within relevant academic sectors to retool political science toward practical political research and to identify democracy with existing institutional arrangements (Seybold, 1980).

The pervasive consequences of the foundation's actions were often hidden from public view. The shaping of the production of knowledge often occurs behind the backs of even those involved in the process. As a network of institutions grows it becomes part of the "natural order of things." The very existence of a center for international affairs or metropolitan politics at a prestigious university tends to define the appropriate boundaries for inquiry. As the institutional base for producing social science research matures, it becomes somewhat independent of the funding sources that gave it life. Ultimately, this independence leads to a drifting away from the founder's mandates, but the research is still infused with the founder's assumptions. The production of social science research thus becomes regularized or routinized, and its connection to sponsoring institutions becomes obscured from the public's view.

Twenty years down the road, a set of institutions exist which are prestigious and prominent, and they are the "natural" organizations to which knowledge consumers turn for new research. The ultimate consequence of Ford's intervention within political science was that it created a series of institutions that were instrumental in defining the agenda for social research in the United States and that continue to define the new agendas in changing political economic circumstances. These institutions also contribute the bulk of the policy analysts who work for the State Department or other relevant government agencies or who are employed by private think tanks.

Viewed in this larger context, the Ford Foundation's role in restructuring political science takes on added significance. It can be seen as example of the transmission and ultimate institutionalization of ruling class interests into the cultural sphere. As David Noble has argued, this is part of a cultural war. "There is no conspiracy, for this is not a secret war. . . . But the forces which shape intellectual discourse in this country are nevertheless too often hidden from public view" (Noble, 1981, p. 336). The social forces involved in the reorganization of the social sciences thus are unnoticed, even though they may have lasting consequences for the nature of political debate in the United States. As this brief history of the transformation of political science indicates, the network of institutions that became the centers of the "new political science" were permanently marked by the interests and concerns of the trustees of the Ford Foundation. In short, they reflected, in a subtle but powerful manner, the agenda that was transmitted to them by members of the ruling class during their period of formation.

NOTES

1. For an excellent overview of the role of private foundations in the production of knowledge in the United States see Arnove (1980).

2. This discussion of the growth of the Ford Foundation relies heavily on the account provided by Nielsen (1972).

3. Ford Foundation, Grant File No. 50-266, "University of North Carolina."

4. Ford Foundation, Grant File No. 55-118, "Russell Sage Foundation."

5. The Committee on Political Behavior during this period included David Truman (1949–1964), Angus Campbell (1949–1958, 1963–1964), Robert Dahl (1955–1962); Oliver Garceau (1949–1964), Alexander Heard (1954–1958); V. O. Key (1949–1963), and Avery Leisersen (1949–1964).

Heard went on to become chairman of the board of trustees of the Ford Foundation.

6. This theory of development has been discredited by recent scholarship. It fails to recognize that present circumstances are vastly different, due to the existence of a complex world economy which distorts the economies of Third World countries. The decidedly Western bias of this model has been an embarrassment to U.S. policy-makers in Latin America, Africa, and Asia, where underdevelopment is viewed as at least partially the result of the overdevelopment of advanced capitalist countries.

For an overview of the criticisms of the "First New Nation" perspective, see Andre Gunder Frank, *Latin America: Underdevelopment or Revolution* (New York: Monthly Review Press, 1969), Chapter 2; K. T. Fann and Donald Hodges (eds.), *Readings in U.S. Imperialism* (Boston: Porter Sargent Publishers, 1971); and Charles Wilber (ed.), *The Political Economy of Development and Underdevelopment* (New York: Random House, 1973).

7. Ford Foundation Grant Files No. 56–83, "Rotating Research Professorship in Governmental Affairs."

PART IV
Conclusion

13

Reagan or Business? Foundations of the New Conservatism

Dan Clawson
Mary Ann Clawson

The 1980 election, and the 1984 consolidation of those results, apparently marked a decisive realignment in American politics. Not only did they represent the most significant electoral shift since the 1930s, they were accompanied by "one of the largest and most comprehensive policy changes in modern times" (Burnham, 1982, p. 268). Reagan's unprecedented success in implementing his policies was matched only by his seeming ability to move the terrain of political debate rightward. Instead of increased polarization, the Republican move rightward produced a Democratic party that accepted substantial parts of the new conservative agenda and sought to shed its identification with traditional constituencies.

At the same time as it constitutes a political watershed, the Reagan phenomenon poses a fundamental challenge to a central argument of this book. The fact that an electoral victory and a change of presidents produced a far-reaching transformation in public policy would seem to reestablish electoral politics as the central arena of political power and the state as the site of public policy formation. In order to retain its credibility, the perspective advanced in this book must be able to provide an alternative explanation for this shift to the right.

Most analyses have indeed remained at the level of electoral politics. The most superficial provide explanations in terms of personal or chance factors: Reagan's charm and media skills as "The Great Communicator," Jimmy Carter and Walter Mondale's ineffectiveness, the state of the economy (bad in 1980, good in 1984) (Adatto, 1984; DiSouza, 1984; Hibbs, 1982). Others find the key in the right-wing populism of the "prolife" and religious fundamentalist movements (Petchesky, 1981). The most insightful approaches to electoral politics focus on the declining participation of less affluent voters and the collapse of the Democratic party (Burnham, 1981, 1982; Edsall, 1984).

Undoubtedly each of these factors has played some part in the political shift to the right. But this chapter will argue that the most basic cause lies elsewhere, in the economic, political, and ideological processes that this book has analyzed. American politics moved rightward because of a concerted corporate mobilization around a conservative agenda. Beginning well before the 1980 election, this mobilization involved the development of a new economic and political agenda and a redirection of corporate resources toward new policy formation institutions and new ways of influencing both the government and the public. It was these prior changes which created the impetus and laid the groundwork for the more visible transformation of 1980–1984.

WHY DID BUSINESS MOBILIZE FOR A CONSERVATIVE AGENDA?

As this book has argued (see Chapter 7), business and the policy organizations it dominates have largely controlled American politics for generations. Even the liberal social policies of the New Deal and Great Society were shaped by business groups in order to meet their needs while simultaneously responding to and defusing popular protests. If the liberal institutions that existed in the late 1960s and early 1970s were created to accord with business priorities, why then would corporate leaders wish to dismantle them? Why did they begin a mobilization to fundamentally change policies and organizations that they had shaped, supported, and in some cases even initiated?

The motivating factors for the rise of corporate conservatism are located in the economic and political changes of the last 30 to 40 years: the growing economic power of other capitalist nations in Europe and Asia, successful challenges to United States hegemony by Third World countries, and the impact of popular movements within the United States, including the black, student, antiwar, women's, labor, environmental, and consumer protection movements. None of these developments were about to topple Americna capitalism, yet it is clear that by the early 1970s many capitalists believed their power and options to be threatened. When, for example, Leonard Silk (*New York Times* economic columnist) and David Vogel (a graduate student) were allowed to sit in on a 1973 series of retreats for top executives, they found a mood of vulnerability and a concern about the long-range implications of recent social and economic policies: "we are fighting for our lives," "we are fighting a delaying action," "we are on the defensive, on the witness stand, forced to justify ourselves." The executives felt that "we must get to problems before they get politically hot," because "if we don't take action now, we will see our own demise. We will evolve into another social democracy" (Silk and Vogel, 1976, pp. 44, 45, 67, 72). Corporate executives, like many other people, may tend to overestimate their problems. Nonetheless, a comparison of the 1940s and 1970s makes it clear that the nature of the problems confronting U.S. capital had changed profoundly.

In international affairs, the initiatives of the 1940s, predicated on the assumption of American economic and political hegemony, had been directed toward two goals: (a) rehabilitating other industrialized capitalist countries so as to create viable political and economic partners for the United States and (b) freeing the Third World from overt colonial relationships, in order to satisfy aspirations for independence, meet the ideological challenge of the Cold War, and open those economies to equal penetration by American goods and capital. In contrast, the 1970s saw American industry outperformed by other capitalist countries. Moreover, popular insurgency in the Third World now focused primarily in the United States as the world's leading imperialist power. Such opposition posed a threat to American political and military primacy even in those cases where the loss of access to markets and investments was economically insignificant.

Domestically, corporate as well as political leaders, shaped by the experience of the thirties, entered the postwar era committed to the maintenance of consumer demand. Thus business came to accept increased government involvement in the economy (Collins, 1981; Stein, 1969). Welfare policies such as unemployment compensation and social security were especially important because they protected consumer purchasing power while helping to assuage popular discontent over the dislocations in the business cycle and the labor market. At the same time, the dominant position of the United States in the world economy enabled large corporations to pay high wages to unionized sectors of the workforce without significant cost to themselves.

By the 1970s these policies looked increasingly problematic to many business leaders. Expenditures for welfare, boosted in response to black insurgency and discontent, increased dramatically as a larger proportion of the poor began to actually collect the welfare for which they were technically eligible (Piven and Cloward, 1971). Expenditures also increased for programs primarily benefiting the stable working class (unemployment compensation, Social Security, Medicare), straining state finances and reducing (but by no means eliminating) workers' incentives to accept the wages and conditions employers chose to offer (Bowles, Gordon, and Weiskopf, 1983). Simultaneously, concern about the increasing level of imports prompted corporate leaders to seek to weaken unions and lower wages to facilitate competition with Europe and Japan. However, the entrenched power of unions meant that this could not be done without a political as well as an economic offensive. Finally, there was dismay over a new generation of government regulation in support of the environment, occupational health and safety, consumer protection, and affirmative action. These new regulatory agencies had been introduced as a result of popular social movements; while business had managed to keep these laws weak, it was concerned at the very existence of such agencies.

On the one hand this concern seems misplaced or exaggerated: the power of an agency like the Occupational Safety and Health Administration (OSHA), for example, was severely compromised by the low budget given for enforcement and the low fines imposed on violators. In 1971 there were 47,000 commercially available chemical compounds. Since OSHA has set legal limits on concentration levels for only about 500 compounds, "thousands of known and suspected toxic chemicals lack exposure standards" (Berman, 1978, p. 82). Most workplaces never get inspected; even when violations are found, the fines imposed are generally nominal—in the early 1970s, for example, only about $25 per violation (Berman, 1978, p. 34).[1] Yet the logic of capitalist concern is clear. Laws gave OSHA the right to set standards for work place pollutants and for safeguards on machinery and equipment, to inspect work places to check compliance, and to fine employers found to be in violation. Properly enforced and funded, such laws could mean a major loss of power by capitalists. Even the weak and underenforced laws of the 1970s meant that in some cases social objectives would determine corporate operations even if this reduced profitability.

Thus capitalists in the early seventies felt threatened—by changes in the world economy, by the decline of American hegemony, and by the consequences and implications of domestic political mobilizations. The business community could, of course, continue to respond to these challenges incrementally, within the basic framework of postwar institutional structures, and this was one response. But, within the business community, expressions of discontent and calls for a more fundamental change had begun to coalesce in the early seventies.

Indeed, what would later become Reagan's agenda was being outlined in *Business Week* as early as 1975. The key problem in America, *Business Week,* argued, was a capital shortage: business needed more money so it could invest and rejuvenate the economy. After considering and rejecting various alternatives, *Business Week* decided that "a policy designed to increase savings is the only one that makes sense" and recommended a three-pronged attack:

> —The growth of government spending must be curbed. . . .
> —The tax structure must be changed so that the cash flow to business increases. . . .
> —Rewards to individual savers and investors must be increased (September 22, 1975, p. 115)

Thus by 1975 the new business agenda was emerging. But its implementation would require changes in both institutional structures and public perceptions. Its adherents had to mobilize, not only to articulate their positions in more practical detail, but to begin the massive job of changing the terms of political debate, reaching influential opinion leaders, and organizing an electoral majority. Thus the conservative mobilization operated in three major areas: policy formation, attempts to influence political and opinion leaders, and campaign funding. In this way business helped not only to change state policy, but the political mood of the country as well.

FORMS OF MOBILIZATION

In the sphere of policy formation, the major change was a shift of resources to conservative institutions. Think tanks are crucial to the policy formation process, providing information, ideas, and proposals to be considered by the government, the mass media, and capitalists themselves. In the 1950s and 1960s, the most important of these business-dominated organizations—the Brookings Institution, the Ford Foundation (see Chapter 12), the Committee for Economic Development (CED), and the Council on Foreign Relations (CFR)—supported and in fact shaped the moderate-to-liberal policies of the times. Explicitly conservative think tanks, such as the Hoover Institute and American Enterprise Institute (AEI), were relatively marginal. In the 1970s and 1980s, the shift to conservatism is evident both in the changed policies recommended by the "liberal" groups (Peschek, 1987) and, still more important, in the creation and expansion of explicitly conservative think tanks. Hoover and the AEI have expanded rapidly; the Heritage Foundation was created in 1973 and has since risen to prominence; and a host of other right-wing think tanks and institutes have appeared or been rejuvenated (Ed Meese's Institute for Contemporary Studies, the Georgetown Center for Strategic and International Studies, university-related centers for the promotion of "free enterprise," and a number of "public interest" conservative law firms that have done such things as pay for Westmoreland's lawsuit charging the media with liberal bias in their accounts of the Vietnam war).

The emergence of these conservative organizations is often attributed to a split in the capitalist class between western new money "Cowboys" and the eastern old money establishment "Yankees" (Davis, 1981; Dye, 1981; Sale, 1976). According to this explanation, the conservative organizations are essentially financed by the former group. For example, Joseph Coors, a Colorado beer manufacturer with little multinational involvement, was the most visible founding patron of the Heritage Foundation. But while theories of splits between "liberal" and "conservative" capitalists are extremely widespread, there is little or no evidence to sustain them. Thus, although Coors has been a major contributor to the New Right, the largest contributor, with amounts estimated at $10 million a year, is Richard Mellon Scaife, who provided far more of the seed money for Heritage than did Coors—and the Mellons are one of the most established old money families in America (Rothmeyer, 1981). Walter Wriston, chairman of the board of Citibank, the largest New York money market bank, is on the board of the American Enterprise Institute. The AEI has over 600 corporate contributors, including Citibank, IBM, Morgan Guaranty Trust, Exxon, Ford, General Motors, Firestone, and Goodyear (Goldstein, 1982; Morgan, 1981), the same corporations that contribute to moderate think tanks. There is simply no systematic evidence for a split; the only effort to test for one found that the hypothesized factors had little or no impact on corporate support for conservative congressional candidates in the 1980 election (Clawson, Kaufman, and Neustadtl, 1985).

Table 19 indicates the extent of the shift in resources for think tanks. If we compare the three leading conservative think tanks with the three leading moderate/liberal groups (AEI, Hoover, and Heritage versus Brookings, CED, and CFR), in both 1965 and 1970 the moderate/liberal groups had more than three times the expenditures of the conservatives. In 1975 moderate/liberal think tanks still had a significant though much-diminished edge over the conservatives, but by 1980 conservatives spent substantially more than the moderate/liberal organizations (about one-third more). The moderate organizations continued to grow throughout this period, but the business mobilization led to an enormous increase in funding for conservatives.

A somewhat different but equally revealing case is the decline of the Ford Foundation as a funding source. In the 1960s and early 1970s the Ford Foundation had functioned as the quintessential liberal and activist foundation. It had provided massive funding for a variety of activities, supporting, for example, pilot projects that played an important role in defining the character of the civil rights movement and the War on Poverty. During this period, the foundation had in fact spent more than its income. But by the mid-seventies, it began to reduce its spending drastically, from a peak of $905 million in 1966 to $114 million in 1980 (in constant 1980 dollars), the year of Reagan's election. Therefore, even if Ford remained just as "liberal" as ever, liberal causes had only one-eighth as much money from this source during the late 1970s as during the mid-1960s.[2]

A second significant type of conservative activity was influencing political decision making through lobbying and public advocacy of probusiness positions. Of crucial importance to these efforts was the formation of the business Roundtable in 1973. Although the roundtable began in the efforts of two groups to break the power of construction unions by encouraging big business to use nonunion contractors, it was soon transformed by its merger with an informal group of top business leaders. It differed from the CED, which had previously been the most important business domestic policy organization, in two ways: first, it was only open to chief executive officers (no academics, no vice presidents); second, it focused primarily on active lobbying rather than on policy formation. In lobbying Congress, business was able to exert enormous leverage, because all congress-people are dependent, to some extent, on the operations of big business within their district. For example, in 1979 when Congress debated federally guaranteed loans for the Chrysler Corporation, Chrysler produced a list of the employment it generated in each congressional district. The list for just one Indiana Republican's district included 436 companies with sales totaling over $29 million (Edsall, 1984, p. 111). Since the Business Roundtable meets to coordinate its lobbying and plan the best approach to each member of Congress, it could multiply such a list by a factor of 100 or more, reflecting the combined employment of all the major companies and their suppliers in

Table 19
POLICY GROUP/THINK TANK EXPENDITURES
(IN MILLIONS OF DOLLARS)

Organization	1965	1970	Year 1975	1980	1983
American Enterprise Institute	.6	.9	4.1	9.7	10.6
Hoover Institution	1.2	1.9	3.0	5.7	8.4
Heritage Foundation	——	——	2.8[a]	5.3	10.6
Total, Three Conservative Organizations	1.8	2.5	9.9	20.7	29.6
Brookings Institution	3.0	5.5	7.8	9.2	11.9
Committee for Economic Development	1.7	2.1	1.9	2.6	3.1
Council on Foreign Relations	1.7	2.1	2.3	3.9	6.5[b]
Total, Three Moderate Organizations	6.4	9.7	12.0	15.7	21.5

SOURCE: Annual reports, phone conversations with relevant officials.

[a] 1978; 1975 data not available

[b] 1984

each district. Business is reported to have spent more than $5 million on the lobbying for just one bill, discussed below, the Labor Law Reform Act of 1978 (Malbin, 1980, p. 179).

Big business has also benefited from, and helped promote, the recent mobilization of small business. The Chamber of Commerce has been revived, with huge increases in membership and effectiveness, and to a lesser extent so have other small business organizations. On several key issues big business has gotten the support of small business. During the Labor Law Reform Bill debate, for example, big business used its corporate jets to fly small business people to meet with Congress. Big business has not been willing to reciprocate, however. For example, in the tax law of 1978, the breaks went almost exclusively to big business. " 'The bigs lobbied against us and squashed us,' James (Mike) McKevitt, head of the National Federation of Independent Business, complained after enactment of the 1978 tax bill." (Edsall, 1984, p. 126).

The seventies also saw the emergence and expansion of advocacy advertising as a means of influencing public opinion. Traditional advertising tries to sell a product: Presta-Glop cleans teeth whiter than Ultra-Goo. Advocacy advertising has no explicit connection with a corporation's products but rather promotes a political message.

Advocacy advertising has been targeted in both style and substance primarily at opinion formers; Mobil's ads appear on the *New York Times* editorial page rather than in the *National Enquirer.* In the case of Mobil, advertisements laid out to resemble op-ed pieces have criticized the media, defended special tax breaks for oil companies, and favored deregulation of gas and oil prices. Union Carbide commissioned public opinion surveys and then took out ads claiming the American people had the same views as Union Carbide ("Americans reject no-growth future") and implying they supported Union Carbide's own recommendations for stimulating growth: less government spending, lower business taxes, and reduced government regulation (Himmelstein, 1980).

While no comprehensive data exist on the extent of corporate advertising, David Vogel claims that "major corporate advertisers are now spending about one-third of their advertising dollars on campaigns aimed at the public in their roles as citizens rather than consumers," and a congressional committee has estimated that issue advertising amounts to $1 billion a year (Vogel, 1979, p. 627; Edsall, 1984, p. 116). Clearly, advocacy advertising must now be recognized as a significant corporate strategy.

Last but not least, business has also mobilized around politics more narrowly defined, using its superior financial resources to make up for its limited numbers. As discussed in Chapter 6, campaign finance laws underwent changes in the early 1970s. Though these changes appeared to restrict the power of money, very similar changes had earlier been recommended by the Committee for Economic Development. By restricting the size of any individual donation and requiring public disclosure, the new laws made it much more difficult for a single source of wealth, whether an individual or a company, to buy special favors. (In 1972, for example, W. Clement Stone gave more than $2 million to Richard Nixon.) In practice this means that money influences politics through the coordinated action of many donors, and generally can only do so for ends that are publicly defensible. Translated, big business is the group able to coordinate hundreds of "small" donations (an average of $500 each), because of the underlying unity of business analyzed in Part I of this book. The new campaign finance laws simply restricted the power of mavericks such as Howard Hughes while reinforcing the structural power of the coordinated business community.

The alterations in campaign finance laws mean that comparisons of changes over time need to be treated cautiously. The new laws explicitly legalized political action committees (PACs) associated with labor unions or businesses: the PAC collects and pools donations from union members or corporation employees while the sponsoring organization contributes the administrative and collection costs. Though the money comes from individuals, it is controlled by the organization. Some part of the increase in business giving may simply be the result of previously hidden disclosures becoming public. What the data indicate, however, is that in 1974 labor PACs outnumbered business PACs by more than two-to-one, while in 1980 business PACs outnumbered labor ones by four-to-one. If we include under the rubric of business PACs of both corporations and trade associations, in 1974 labor gave substantially more than business ($6.3 million to $4.8 million), while by 1980 business contributed well over twice as much as labor ($35.3 million to $13.1 million) (Ashford, 1985). This business money comes from the very largest corporations: 70 of the 100 largest industrial corporations have PACs, but only 34 of the second 500 largest industrials do. While only one corporate

PAC in five spends more than $25,000, the PACs of the 10 largest corporations spent about $70,000 each (Useem, 1984; Ashford, 1985).

Business not only gave more money to electoral politics, it also changed the character of its giving. Traditionally, business campaign contributions were primarily pragmatic, given to buy access to incumbents. Corporations were relatively unconcerned with a person's politics, and contributed to almost any incumbent, including liberals. Ideological commitments were not important enough to risk offending a powerful incumbent (given that almost no incumbents seriously challenged business). As a result, incumbents received far more business money than challengers—six times as much in 1972. In recent years, however, business has become more and more ideological, willing to oppose even powerful incumbents in order to alter the political composition of the Congress. In 1976, incumbents received only 3.9 times as much as challengers, and in 1980, only 1.9 times as much.

The change is not in the races pitting Republican incumbents against Democratic challengers. In those races both the pragmatic concern to gain access to incumbents and the ideological commitment to conservatism argued in favor of donating to the Republican incumbents, and as a result in both 1976 and 1980 they received more than 20 times as much as their Democratic challengers. But there has been a dramatic shift in races pitting Democratic incumbents against Republican challengers. In 1972 Democratic incumbents received almost four (3.89) times as much business money as their Republican challengers; in 1976 they received a little over twice (2.14) as much; and by 1980 they actually received *less* ($21,755 to $22,424) (Common Cause, 1973, 1977; Federal Election Commission, 1981).

There are few races in which business divides its money between the candidates equally; in practice there are some races where business unifies around the Democratic incumbent (because he or she is unbeatable or has political views that are unequivocally conservative) and other races in which business unifies behind the Republican challenger (Clawson, Neustadtl, and Bearden, 1986). Since studies show that the key impact of campaign money is in making challengers viable candidates, this major shift in corporate giving has contributed significantly to recent Republican strength (Jacobson, 1980, 1983).

For each of these forms of mobilization—conservative and tanks, the Business Roundtable, advocacy advertising, and electoral politics—the question can reasonably be asked: if corporate capital dominated the political system, why should business need to create new institutions to promote its views rather than changing the already existing ones? Organizations tend to take on a life of their own, as the professionals who work within them defend their own occupational interests, even vis-à-vis the capitalists who fund them. Corporate and individual donors, through their control of the board of directors, could have fired the liberal academics who had spent their life at Brookings and replaced them with the conservatives who now staff the American Enterprise Institute or the Heritage Foundation, but doing so would have involved a major public confrontation and an admission of the ideological purpose behind this move. It is both simpler and more effective to simply establish, or increase the funding for, a parallel institution.

REAGANISM BEFORE REAGAN

This mobilization had begun to redefine the contours of American politics well before Reagan's election or Jerry Falwell's rise to political prominence. The decisive shift to conservatism came during the Carter administration (and before the 1978 elections), not as a result of the 1980 election—though that certainly extended and consolidated the reaction already in process. In important ways the 1980 election only provided electoral confirmation of a power shift that had already taken place in the economic and ideological spheres.

Because business has such enormous economic and social power, it does not need majority support in electoral politics to carry through a change in power relationships. In a capitalist system business has the power and the "right" to make hundreds of vital decisions—about employment levels, wages, hours, sex and race discrimination, pollution, prices, the safety and quality of products, the location of factories, whether flextime is permissible, the nature of advertising, retirement ages—on its own, without even a pretense at democracy, unless a specific law has been passed to the contrary. Thus, the fact that there are 47,000 commercially available chemical compounds but OSHA has set limits on worker exposure levels for only 500 of them (Berman, 1978, p. 82) means that for the other 46,500 (including thousands of toxic chemicals) business may decide what it considers appropriate. As if this isn't enough, most laws allow business's decision to stand until all appeals are exhausted, giving business the ability to effectively resist, or even change, the law through aggressive appeals and delaying tactics.

Take the area of labor relations. For many years after World War II, business accepted unions' right to exist (or the inadvisability of trying to defeat them) and generally lived with them in a relatively peaceful accord. From the mid 1970s on, corporations became increasingly antiunion and often intentionally violated the law. Labor then had to go to court for redress, and business stalled as long as it could, until the redress ordered by the courts was meaningless.

An excellent example of this is union organizing drives. When a union has signed support of 30 percent of the eligible workers, a representation election is held to decide if the union has majority support and can therefore be certified as a bargaining agent. It is illegal for employers to discriminate against workers for their union activity, but it nonetheless happens all the time, since the penalties are so minimal: an employer convicted of having illegally discharged a worker must make up his or her wages, less whatever the person has earned in the interim. If we compare the number of people illegally fired for their union activity (as determined by their having won their case before the National Labor Relations Board) with the number of workers who favored the union (as determined by the number who voted for unions in NLRB representation elections), we get "a remarkable result: one in twenty workers who favored the union got fired" (Richard B. Freeman, quoted in Edsall, 1984, p. 152). Employers found this penalty well worth the cost, because firing a few union activists often stopped an organizing drive dead in its tracks. The illegal firing helped the union only if workers were actually reinstated before the representation election, but given the way the law was enforced employers could virtually always avoid this through delaying tactics.

Minimal penalties and lengthy delays in enforcement meant that employers had in practice changed the law, since a worker or union whose rights were violated had no meaningful recourse. Unions responded with a very mild bill, the Labor Law Reform Bill of 1978, intended to do little more than restore the initial intent of the law. The reform bill required that decisions be rendered within specified time periods, that the judge's ruling stand during the appeal process, and that the penalties for violating the law be increaed slightly. For example, employees found to have been illegally discharged for union activity were to receive not simply the wages they had lost, but 150 percent of lost wages.

Labor saw the bill as an attempt to isolate a few corporations that had been systematically violating the law, and expected that most large corporations would either support the bill or offer only token opposition. This mild reform bill was labor's number one priority; the Democratic party was heavily dependent on labor money to finance its election campaigns; Democrats occupied the White House and had strong majorities in both houses of Congress. It appeared that the bill should pass easily. But President Carter's first priority at this time was to secure the adoption of the Panama Canal treaty, and for the most part he left labor to fend for itself. Then, big business began an unprecedented mobilization against the bill, and labor was caught off guard.

> What galled labor beyond measure, oddly enough, was not the treason of politicians who had taken labor's shilling at election time. It was the defection to the anti-union camp of a raft of chief executives from the Fortune 500—men whom the unions had come to think of almost as allies. As many labor leaders see it, that crucial battle marked the end of a thirty-year entente cordiale. (A. H. Raskin, quoted in Edsall, 1984, p. 156)

Business interests spent more than $5 million lobbying on this one bill. The Business Roundtable served as a coordinating and directing force of the efforts by the inner circle to stop the measure. Heavy lobbying efforts focused on members of Congress whose votes seemed in doubt, with the Roundtable arranging a series of visits by the businesspeople from the district. Such lobbying was of considerably greater importance than the several million postcards sent out by the National Right to Work Committee (Ferguson and Rogers, 1979; Guzzardi, 1978; McQuaid, 1982). The bill was eventually stopped in the Senate by a filibuster; repeated attempts to invoke cloture failed by narrow margins. Its defeat dramatically signaled a major political shift: the dominance of an aggressively conservative, big business posture.

The same story could be told of other issues. The proposed Consumer Protection Agency was defeated. The tax bill of 1978 began with a mildly progressive proposal from Carter, but the eventual result was "the first major tax bill since the 1930s that did not skew benefits toward those at the bottom and middle of the income spectrum" (Edsall, 1984, p. 150). Despite strong Democratic majorities in both houses of Congress and a Democratic president, the final tax bill involved a major cut in the capital gains tax (from 48 percent to 28 percent), a tax paid almost exclusively by the rich, along with increases in the most regressive federal tax, Social Security (Edsall, 1984, p. 65).

A range of other "Reagan" policies in fact began under Carter. One such policy was that of military buildup. Military spending as a percentage of GNP had declined fairly steadily from the late 1950s onward, from 9 percent in the late 1950s to 5 percent in 1978 and 1979. In 1979, however, this decline was halted, as Carter insisted on substantial increases in the 1980 military budget. Iran (and to a lesser extent, Afghanistan) seems to have been the crucial factor here.

Under the Shah, Iran had been regarded as the most stable and trustworthy U.S. ally; its wealth even allowed it to pay for most of the military equipment it received, and the Shah's unpopularity made it in his interest to have a strong military. The Middle East was a key to control of the world economy. When the Shah's power crumbled it seemed that nowhere in the world was safe: one day Iran was "an island of security in a troubled area of the world" (Jimmy Carter), the next month the Shah was out of power and the United States couldn't even find any "moderates" to quietly carry out its wishes. Iran underscored the problems inherent in relying on Third World dictatorships to protect U.S. interests. The idea that the United States must rely on itself led to both the reintroduction of registration for the draft and substantial increases in U.S. military spending. Carter proposed that the military budget be increased not only to match inflation, but also by an additional 3 percent a year.

Thus it would seem that not only had the ideological and institutional groundwork for a shift to the right been laid, but that actual policy changes had begun to be implemented. What then caused business's defection to Reagan? It is true that Carter was widely perveived as an ineffectual president. While his failures are most often attributed to his personal weaknesses, they must also be related to the inherent conflicts between the new (business) agenda and the traditional constituencies (labor, minorities) and programs to which a Democratic president and Congress were linked, conflicts which often compromised the ability to do what business wanted.

In 1974, *Business Week* had anticipated the political difficulties in the new program, and the consequent need for a Great Communicator: "It will be a hard pill for many Americans to swallow—the idea of doing with less so that big business can have more. . . . Nothing that this nation, or any other nation, has done in modern economic history compares in difficulty with the selling job that must now be done to make people accept the new reality" (October 12, 1974, p. 120). The selling campaign began with advocacy advertising and new think tank studies, but it culminated six years later in the campaign and election of Ronald Reagan.

THE "REAGAN REVOLUTION"

In important ways Ronald Reagan in 1979 resembled Barry Goldwater in 1963. Both were extreme ideological conservatives with a large core of devoted supporters, and both seemed unlikely to attract the support of a majority of voters, let alone be able to carry through on their campaign platforms. But although in 1964 Goldwater lost by a landslide, 16 years later Reagan won by a landslide.

The differing outcomes of these elections are due to many different factors—the mood of the country, the economic situation, the United States' ability to militarily dominate the rest of the world, the basic competence of the two incumbent presidents. Probably no difference is as crucial, however, as the contrast in the extent of their support from big business. In 1964 the largest corporations and the most important inner circle capitalists abandoned the Republicans and Goldwater for the Democrats and Johnson. Without the support of big business Goldwater remained simply an extremist, and the press focused on his occasional problematic statements.

Reagan, on the other hand, although starting out without much support from business's inner circle or from the largest companies, by election day had the solid support of most of the big business community (Ferguson and Rogers, 1981). Big business didn't just support Reagan, they supported a complete conservative slate. In 1980 congressional races, corporate donors rejected their traditional strategy of support for incumbents. Most business PACs gave some money to conservative challengers, and about 40 percent of the largest corporate PACs essentially replicated the behavior of conservative ideological PACs, supporting ideological conservative challengers even where they were running against powerful moderate incumbents (Clawson, Kaufman, and Karson, 1986). These corporate PACs provided much more money to Republican challengers than did the more highly publicized ideological PACs. In a number of key races business money clearly made the difference. For example, Frank Church, an incumbent senator with 24 years seniority, received $32,000 from corporate PACs; his victorious conservative challenger Steve Symms received over $400,000 from corporate PACs in an election decided by 4,000 votes.

On the one hand, Reagan had to make certain concessions to gain this support from business. On the other hand, once Reagan had business support, that very fact guaranteed that he would no longer be seen as an extremist. However implausible some of his assertions may have been, they were treated with respect. Thus the media did not embarrass Reagan by adding up the numbers when he insisted that he would balance the budget by 1984 while simultaneously introducing massive tax cuts and huge increases in military spending. Compare this to the careful accounting that was given to George McGovern's 1972 proposal for a guaranteed annual income once it became apparent that he was a serious candidate. Questions about its financial viability were used not only to discredit the program itself but to raise more serious questions about McGovern's general competence and responsibility. Reagan could claim that there was a "window of vulnerability" such that the Soviets could successfully launch an unanswerable first strike against United States, and no one laughed him out of court (Scheer, 1983). Reagan could even question the theory of evolution, claiming that "recent discoveries over the years have pointed out great flaws in it" (quoted in Ferguson and Rogers, 1981, p. 3) without any of the press asking him what effect these views would have on his science policy or appointments. Solid support from big business is perhaps the single most important factor making Reagan a viable candidate, though the weakness of Carter and the Democrats was also necessary. Without business support Reagan would not have been in a position to benefit from Carter's weakness; with business support Carter would not have been as weak and ineffective as he was.

The 1980 election involved a stunning political shift to the right, probably the most important political shift since the 1930s. It brought the first defeat of an elected incumbent president since the 1930s, the most ideologically conservative president since the 1920s, Republican control of the Senate for the first time in more than a quarter century, and large Republican gains in the House. Nonetheless, these changes would normally not have been enough to carry through the sorts of policy shifts Reagan had promised. The Democrats still controlled the House, and the American political system gives many advantages to the forces resisting change. After the 1980 election most analysts thought Reagan would be unable to enact his tax cut and budget changes. In fact, however, he was able to get Congress to adopt an essentially intact version of his basic program.

Why was Reagan able to get his program enacted? The most commonly offered explanation focuses on Reagan's personal popularity and his skills as the Great Communicator. His background as an actor supposedly makes him able to get his message across on TV; when people hear this message they support it; by mobilizing popular support, Reagan pressures a reluctant Congress to adopt his program.

There is no doubt that Reagan makes effective use of television, but this cannot explain his success. The polls, in fact, indicate that during the first two years when Reagan's crucial policy changes were enacted, he was *not* a popular president. Most presidents are popular right after they are first elected, but Reagan received the lowest first- and second-year ratings of any president elected in the fifty-year period during which public opinion surveys have measured presidential popularity. Reagan was substantially less popular than Carter, Nixon, Kennedy, or Eisenhower. Later in his term Reagan's approval ratings increased—but during the time he had high approval ratings he was unable to enact any significant new elements of his program. Given that Reagan's approval was low while he was getting his program adopted, and high during the time he could not enact legislation, it seems that public approval or personal popularity cannot explain the adoption of the dramatic and significant policy shifts favored by Reagan.

Reagan's success is instead to be explained by the fact that his program was supported by a virtually unanimous business community. This support, combined with a less explicit consensus among leaders of both parties, made it possible to get his program through even without a popular mandate.[4] In the spring of 1981, for example, both business and political leaders strongly supported some kind of major tax cut for business. The Democratic leadership agreed on the need to cut business taxes (this had also been part of Carter's platform), differing primarily in their opposition to cuts in personal income taxes. Similarly, the Democratic leadership agreed on the need to increase military spending, though there were clear differences on the extent of the increases.

Reagan was able to enact three major changes: a reduction in many areas of government spending, a tax cut for business, and a tax cut for individuals with benefits heavily weighted toward the wealthier individuals most likely to save. A fourth major Reagan initiative, an increase in military spending, actually began under Carter, though Reagan accelerated it. The three major changes in government policy that are specific to Reagan are identical to the changes *Business Week* had demanded five years earlier (see p. 204 above). On the other hand, there have been few changes in the areas of most importance to many of Reagan's New Right supporters, social issues such as abortion, race, and school prayer. This is not to say that Reagan would not like to make changes in those areas, and has not attempted to do so, but the actual changes have been slight. Key elements of the New Right have in fact complained that it is their issues that get Republicans elected and yet the business agenda is implemented while theirs gets shunted aside (Phillips, 1982).

MEANING AND CONSEQUENCES

Pluralist analysts agree that business has vast resources and therefore a unified business community would have enormous power. However, they argue that in practice business is rarely able to unify, since businesses compete against each other in the marketplace and different companies have different interests (the steel industry wants high prices for steel, the auto industry wants low prices, etc.) (Dahl, 1958). Individual businesses may and do buy influence, but "to the extent that the groups are buying anything, therefore, they seem to be canceling each other out" (Malbin, 1980, p. 175) and thus lack significant political impact.

This book has argued, however, that corporate capital is unified as well as divided. This unity, moreover, is not simply at the level of ideology; nor is it achieved solely by the efforts of a semiautonomous state, as theories of Marxist structuralism would maintain. We offer an alternative position which combines elements of both "instrumentalist" and "structuralist" theories of the state.

Instrumentalism, a position incorrectly attributed to G. William

Domhoff, locates capitalist control of the state in a variety of day-to-day influences, achieved through mechanisms such as lobbying and personnel transfers. Structuralists argue that these activities are comparatively unimportant, since what matters is the way the state itself is organized institutionally to pursue long-term capitalist interests. Capital's well-being is served because of the structure of the state, not because of day-to-day capitalist interventions in politics. This book, building on Domhoff's work, finds both perspectives inadequate: long-term capitalist interests are not secured merely through the visible interventions of daily political practice, but neither are they left to the structure of the state.

As Part I revealed, on an economic level big business is tied together in myriad ways, tied together not simply by episodic exchanges between marketplace equals, but by long-term power relationships. If members of the capitalist inner circle serve on the boards of several giant corporations, this both expresses and solidifies their dependence and working relationship. The inner circle helps the capitalist class to develop, and *enforce,* a unified perspective (see Chapter 9). Similarly, when banks lend money to a corporation they develop a material interest in its policies and programs and their financial involvement gives them the leverage to insure their wishes receive serious consideration. All these underlying *material* relations, which are simultaneously *social* relations, make it possible for capitalist leaders to develop a range of organizations and processes through which they discuss, argue about, and eventually agree on policies to serve the long-range interests of capital. Thus, capitalists develop a class-conscious understanding of their long-range interests *outside* the state; only later are these policies brought to the state itself. The structure of the state does not serve capitalist interests through the automatic operation of mechanical laws; deliberate and continuing process of capitalist activity is required.

Neither Reagan nor the 1980 election can explain Reaganism: the bases of this political transformation are to be found in the changing interests and perceptions of business as it responded to a changing world. Business concern about the political and economic climate seems to have crystallized around 1973, and with this crystallization began the key period of mobilization. It is important to note that the various forms of business mobilization described here—new policy organizations, new think tanks, advocacy advertising—emerge *before* there is any shift in popular opinion or election results. The Congresses elected in 1974 and 1976, as the mobilization was developing, were among the most Democratic ever elected. Clearly the business mobilization is not a consequence but a cause of the shift to conservatism.

Nor did business initiate its offensive through changes in state policy. It began by creating new policy organizations (the Business Roundtable), by founding or expanding think tanks (the American Enterprise Institute, the Heritage Foundation), by advocacy advertising, and (presumably) by the exchange of ideas at corporate board meetings. Only after an extensive process of this kind had taken place *outside* the state was it possible to change state policy. The changes in state policy began well before they had received any significant electoral support: the first tax cut favoring the rich and the defeat of the Labor Law Reform Bill actually occurred before the 1978 election, with a Democratic president and heavy Democratic majorities in both houses of Congress. The 1980 triumph of Reagan and the Republicans was a watershed, but it did not begin the process. The policy changes that Reagan then enacted were crucial; they resulted, however, not from widespread public demand, but from a unified business community and a public willingness to tolerate such changes.

NOTES

1. A 1985 study by the Congressional Office of Technology Assessment makes it clear that nothing has changed: less than 4 percent of work places are inspected each year; a "serious violation" is defined as one that creates a "substantial probability of death or serious physical harm"—but the average fine for such a violation is only $172 (*New York Times*, April 18, 1985, p. A18).

2. The decline of expenditures by Ford seems to typify a pattern in business political activity. Major sectors of the business community rarely oppose each other publicly and directly on important political issues. Rather, at some time periods or for some issues, one part of business mobilizes, while other sectors maintain a low profile; at another time, or for another issue, the first sector reduces its activity and visibility while a previously quiescent sector leads the business community (Whitt, 1982; Clawson, Neustadtl, and Bearden, 1986). Here as well, the Ford Foundation, a well-known supporter of "liberal" causes, reduced its funding at the same time that other parts of business were increasing the funding of conservatives.

3. For discussion of the Business Roundtable see Burch (1981), McQuaid (1982), Ferguson and Rogers (1979), and Guzzardi (1978).

4. Reagan's election mandate was itself weak. On the one hand, he won the 1980 election by a landslide, but on the other hand relatively few people voted. In fact, a smaller proportion of the eligible electorate voted for Reagan in 1980 than voted for Willkie in 1940, even though Willkie lost as decisively as Reagan won. Business had not so much succeeded in persuading the population to accept their program as created a situation where no alternative seemed viable and appealing. Therefore many people stayed home on election day (Burnham, 1981).

BIBLIOGRAPHY

Adatto, Kiku
  1984 "How the White House Was Won." *New Republic* (November 12): 22.
Aiken, Michael and Pasul E. Mott
  1970 *The Structure of Community Power.* New York: Random House.
Aldrich, Howard
  1979 *Organizations and Environments.* Englewood Cliffs, NJ: Prentice-Hall.
Aldrich, Howard and Jeffrey Pfeffer
  1976 "Environment of Organizations." In Alex Inkeles (ed.), *Annual Review of Sociology* 2: 79–105. Palo Alto: Annual Reviews.
Alexander, Herbert E.
  1976 *Financing the 1972 Election.* Lexington, MA: Lexington Books.
Allen, Gar
  1976 "A History of Eugenics in the Class Struggle." In Science for the People, *IQ: Scientific or Social Controversy,* Somerville, MA: Science for the People.
Allen, Michael P.
  1978 "Economic Interest Groups and the Corporate Elite Structure." *Social Science Quarterly* 58: 597–615.
  1976 "Management Control in the Large Corporation: Comment on Zeitlin." *American Journal of Sociology* 81: 885–894.
  1974 "The Structure of Interorganizational Elite Cooptation: Interlocking Corporate Directors." *American Sociological Review* 39: 393–406.
Altschuler, A.
  1980 *Urban Transportation Policy.* Cambridge, MA: MIT Press.
Angell, D. R.
  1961 "James Rowland Angell." In C. Murchison (ed.), *A History of Psychology in Autobiography.* New York: Russell and Russell.
Arnove, Robert F.
  1980 *Philanthropy and Cultural Imperialism: The Foundations at Home and Abroad.* Boston: G. K. Hall.
Arthur Anderson and Company
  1979 *Cost of Government Regulation Study.* New York: Business Roundtable.

Ashford, Kathryn L.
    1985   "The Role of Corporations in the U.S. Congressional Elections."
          Paper presented at the annual meeting of the American
          Sociological Association, Washington, D.C.
Austin, Peter
    1973   "Annals of Finance: The Go-Go Years." Part 3, *New Yorker*
          (August 13): 34–53.

Bache, R. M.
    1895   "Reaction Time with Reference to Race." *Psychological Review*
          2: 474–486.
Bachrach, Peter
    1967   *The Theory of Democratic Elitism*. Boston: Little Brown.
Bachrach, Peter and Morton Baratz
    1962   "The Two Faces of Power." *American Political Science Review*
          56: 947–952. Reprinted in William Connolly, *The Bias of*
          Pluralism (New York: Lieber-Atherton, 1969.
Bagley, W. C.
    1922   "Educational Determinism; or Democracy and the IQ." *School*
          and Society 15: 373–384.
Balbus, Isaac
    1971   "Power Elite Theory vs. Marxist Class Analysis." *Monthly*
          Review 22 (May: 36–46.
Baltzell, E. Digby
    1958   *Philadelphia Gentlemen: The Making of a National Upper*
          Class. New York: Free Press.
    1966   " 'Who's Who in America' and 'The Social Register': Elite and
          Upper Class Indexes in America." In R. Bendix and S. M.
          Lipset (eds.), *Class, Status, and Power*. New York: Free
          Press.
Baran, Paul and Paul Sweezy
    1966   *Monopoly Capital: An Essay on the American Economic and*
          Social Order. New York: Monthly Review Press.
Barnet, Richard J. and Ronald E. Mueller
    1974   *Global Reach: The Power of the Multinational Corporation*,
          Parts 1 and 2. New York: Simon and Schuster.
Barrett, P. F.
    1976   *Mass Transit, the Automobile, and Public Policy in Chicago,*
          1920–1930. Ph.D. dissertation, University of Illinois.
Bauer, Raymond A., Ithiel de Sola Pool, and Lewis Dexter
    1972   American Business and Public Policy: *The Politics of Foreign*
          Trade. New York: Aldine-Atherton.
Baum, D. J. and N. B. Stiles
    1965   *The Silent Partners: Institutional Investors and Corporate*
          Control. Syracuse: Syracuse University Press.
Baumol, William J.
    1967   *Business Behavior, Value and Growth*. (Rev. Ed.), New York:
          Macmillan.
Bean, W.
    1968   *Boss Ruef's San Francisco*. Berkeley and Los Angeles:
          University of California Press.

Bearden, James
    1982   *The Board of Directors in Large U.S. Corporations.* Ph.D.
                dissertation, Department of Sociology, State University of
                New York, Stony Brook.
Bearden, James, William Atwood, Peter Freitag, Carolyn Hendricks, Beth
    Mintz, and Michael Schwartz
    1975   "The Nature and Extent of Bank Centrality in Corporate
                Networks." Paper presented at the annual meeting of the
                American Sociological Association, San Francisco.
Bearden, James and Beth Mintz
    1987   "Inner Group Membership and the Cohesion of the Network."
                In Mark S. Mizruchi and Michael Schwartz (eds.),
                Structural Analysis of Business. New York: Cambridge
                University Press.
Beckmann, George
    1964   "The Role of Foundations." *Annals of the American Academy of
                Political and Social Science* 4 (November): 22–44.
Bell, Daniel
    1961   "The Break-up of Family Capitalism." In Daniel Bell, *The End of
                Ideology.* New York: Collier.
    1973   *The Coming of Post-Industrial Society: A Venture in Social
                Forecasting.* New York: Basic.
Berelson, Bernard
    1960   "The Place of Foundation." Paper presented at the annual
                meeting of Sociological Association.
Berle, Adolf
    1947   *Economic Power and the Free Society.* Santa Barbara, CA: Fund
                for the Republic.
Berle, Adolf and Gardiner Means
    1932   *The Modern Corporation and Private Property* (reprinted,
                1968). New York: Harcourt, Brace and World.
Bernstein, J.
    1960   *The Lean Years: A History of the American Worker, 1920–1933.*
                Baltimore: Penguin.
Bluestone, Barry and Bennett Harrison
    1982   The Deindustrialization of America. New York: Basic Books.
Blum, J. M.
    1978   *Pseudoscience and Mental Ability: The Origins and Fallacies of
                the IQ Controversy.* New York: Monthly Review Press.
Bonacich, Phillip
    1972   "Technique for Analyzing Overlapping Memberships." In
                Herbert Costner (ed.), *Sociological Methodology.* San
                Francisco: Jossey-Bass, 176–85.
Bonacich, Phillip and G. William Domhoff
    1977   "Overlapping Memberships among Clubs and Policy Groups of
                the American Ruling Class: A Methodological and
                Empirical Contribution to the Class Hegemony Paradigm
                of Power Structures." Paper presented at the annual
                meeting of the American Sociological Association.
Boring, E. G.
    1957   *A History of Experimental Psychology* (2d ed.). New York:
                Appleton-Century-Crofts.

Bowles, Samuel and Herbert Gintis
  1976   *Schooling in Capitalist Society.* New York: Basic.
Bowles, Samuel, David. M. Gordon, and Thomas E. Weiskopf
  1983   *Beyond the Waste Land: A Democratic Alternative to Economic Decline.* Garden City, N.Y.: Doubleday.
Boyer, R. O. and H. M. Morais
  1972   *Labor's Untold Story* (3d ed.). New York: United Electrical, Radio and Machine Workers of America.
Bradford, Calvin and Dennis R. Marino
  1977   "Redlining and Disinvestment as a Discriminatory Practice in Residential Mortgage Loans." Prepared for U.S. Department of Housing and Urban Development. Washington, D.C.: U.S. Government Printing Office.
Brandeis, Louis
  1913   "The Endless Chain: Interlocking Directorates." *Harper's Weekly* (December 6): 13–15.
  1914   *Other People's Money.* New York: Frederick A. Stokes. Reprinted, New York: Harper & Row, 1967.
Brantley, Peter S.
  1985   "The Impact of Deindustrialization on Welfare: New York State." Typescript, Department of Sociology, State University of New York, Stony Brook.
Breiger, Ronald
  1974   "The Duality of Persons and Groups." *Social Forces* 53: 181–190.
Brigham, Charles C.
  1922   *A Study of American Intelligence.* Princeton: Princeton University Press.
Brown, Stanley H.
  1972   *Ling: The Rise, Fall and Return of a Texas Titan.* New York: Atheneum.
Buckingham, B. R.
  1941   "Our First Twenty-Two Years." In *Addresses and Proceedings of the National Education Association* 79.
Bunting, David
  1976   "The Separation of Ownership and Control before Berle and Means." Department of Economics, Eastern Washington University.
Bunting, David and Jeffrey Barbour
  1971   "Interlocking Directorates in Large American Corporations, 1896–1964." *Business History Review* 45: 317–335.
Bunting, David and Tsung-Hua Lai
  1977   "Economic and Social Aspects of Interlocking." Paper presented at the meeting of the American Political Science Association, Washington, D.C., September 1977.
Burch, Philip H., Jr.
  1972   *The Managerial Revolution Reassessed.* Lexington, MA: D. C. Heath.
  1981   "The Business Roundtable: Its Make-up and External Ties." *In Paul Zarembka (ed.), Research in Political Economy* 4: 101–127.

Burck, Charles G.
　　1976　"A Group Profile of the Fortune 500 Chief Executive." *Fortune*
　　　　　　93: 173–177, 308, 311–312.
Burnham, James
　　1941　*The Managerial Revolution*. New York: John Day.
Burnham, Walter Dean
　　1981　"The 1980 Earthquake: Realignment, Reaction, or What?" In
　　　　　　Thomas Ferguson and Joel Rogers (eds.), *The Hidden
　　　　　　Election*. New York: Pantheon.
　　1982　*The Current Crisis in American Politics*. New York: Oxford
　　　　　　University Press.
Burt, Ronald S.
　　1978　"A Structural Theory of Interlocking Corporate Directorates."
　　　　　　Survey Research Center Working Paper #13, University
　　　　　　of California, Berkeley.
　　1980a "Anatomy in a Social Topology." *American Journal of Sociology*
　　　　　　85: 892–925.
　　1980b "Cooptive Corporate Actor Networks: A Reconsideration of
　　　　　　Interlocking Directorates Involving American
　　　　　　Manufacturing." *Administrative Science Quarterly* 25:
　　　　　　557–582.
　　1983　*Corporate Profits and Cooptation: Networks of Market
　　　　　　Constraints and Directorates Involving American
　　　　　　Manufacturing*. New York: Academic Press.
Burt, Ronald S., Kenneth P. Christman, and Harold C. Kilborn, Jr.
　　1980　"Testing a Structural Theory of Corporate Cooptation:
　　　　　　Interorganization Directorate Ties as a Strategy for
　　　　　　Avoiding Market Constraints on Profits." *American
　　　　　　Sociological Review* 45: 821–841.

Caddy, Douglas
　　1975　*How They Rig Our Elections*. New York: New Rochelle.
Camfield, T. M.
　　1970　*Psychologists at War: The History of American Psychology and
　　　　　　the First World War*. Ph.D. dissertation, University of
　　　　　　Texas (University Microfilms No. 70-10-766).
Carnegie Commission of Higher Education
　　1971　*Less Time, More Options: Education Beyond the High School*.
　　　　　　New York: McGraw-Hill.
Carson, Claybourne
　　1981　*In Struggle: SNCC and the Black Awakening of the 1960s*.
　　　　　　Cambridge, MA: Harvard University Press.
Carter, Jimmy
　　1977　*Weekly Compilation of Presidental Documents, XIII*.
　　　　　　Washington, D.C.: U.S. Government Printing Office.
Chandler, Alfred
　　1968　*Strategy and Structure*. Garden City, NY: Doubleday.
　　1977　*The Visible Hand: The Managerial Revolution in American
　　　　　　Business*. Cambridge, MA: Harvard University Press.
Chandler, Alfred and H. Daems
　　1974　"The Rise of Managerial Capitalism and Its Impact on

Investment Strategy in the Western World and Japan." In H. Daems and H. Van der Wee (eds), *The Rise of Managerial Capitalism*. The Hague: Martinus Nijhoff.

Chase, Allen
 1976 *The Legacy of Malthus: The Social Costs of the New Scientific Racism*. New York: Knopf.

Chase, J.
 1927 *New York At School*. New York: Public Education Association.

Cheaper, C.
 1980 *Moving the Masses*. Cambridge, MA: Harvard University Press.

Chevalier, Jean Marie
 1970 *La Structure financiere de l'industrie americaine*. Paris: Editions Cujas.

Clark, Terry Nichols
 1975 "Community Power." In Alex Inkeles, James Coleman, and Neil Smelser (eds.), *Annual Review of Sociology 1*. Palo Alto: Annual Reviews.

Clawson, Dan and Mary Ann Clawson
 1985 "The Logic of Business Unity: Corporate Contributions in the 1980 Election." Paper presented at the meeting of the American Sociological Association, Washington, D.C.

Clawson, Dan, Karen Johnson, and John Schall
 1982 "Fighting Union Busting in the 1980s." *Radical Review* 16 (4–5): 45–64.

Clawson, Dan, Allen Kaufman, and Marvin Karson
 1986 "The Corporate PACt for a Conservative America: A Data Analysis of 1980 Corporate PAC Donations in Sixty-Six Conservative Congressional Elections." In James Post (ed.), *Research in Corporate Social Policy and Performance*. Greenwich, Ct.: JAI Press, 1986.

Clawson, Dan, Allen Kaufman, and Alan Neustadl
 1983 "Which Class Fractions Fund the New Right?" Paper presented at the meeting of the American Sociological Association, Detroit.
 1985 "Corporate PACs for a New Pax Americana." *Insurgent Sociologist* 13 (1–2): 63–77.

Clawson, Dan, Alan Neustadtl, and James Bearden
 1986 "The Logic of Business Unity: Corporate Contributions to the 1980 Congressional Elections." *American Sociological Review* 51 (6): 797–811.

Cockburn, Alexander and James Ridgeway
 1981 "The World of Appearance: The Public Campaign." In Thomas Ferguson and Joel Rogers (eds.), *The Hidden Election: Politics and Economics in the 1980 Presidential Campaign*. New York: Pantheon.

Cohen, Robert B.
 1980 "Structure Change in International Banking and its Implications for the U.S. Economy." In Joint Economic Committee of the U.S. Congress, *Special Study of Economic Change* 9 (International Economy U.S. Role in a World Market), 96th Cong. 2d session pp. 501–555.

Collins, Randall
1971 "Functional and Conflict Theories of Educational Stratification."
American Sociological Review 36: 1002–1019.
1979 *The Credential Society: An Historical Sociology of Education
and Stratification.* New York: Academic.
Collins, Robert M.
1981 *The Business Response to Keynes, 1929–1964.* New York:
Columbia University Press.
Committee for Economic Development
1968 *Financing a Better Election System.* New York: Research and
Policy Committee of the Committee for Economic
Development.
Common Cause
1973 *1972 Federal Campaign Finances.* Washington, D.C.: Common
Cause.
1977 *1976 Federal Campaign Finances.* Washington, D.C.: Common
Cause.
Conference Board
1973 *Corporate Directorship Practices* (report no. 588). Washington,
D.C.: Conference Board.
Corey, Louis
1930 *The House of Morgan: A Social Biography of the Masters of
Money.* New York: Grosset & Dunlop.
Corporate Data Exchange
1977 *CDE Stock Ownership Directory: Transportation.* New York:
Corporate Data Exchange.
1978 *CDE Stock Ownership Directory: Agribusiness.* New York:
Corporate Data Exchange.
Corson, William
1978 *The Armies of Ignorance.* New York: Dial.
Cremin, A. A., D. A. Shannon, and M. E. Townsend
1954 *A History of Teachers College, Columbia University.* New York:
Columbia University Press.
Crooks, J. B.
1968 *Politico and Progress: The Rise of Urban Progressivism in
Baltimore, 1895–1911.* Baton Rouge: Louisiana State
University Press.
Cumings, Bruce
1981 "Chinatown: Foreign Policy and Elite Realignment." In Thomas
Ferguson and Joel Rogers (eds.), *The Hidden Election:
Politics and Economics in the 1980 Presidential
Campaign.* New York: Pantheon.
Cyert, Richard M. and James G. March
1963 *A Behavioral Theory of the Firm.* Englewood Cliffs, NJ:
Prentice-Hall.

Dahl, Robert A.
1958 "A Critique of the Ruling Elite Model." *American Political
Science Review* 52:463–469.
1961a *Who Governs? Democracy and Power in an American City.* New
Haven: Yale University Press.

1961b "The Behavioral Approach to Political Science: Epitaph for a
            Movement to a Successful Protest." *American Political
            Science Review* 55 (December): 765–66.
1966   *Preface to Democratic Theory.* New Haven: Yale University
            Press.
Dahrendorf, Rolf
1959   *Class and Class Conflict in Industrial Society.* Stanford:
            Stanford University Press.
Data Resources
1979   *The Macroeconomic Impact of Federal Pollution Control
            Programs, 1978 Assessment.* Washington, D.C.: Council
            on Environmental Quality.
Daughan, Joseph R. and Peter Binzen
1971   *Wreck of the Penn Central.* Boston: Little Brown.
Davies, C. S. and M. Albaum
1976   "The Mobility Problem of the Poor in Indianapolis." *Antipode*
            1:67–86.
Davis, Mike
1981   "The New Right's Road to Power." *New Left Review* 128:28–49.
DeFina, Robert
1977   *Public and Private Expenditures for Federal Regulation of
            Business.* St. Louis: Washington University, Center for
            the Study of American Business.
Defty, Sally Bixby
1975   "New Jobs Called Top Area Need." *St. Louis Post-Dispatch*
            (special supplement: "Toward 2000: St. Louis Horizons").
Dewees, D.
1970   "The Decline of the American Street Railways." *Traffic
            Quarterly* 24: 563–82.
DiDonato, Donna, Davita Silfen Glasberg, Beth Mintz, Michael Schwartz
        Forthcoming   "The Social History of Interlock Research." In
            Sam Bacharach (ed.), *Perspectives in Organizational Sociology.*
            Greenwich, CT: JAI Press.
DiMaggio, Paul and Michael Useem
1981   "The Arts in Class Reproduction." In Michael Apple (ed.),
            Cultural and Economic Reproduction in Education.
            London: Routledge and Kegan Paul.
Disouza, Dinesh
1984   "Mondale's Effeminate Style." *Prospect* (November).
Domhoff, G. William
1967   *Who Rules America?* Englewood Cliffs, NJ: Prentice-Hall.
1970a   *The Higher Circles: The Governing Class in America.* New
            York: Random House.
1970b   "How the Power Elite Set National Goals." In Ken Chen (ed.),
            National Priorities. San Francisco: San Francisco Press.
            Reprinted in Robert Perucci and Marc Pilisuk (ed.), *The
            Triple Revolution Emerging* (Boston: Little Brown).
1974   *The Bohemian Grove and Other Retreats.* New York: Harper &
            Row.
1975   "Social Clubs, Political Groups and Corporations: A Network
            Study of Ruling Class Cohesivensss." *Insurgent
            Sociologist,* Spring 1975.

1979   *The Powers That Be: Process of Ruling Class Domination in America.* New York: Random House.
1983   Who Rules America Now? Englewood Cliffs, NJ: Prentice-Hall.
Domhoff, G. William and Hoyt Ballard (eds.)
1968   *C. Wright Mills and the Power Elite.* Boston: Beacon.
Dooley, Peter
1969   "The Interlocking Directorate." *American Economic Review* 59: 314–323.
Downey, M. T.
1965   *Ben D. Wood: Educational Reformer.* Princeton: Educational Testing Service.
DuBois, P. H.
1970   *A History of Psychological Testing.* Boston: Allyn and Bacon.
Duncan, B. and S. Lieberson
1970   *Metropolis and Region in Transition.* Beverly Hills, CA: Sage.
Dunn, J. A.
1981   *Miles to Go.* Cambridge, MA: MIT Press.
Dunn, Marvin G.
1980   "The Family Office: Coordinating Mechanism of the Ruling Class." In G. William Domhoff, *Power Structure Research.* Beverly Hills, CA: Sage.
Dye, Thomas
1981   *Who's Running America? The Reagan Years.* Englewood Cliffs, NJ: Prentice-Hall.

Eckberg, Douglas L.
1979   *Intelligence and Race: The Origins and Dimensions of the IQ Controversy.* New York: Praeger.
Edsall, Thomas Byrne
1984   *The New Politics of Inequality.* New York: W. W. Norton.
Eulau, Heinz
1976   "Understanding Political Life in America: The Contribution of Political Science." *Social Science Quarterly* 57: 112–153.

Federal Election Commission
1981   Computer tape of PAC contributions of candidates for federal office.
Federal Electric Railways Commission [FERRC]
1920   *Commission Proceedings.* Washington, D.C.: Government Printing Office.
Federal Trade Commission
1951   *Report on Interlocking Directorates.* Washington, D.C.: U.S. Government Printing Office.
Fellmuth, Robert
1970   *The Interstate Commerce Commission.* New York: Grossman.
Fennema, Meindert
1982   *International Networks of Banks and Industry.* Boston: Martinus Nijhoff.
Ferguson, Thomas and Joel Rogers
1979   "The Knights of the Roundtable." *Nation* (December 15): 620–625.

1980 "Labor Law Reform and Its Enemies." In Mark Green and Robert Massie, Jr. (eds.), *The Big Business Reader.* New York: Pilgrim Press.

1981 "The Reagan Victory: Corporate Coalitions in the 1980 Campaign." In Thomas Ferguson and Joel Rogers (eds.), *The Hidden Election: Politics and Economics in the 1980 Presidential Campaign.* New York: Pantheon.

Fitch, Robert and Mary Oppenheimer
1970 "Who Rules the Corporations?" *Socialist Revolution* 1, Parts I–III: 73–108, 61–114, 33–94.

Flink, J. J.
1970 *America Adopts the Automobile,* 1895–1910. Cambridge, MA: MIT Press.

1975 *The Car Culture.* Cambridge, MA: MIT Press.

Ford Foundation
1949 *Report of the Study for the Ford Foundation on Policy and Program.* New York: Ford Foundation.

1953 *Behavioral Science Division Report.* New York: Ford Foundation.

1958 *Final Report of the Behavior Science Division.* New York: Ford Foundation.

1976 *Current Interests of the Ford Foundation.* New York: Ford Foundation.

Forman, James
1972 *The Making of Black Revolutionaries.* New York: Macmillan.

Freeman, F. S.
1926 Mental Tests. Boston: Houghton Mifflin.

1962 *Theory and Practice of Psychological Testing* (3d ed.). New York: Holt, Rinehart and Winston.

Freitag, Peter J.
1975 "The Cabinet and Big Business." *Social Problems* 23 (December): 137–152.

1979 *Class Struggle and the Rise of Government Regulation.* Ph.D. dissertation, State University of New York, Stony Brook.

1983 "The Myth of Corporate Capture: Regulatory Commissions in the United States." *Social Problems* 30 (April): 480–491.

Friedland, Roger and Donald Palmer
1984 "Park Place and Main street: Business and the Urban Power Structure." *Annual Review of Sociology* 10: 393–460.

Frenzel, William
1973 Tape-recorded speech. Washington, D.C.

Galbraith, John K.
1967 *The New Industrial State.* New York: New American Library.

Gardner, John
1972 *In Common Cause.* New York: W. W. Norton.

Garis, M.
1927 *Immigration Restriction.* New York: Macmillan.

Genovese, Eugene
1972 *Roll, Jordan, Roll.* New York: Random House.

Georgine, Dan
1980 "From Brass Knuckles to Briefcases: The Modern Art of Union

Busting." In Mark Green and Robert Massie Jr. (eds.), *The Big Business Reader.* New York: Pilgrim Press.

Gersh, D. A.
  1981   *The Development and Use of IQ Tests in the United States from 1900 to 1930.* Ph.D. dissertation, State University of New York at Stony Brook. (*Dissertation Abstracts International* 42, 2599B).

Glasberg, Davita Silfen
  1981   "Corporate Power and Control: The Case of Leasco Corporation versus Chemical Bank." *Social Problems* 29 (December): 104–116.
  1982   *Corporations in Crisis: The Significance of Interlocking Directorates.* Ph.D. dissertation, State University of New York, Stony Brook.

Glasberg, Davita Silfen and Michael Schwartz
  1983   "Corporate Power." *Annual Review of Sociology* 9, Palo Alto, CA: Annual Reviews.

Goddard, H. H.
  1911   "Heredity of Feeble-Mindedness." *Eugenics Record Office Bulletin* 1.
  1917   "Mental Tests and the Immigrant." *Journal of Delinquency* 2: 243–277.
  1920   *Human Efficiency and Levels of Intelligence.* Princeton: Princeton University Press.

Gogel, Robert
  1977   *Interlocking Directorships and the American Corporate Network.* Ph.D. dissertation, University of California, Santa Barbara.

Gogel, Robert and Thomas Koenig
  1981   "Commercial Banks, Interlocking Directorates and Economic Power: An Analysis of the Primary Metals Industry." *Social Problems* 29 (December): 117–128.

Gold, David, Clarence Lo, and Erik Olin Wright
  1975   "Recent Developments of Marxist Theories of the State," Parts I and II. *Monthly Review* 27 (October and November: 27–43; 36–51.

Goldstein, Richard
  1982   "The War for America's Mind." *Village Voice* (June 8): 1, 11–20.

Goleman, D.
  1980   "1,538 Little Geniuses and How They Grew." *Psychology Today* 13 (February): 28–43.

Goodwyn, L.
  1976   *Democratic Promise: The Populist Movement in America.* New York: Oxford University Press.

Gordon, R. A.
  1945   *Business Leadership in the Large Corporation.* Washington, D.C.: Brookings Institute.

Gould, Stephen J.
  1980   "Science and Jewish Immigration." *Natural History* 89 (December): 14–19.

Gramsci, Antonio
  1971   *Selections from the Prison Notebooks.* New York: International Publishers.

Green, Mark and Andrew Buchsbaum
  1980   *The Corporate Lobbies: Political Profiles of the Business
          Roundtable and the Chamber of Commerce.* Washington
          D.C. Public Citizen.
Green, Mark and Norman Waitzman
  1980   "Cost, Benefit, and Class." *Working Paper for a New Society* 7
          (May/June): 39–50.
Guerin, Daniel
  1979   *100 Years of American Labour.* London: Ink Links.
Guzzardi, Walter, Jr.
  1978   "Business Is Learning How to Win in Washington." *Fortune*
          97(6): 52–58.

Haller, M. H.
  1963   *Eugenics: Hereditarian Attitudes in American Thought.* New
          Brunswick, NJ: Rutgers University Press.
Harris, James F. and Anne Klepper
  1977   "Corporate Philanthropic Public Service Activities." In
          Commission on Private Philanthropy and Public Needs
          (ed.). *Research Papers.* Washington, D.C.: U.S.
          Department of Treasury.
Harris, Louis and Associates
  1977   *A Survey of Outside Directors of Major Publicly Owned
          Corporations.* New York: Louis Harris.
Harris, Richard
  1964   The Real Voice. New York: Macmillan.
Hartman, Chester
  1974   *Yerba Buena: Land Grab and Community Resistance in San
          Francisco.* San Francisco: Glide.
Hartz, Louis
  1955   *The Liberal Tradition in America.* New York: Harcourt, Brace,
          and World.
Harvey, David
  1975   "The Political Economy of Urbanization in Advanced Capitalist
          Societies: The Case of the United States." In Gary
          Gappert and Harold M. Rose (eds.), *The Social Economy
          of the Cities.* Beverly Hills: Sage.
Hayes, Edward C.
  1972   *Power Structure and Urban Policy: Who Rules in Oakland?*
          New York: McGraw-Hill.
Herman, Edward S.
  1973   "Do Bankers Control Corporations?" *Monthly Review* 25 (June):
          12–25.
  1981   *Corporate Control, Corporate Power: A Twentieth Century Fund
          Study.* New York: Cambridge University Press.
Hibbs, Douglas A., Jr.
  1982   "President Reagan's Mandate from the 1980 Elections: A Shift
          to the Right?" *American Politics Quarterly* 10: 387–420.
Hilferding, Rudolph
  1910   *Das Finanzkapital.* Munich: Literarische Agentur Willi
          Weisman. English-language edition (Tom Bottomore,
          trans.). London: Routledge and Kegan Paul, 1981.

Hilton, G.N. and J.E. Due
    1960   *The Electric Interurban Railways in America.* Stanford, CA:
            Stanford University Press.
Himmelstein, Jerome
    1980   "The New Corporate Activism: Union Carbide's Misleading
            Ads." Unpublished manuscript, University of
            Massachusetts, Amherst.
Holli, M.
    1969   *Reform in Detroit: Hazen Pingress and Urban Progress.* New
            York: Oxford University Press.
Holmes, E. H.
    1973   "The State of the Art in Urban Transportation Planning."
            Tranportation 4 : 379–402.
Hunt, E. K.
    1972   *Property and Prophets.* New York: Harper Row.

Jacobson, Gary
    1980   *Money in Congressional Elections.* New Haven: Yale University
            Press.
    1983   *The Politics of Congressional Elections.* Boston: Little Brown.
Jackson, J.J.
    1969   *New Orleans in the Guilded Age: Politics and Urban
            Progressivism, 1880–1896.* Baton Rouge: Louisiana State
            University Press.
Jensen, G.
    1956   *The National Civic Federation: American Business in an Age of
            Social Change and Reform, 1900–1910.* Ph.D.
            dissertation, Princeton University.
Joncich, G.
    1968   *The Sane Positivist: A Biography of Edward L. Thorndike.*
            Middletown, CT: Wesleyan University Press.
Joseph, Paul
    1979   "American Policy and the Italian Left." In Carl Boggs and David
            Plotke, *The Politics of Eurocommunism.* Boston: South
            End Press.

Kamin, Leon J.
    1974   *The Science and Politics of IQ.* Hillsdale, NJ: Erlbaum.
Katona, George
    1957   *Business Looks at the Banks.* Ann Àrbor: University of
            Michigan Press.
Kaysen, Karl
    1957   "The Social Significance of the Modern Corporation." *American
            Economic Review* 47: 313.
Kennedy, E.D.
    1941   *The Automobile Industry.* New York: Reynal & Hitchkock.
Keules, D. J.
    1968   "Testing the Army's Intelligence: Psychologists and the Military
            in World War I." *Journal of American History* 55 : 565–
            581.
    1985   *In the Name of Eugenics: Genetics and the Uses of Human*

Heredity. Berkeley and Los Angeles: University of California Press.

Knowles, James C.
1973 Superconcentralian/Supercorporation, ed. R.L. Andreano. Warner Modular Publications, Book 1, Module 343, pp. 1–30.

Koenig, Thomas
1979 "Social Networks and the Political Role of Big Business." Ph.D. dissertation, University of California at Santa Barbara.

Koenig, Thomas and Robert Gogel
1981 "Interlocking Directorates as a Social Network." *American Journal of Economics and Sociology* 40 : 37–50.

Koenig, Thomas, Robert Gogel, and John Sonquist
1979 "Models of the Significance of Corporate Interlocking Directorates." *American Journal of Economics and Sociology* 38 : 173–188.

Kohlmeier, Herbert
1969 *The Regulators: Watchdog Agencies and the Public Interest.* New York: Harper & Row.

Kolko, Gabriel
1963 *The Triumph of Conservatism.* Chicago: Quadrangle.

Korbin, Stephen J.
1979a "Political Risk: A Review and Reconsideration." *Journal of International Business Studies* (Spring): 67–80.
1979b "The Assessment and Evaluation of Non-Economic Environments by American Firms: A Preliminary Report." Unpublished manuscript.

Kotz, David
1978 *Bank Control of Large Corporations in the United States.* Berkeley: University of California Press.

Kraier, Clarence J.
1972 "Testing for Order and Control in the Corporate Liberal State." *Educational Theory* 22: 154–180.

Kuhn, A.
1952 *Arbitration in Transit.* Philadelphia: University of Pennsylvania Press.

Larner, Robert J.
1970 *Management Control and the Large Corporations.* New York: Dunellen.

Leinsdorf, David and Donald Etra
1973 *Citibank: Ralph Nader's Study Group Report on First National City Bank.* New York: Grossman.

Lenin, V. I.
1971 *Imperialism: The Highest Stage of Capitalism.* Reprinted, Peking: Foreign Languages Publishing, 1965.

Levine, Joel
1972 "The Sphere of Influence." *American Sociological Review* 37: 14–27.
1977 "The Network of Corporate Interlocks in the United States: An

Overview." Paper presented at the Advanced Symposium
on Social Networks, Dartmouth College.

Levitt, Theodore
1960   "Business Should Stay out of Politics." *Business Horizons* 3
(Summer): 45–51.

Leiberson, Stanley
1971   "An Empirical Study of Military-Industrial Linkages." *American
Journal of Sociology* 76 (January): 526–584, 77 (July:
138–142.

Lindblom, Charles E.
1977   *Politics and Markets: The World's Political-Economic System.*
New York: Basic. Part V: The Close but Uneasy Relation
between Private Enterprise and Democracy.

Lintner, John
1959   "The Financing of Corporations." In E. S. Mason, *The
Corporation and Modern Society.* New York: Atheneum.

Lippman, Walter
1922   "The Mental Age of Americans." New Republic (October 25):
213–215.

Lipset, Seymour Martin
1963   *The First Nation,* Glencoe, Ill: Free Press.

Lomax, E.
1977   "The Laura Spelman Rockefeller Memorial: Some of Its
Contributions to Early Research in Child Development."
Journal of the History of the Behavioral Sciences 13: 283–
293.

Lowi, Theodore J.
1969   *The End of Liberalism.* New York: W. W. Norton.

Lundberg, Ferdinand
1936   *The Rich and the Super Rich.* Reprinted, New York: Lyle
Stuart, 1968.
1937   *America's 60 Families.* New York: Halcyon House.

Mace, Myles
1971   *Directors: Myth and Reality.* Cambridge, MA: Harvard
University Graduate School of Business Administration.
Chapters 2–4.

MacShane, C.
1975   *American Cities and the Coming of the Automobile in the 19th
Century.* Ph.D. dissertation, University of Wisconsin,
Madison.

Magrass, Yale
1981   *Thus Spake the Moguls.* Boston: Shenkman.

Malbin, Michael J. (ed.)
1980   *Parties, Interest Groups, and Campaign Finance Laws.*
Washington, D.C.: American Enterprise Institute.

Mann, Dean E.
1965   *The Assistant Secretaries.* Washington, D.C.: Brookings,
Institution.

Mariolis, Peter
1975   "Interlocking Directorates and the Control of Corporations."
Social Science Quarterly 56: 425–439.

1977 "Interlocking Directorates and Financial Groups: A Peak Analysis." Paper presented at the annual meeting of the American Sociological Association.

Mariolis, Peter, Beth Mintz, Michael Schwartz, and Mark Mizruchi
1979 "Centrality Analysis: A Methodology for Social Networks." Paper presented at the annual meeting of the American Sociological Association, Boston.

Marks, Russell
1976-1977 "Providing for Individual Differences: A History of the Intelligence Testing Movement in North America." *Interchange* 7 (3): 3–16.

Marquis, A. N. (ed.)
1916 *Who's Who in America 1916–1917* (Vol. 9). Chicago: Marquis' Who's Who.

1922 *Who's Who in America, 1922–1923* (Vol. 12). Chicago: Marquis' Who's Who.

Marx, Karl
1967 *Capital: A Critique of Political Economy* (3 vols.). New York: International.

McConnell, Grant
1962 *Steel and the Presidency.* New York: W. W. Norton.

McConnell, Grant
1966 *Private Power and American Democracy.* New York: Knopf.

McCue, Dennis
1977 "An Economy in Conflict with Democracy: A Case Study of the Financial Crisis in New York City." Honors thesis, State University of New York, Stony Brook.

McKay, J.
1976 *Tramways and Trolleys: The Rise of Urban Mass Transit.* Princeton, NJ: Princeton University Press.

McQuaid, Kim
1980 "Big Business and Public Policy in Contemporary United States." *Quarterly Review of Economics and Business* 20: 57–68.

1982 *Big Business and Presidential Power.* New York: William Morrow.

Means, Gardiner C.
1968 "Implications of the Corporate Revolution for Economic Theory." In Adolf A. Berle and Gardiner C. Means, *The Modern Corporation and Private Property.* New York: Harcourt, Brace and World.

1972 "Business Concentration in the American Economy." In Richard C. Edwards, Michael Reich, and Thomas E. Weiskopf (eds.); *The Capitalist System.* Englewood Cliffs, NJ: Prentice-Hall.

Menshikov, Sergei
1969 *Millionaires and Managers.* Moscow: Progess Publishers.

Meyers, Herbert
1981 "The Decline of Strikes." *Fortune* 104(9): 66–70.

Meyer J.R., J.F. Kain, and M. Wohl
1972 *The Urban Transportation Problem.* Cambridge, MA: Harvard University Press.

Miliband, Ralph
    1969   *The State in Capitalist Society.* New York: Basic.
Miller, J.A.
    1960   *Fares Please!* New York: Dover Press.
Mills, C. Wright
    1956   *The Power Elite.* New York: Oxford University Press.
Mintz, Beth A.
    1975   The President's Cabinet, 1897–1972. *Insurgent Sociologist* 5
            (Spring): 131–148.
Mintz, Beth and Michael Schwartz
    1977   "The Structure of Power in American Business." Paper
            presented at the annual meeting of the American Political
            Science Association, Washington, D.C.
    1981a   "Interlocking Directorates and Interest Group Formation."
            American Sociological Review 46: 851–869.
    1981b   "The Structure of Intercorporate Unity in American Business."
            Social Problems 29: 87–103.
    1986   "Capital Flows and the Process of Financial Hegemony." *Theory
            and Society* (December): 77–101.
    1983   "Financial Interest Groups in American Business." *Social
            Science History* 7(February): 183–204.
    1985   *The Power Structure of American Business.* Chicago: University
            of Chicago Press.
Mizruchi, Mark
    1983   *The American Corporate Network, 1904–1974.* Beverly Hills,
            CA: Sage.
Mokken, R. J. and F. N. Stokman
    1974   "Traces of Power, I: Power and Influence as Political
            Phenomena." Paper delivered to Joint Sessions of
            European Consortium for Political Research, Strasbourg,
            France.
    1979   "Corporate Government Networks in the Netherlands." *Social
            Networks* 1:333–358.
Morehouse, T. A.
    1965   *The Determinants of Federal Policy for Urban Transportation
            Planning under the Federal Highway Act of 1962.* Ph.D.
            dissertation, University of Minnesota.
Morgan, Dan
    1981   "Conservatives: A Well-financed Network." *Washington Post*
            (January 4):A1, A14
Mulherin, J.P.
    1980   *The Sociology of Work and Organization: Historical Context
            and Patterns of Development.* Ph.D. dissertation,
            University of California at Berkeley (*Dissertation
            Abstracts International* 41, 424A–425A).
NACLA (North American Committee on Latin America)
    1971   *Latin America and Empire Report* 5 (November). Council for
            Foreign Relations.
National Research Council
    1916   "Preliminary Report of the Organizing Committee to the
            President of the Academy." *Proceedings of the National
            Academy of Sciences* 2:507–510.

1918   *Report of the National Research Council.* (Senate Document
           192, 65th Cong., 2d Sess.) Washington, D.C.:
           Government Printing Office.
1920a *Fourth Annual Report.* Washington, D.C.: Government Printing
           Office.
1920b *National Intelligence Tests* (Scale A-Form 1). Yonkers: World
           Book.
1921   *Fifth Annual Report.* Washington, D.C.: Government Printing
           Office.
1923   *Report of the National Research Council for the Year July 1,
           1921–June 30, 1922.* Washington, D.C.: Government
           Printing Office.

National Resources Committee
   1939   *The Structure of the American Economy.* Washington, D.C.:
           U.S. Government Printing Office.
Neilson, Waldemar
   1972   *The Big Foundations.* New York: Columbia University Press.
Noble, David F.
   1981   "Corporate Culture Ministries: The Foundation Trap." *The
           Nation* (March 21): 335–340.
Norich, Samuel
   1980   "Interlocking Directorates, the Control of Large Corporations,
           and Patterns of Accumulation in the Capitalist Class." In
           Maurice Zeitlin (ed.), *Classes, Class Conflict and the
           State.* Cambridge, MA: Winthrop.

O'Connor, James
   1968   "Finance Capital or Corporate Capital." *Monthly Review* 20
           (June): 30–35.
   1972   "Question: Who Rules the Corporations? Answer: The Ruling
           Class." *Socialist Revolution* 2 (January–February): 117–
           150.
Offe, Klaus
   1973   "The Abolition of Market Control and the Problem of
           Legitimacy, I." *Kapitalistate* 1:109–116.
Office of Technology Assessment
   1975   *Energy, the Economy, and Mass Transit.* Washington, D.C.:
           Government Printing Office.
Ornati, O.
   1968   *Transportation and the Poor.* New York: Praeger.
Ornstein, Michael D.
   1982   "Interlocking Directorates in Canada: Evidence from
           Replacement Patterns." *Social Networks* 4: 3–25.
   1984   "Interlocking Directorates in Canada: Intercorporate or
           Intraclass Alliance?" *Administrative Science Quarterly*
           29: 210–231.

Palmer, Donald
   1980   *Broken Ties: A Theoretical and Methodological Critique of
           Interlock Research.* Ph.D. dissertation, State University of
           New York, at Stony Brook.
   1983a "Broken Ties: Interlocking Directorates, the

Interorganizational Paradigm, and Intercorporate
Coordination." *Administrative Science Quarterly* 28
(March): 40–55.

1983b "On the Significance of Interlocking Directorates." *Journal of
Social Science History* 7 (Spring).

Palmer, Donald and Roger Friedland

1986   "The Organizational and Class Politics of Corporate
Combination." Unpublished paper, Graduate School of
Business, Stanford University.

Palmer, Donald, Roger Friedland, and Jitandra Singh

1986   "The Ties That Bind: Organizational and Class Bases of
Stability in a Corporate Interlock Network." *American
Sociological Review* (December): 781–96.

Palmer, Donald, Roger Friedland, P. Devereaux Jennings, and Melanie
Powers

1986   "The determmminants of the Multidivisional Form among Large
U.S. Corporations." Unpublished paper, Graduate School
of Business, Stanford University.

Parsons, Talcott

1968   "The Distribution of Power in American Society." In G. William
Domhoff and Hoyt Ballard (eds.), *C. Wright Mills and the
Power Elite*. Boston: Beacon.

Passer, H.

1953   *The Electrical Manufacturing Industry*. Cambridge, MA:
Harvard University Press.

Pearson, Drew and Jack Anderson

1968   *The Case against Congress: A Compelling Indictment of
Corruption on Capitol Hill*. New York: Simon and
Schuster.

Pennings, Johannes

1978   "Interorganizational Relationships: The Case of Interlocking
Directorates." Paper presented to the annual meeting of
the American Sociological Association, San Francisco.

1980   *Interlocking Directorates: Origins and Consequences of
Connections among Organizations' Boards of Directors*.
San Francisco: Jossey-Bass.

Perlo, Victor

1957   *The Empire of High Finance*. New York: International.

Perrow, Charles

1979   *Complex Organizations: A Critical Essay*. Glenview, Ill: Scott,
Foresman.

Peschek, Joseph G.

*Policy-Planning Organizations: Elite Agendas and America's
Rightward Turn*. Philadelphia: Temple University Press, 1987.

Petchesky, Rosalind Pollack

1981   "Anti-abortion, Anti-feminishm, and the Rise of the New Right."
Feminist Studies 7: 206–246.

Pfeffer, Jeffrey

1972a "Size and Composition of Corporate Boards of Directors."
Administrative Science Quarterly 17: 218–228.

1972b "Merger as a Response to Organizational Interdependence."
Administrative Science Quarterly 17: 382–394.

Pfeffer, Jeffrey and Phillip Nowak
1976 "Joint Ventures and Interorganizational Interdependence." *Administrative Science Quarterly* 21: 398–418.
Pfeffer, Jeffrey and Gerald Salancik
1978 *The External Control of Organizations: A Resource Dependence Perspective.* New York: Harper & Row.
Phillips, Kevin
1982 *Post-Conservative America.* New York: Random House.
Piven, Frances Fox and Richard A. Cloward
1971 *Regulating the Poor: The Functions of Public Welfare.* New York: Pantheon.
Porter, John
1965 *The Vertical Mosaic: An Analysis of Social Class and Power in Canada.* Toronto: University of Toronto Press.
Progressive Labor Party
1973a "Eugenics: Survival of the Bosses. Revolution: Survival of the Workers." *Progressive Labor* (April): 78–96.
1973b "Behind the Racist Eugenics Movement: A Century of Ruling Class Effort." *Progressive Labor* (July):63–70.
Pye, Lucien and Ryland Pye
1971 *Report of the Committee on Comparative Politics.* New York: Social Science Research Council.
1974 *Items* (Social Science Research Council) 5 (September).

Quinney, Richard
1974 *Critique of Legal Order.* Boston: Little, Brown.
Ratcliff, Richard E.
1977 "Mortgage Investment and Disinvestment: The Record of Savings and Loan Associations in the St. Louis Area." In *Housing and Neighborhood Investment in Missouri.* Housing Development Commission, St. Louis, MO
1980a "Banks and the Command of Capital Flows: An Analysis of Capitalist Class Structure and Mortgage Disinvestment in a Metropolitan Area." In Maurice Zeitlin (ed.), *Classes, Class Conflict, and the State.* Cambridge, MA: Winthrop.
1980b "Banks and Corporate Lending: An Analysis of the Impact of the Internal Structure of the Capitalist Class on the Lending Behavior of Banks." *American Sociological Review* 45: 553–570.
1980c "Declining Cities and Capitalist Class Structure." In G. William Domhoff (ed.), *Power Structure Research.* Beverly Hills, CA: Sage.
Ratcliff, Richard E., Mary Elizabeth Gallaher, and David Jaffee
1980 "Political Money and Ideological Clusters in the Capitalist Class: An Analysis of Political Contest as a Determinant of Campaign Contributions among Bank Directors." Paper presented at the annual meeting of the American Sociological Association.
Ratcliff, Richard E., Mary E. Gallagher, and Kathryn Strother Ratcliff
1979 "The Civic Involvement of Business Leaders: An Analysis of the Influences of Economic Power and Social Prominence in

the Command of Civil Policy Positions." *Social Problems*
26:298–313.
Reed, Edward F., Richard V. Cotter, Edward K. Gill, and Richard K. Smith
1976   *Commercial Banking.* Englewood, NJ: Prentice-Hall.
Reich, Michael
1973   "The Economics of Racism. In R. Edwards, M. Reich, and T.
       Weisskopf (eds.), *The Capitalist System* (2d ed.).
       Englewood Cliffs, N.J.: Prentice-Hall, 110–25.
Riesman, David
1953   *The Lonely Crowd.* Garden City, NY: Anchor.
Rifkin, Jeremy and Randy Barber
1980   *The North Will Rise Again: Pensions, Politics and Power in the
       1980's.* Boston: Beacon.
Rochester, Anna
1936   *Rulers of America.* New York: International.
Rose, Arnold
1967   *The Power Structure.* New York: Oxford University Press.
Rothmeyer, Karen
1981   "Citizen Scaife." *Columbia Journalism Review* 20(2): 41–50.
Roy, William G.
1983   "Interlocking Directorates and the Corporate Revolution." *Social
       Science History* 7 (February): 143–164.
Russell, J. E.
1937   *Founding Teachers College.* New York: Teachers College.

Sale, Kirkpatrick
1976   *Power Shift: The Rise of the Southern Rim and Its Challenge to
       the Eastern Establishment.* New York: Random House.
Schechter, Jerry
       Forthcoming "The Origins of the Educational Testing Service."
       Ph.D. dissertation, State University of New York at Stony
       Brook.
Scheer, Robert
1983   *With Enough Shovels: Reagan, Bush, and Nuclear War.* New
       York: Random House.
Schlesinger, Arthur M., Jr.
1965   *A Thousand Days.* Boston: Houghton Mifflin.
Schmidt, E. P.
1935   *The Development of the Street Railway.* Ph.D. dissertation,
       University of Wisconsin, Madison.
Schriftgiesser, Karl
1964   *Busiess and the American Government.* Washington, D.C.:
       Robert B. Luce.
Schuessler, Karl
1971   *Analyzing Social Data.* Boston: Houghton Mifflin.
Schwartz, Michael, Hyman Korman, and Sen-Yuan Wu
1985   "Capital Flows, Disinvestment and Plant Closing: The
       Economic Background to Local Fiscal Crisis." Invited
       Lecture, Department of Sociology, Syracuse University.
Scott, John P.
1979   *Corporations, Classes and Capitalism.* London: Hutchinson.

Seltzer, L. H.
   1928   *A Financial History of the American Automobile Industry.*
            Boston: Houghton-Mifflin.
Seybold, Peter
   1978   *The Development of American Political Sociology.* Ph.D.
            dissertation, State University of New York at Stony Brook.
   1980   "The Ford Foundation and the Triumph of Behavioralism in
            American Political Science." In Robert F. Arnove (ed,),
            Philanthropy and Cultural Imperialism. Chicago: G.K.
            Hall.
Sharp, Evelyn
   1972   *The IQ Cult.* New York: Coward, McCann and Geoghegan.
Sheehan, Neil, Hedrick Smith, E. W. Kenworth, and Fox Butterfield (eds.)
   1971   *The Pentagon Papers: As Published in the New York Times,*
            New York: Bantam.
Shoup, Laurence H.
   1975   "Shaping the Post War World: The Council on Foreign Relations
            and United States War Aims during World War Two."
            Insurgent Sociologist 5 (Spring): 9–52.
   1977   "The Council on Foreign Relations and American Policy in
            Southeast Asia, 1940–1973." *Insurgent Sociologist* 7
            (Winter): 19–30.
   1980   The Carter Presidency and Beyond: Power and Politics in the
            1980's. Palo Alto, CA: Ramparts.
Shoup, Lawrence H. and William Minter
   1977   *Imperial Brain Trust: The CFR and United States Foreign
            Policy.* New York: Monthly Review.
Silk, Leonard and David Vogel
   1976   *Ethics and Profits: The Crisis of Confidence in American
            Business.* New York: Simon and Schuster.
Sinclair, U.
   1922   *The Goose-Step: A Study of American Education.* Pasadena:
            author.
   1924   *The Goslings: A Study of American Schools.* Pasadena: author.
Sklar, Holly (ed.)
   1980   *Trilateralism: The Trilateral Commission and Elite Planning for
            World Management.* Boston: South End Press.
Sloan, Alfred P., Jr.
   1965   *My Years at General Motors.* Edited by John McDonald with
            Catherine Stevens. New York: Macfadden.
Smerk, G.
   1975   *Urban Transportation Policy.* Bloomington: Indiana University
            Press.
Smithe, Ephraim P. and Louis R. Desfosses
   1972   "Interlocking Directorates: A Study of Influence." *Mississippi
            Valley Journal of Business and Economics* 7 (Spring): 57–
            69.
Snell, B. C.
   1974   *American Ground Transport.* Washington, D.C.: U.S. Senate,
            Judiciary Committee, Subcommittee on Anti-trust and
            Monopoly.

Sonquist, John and Thomas Koenig
    1975   "Interlocking Directorates in the Top U.S. Firms." *Insurgent Sociologist* 5 (Spring): 196–229.
Soref, Michael
    1976   "Social Class and a Division of Labor within the Corporate Elite: A Note on Class, Interlocking and Executive Committee Membership of Directors of U.S. Industrial Firms." *Sociological Quarterly* 17: 360–368.
    1979   "Research on Interlocking Directorates: An Introduction and a Bibliography of North American Sources." *Connections* 2 (Spring): 84–86.
    1980   "The Finance Capitalist." In Maurice Zeitlin (ed.), *Classes, Class Conflict and the State.* Cambridge, MA: Winthrop.
Stanworth, Philip and Anthony Giddens
    1975   "The Modern Corporate Economy: Interlocking Directorships in Britain, 1906–1970." *Sociological Review* 23:5–28.
Starr, Roger
    1975   *Housing and the Money Market.* New York: Basic.
St. Clair, D. J.
    1980   "The Motorization and Decline of Urban Transit, 1935–50." *Journal of Economic History* 41: 579–600.
Stearns, Linda Brewster
    1982   *Corporate Dependency and the Structure of the Capital Market.* Ph.D. dissertation, Department of Sociology, State University of New York at Stony Brook.
    1983   "Capital Markets Effects on External Control of Corporations." Paper delivered to American Sociological Association, Detroit, Michigan, August.
Stein, Herbert
    1969   *The Fiscal Revolution in America.* Chicago: University of Chicago Press.
Stetson, G. R.
    1897   "Some Memory Tests of Whites and Blacks." *Psychological Review* 4:285–389.
Sweezy, Paul
    1942   *The Theory of Capitalist Development.* New York: Monthly Review Press.
    1953   "Interest Groups in the American Economy," In *The Present as History.* New York: Monthly Review Press.
    1972   "The Resurgence of Finance Capital: Face or Fancy?" *Socialist Revolution* 2: 157–190.
Sweezy Paul and Harry Magdoff
    1975   "Banks: Skating on Thin Ice." *Monthly Review* 26:1–21.

Tarr, J.
    1973   "From City to Suburb: The 'Moral' Influence of Transportation Technology." In A. B. Callow, Jr., (ed.), *American Urban History.* New York: Oxford University Press.
Taylor, Tabb
    1978   *Management Succession under Conditions of Crisis: The Role of the Board of Directors.* DBA dissertation, Harvard University.

Terman, L. M.
   1916   *The Measurement of Intelligence: An Explanation of and a Complete Guide for the Use of the Stanford Revision and Extension of the Binet-Simon Intelligence Scale.* Boston: Houghton-Mifflin.
   1922a   "Were We Born That Way?" *World's Work* 44:655–660.
   1922b   "The Great Conspiracy of the Impulse Imperious of Intelligence Testors, Psychoanalyzed and Exposed by Mr. Lippman." *New Republic* (December 27):116–120.
   1961   "Lewis M. Terman: Trails to Psychology." In C. Murchison (ed.), *A History of Psychology in Autobiography* (Vol. 2). New York: Russell & Russell.
Terman, L. M., G. Lyman, G. Ordahl, L. E. Ordahl, N. Galbreath, and W. Talbert
   1917   *The Stanford Revision and Extension of the Binet-Simon Scale for Measuring Intelligence.* Baltimore: Warwick and York.
Thompson, James
   1967   *Organizations in Action,* New York: McGraw-Hill.
Tinnin, David B.
   1973   *Just About Everybody vs. Howard Hughes.* Garden City, NY: Doubleday.
Tobias, Andrew
   1976   "The Merging of the 'Fortune 500'." *New York Magazine* (December 20).

U.S. Department of Transportation
   1976   *Urban System Study.* Washington, D.C.: Government Printing Office.
U.S. House of Representatives (Committee on Banking and Currency)
   1913   *Investigation of Concentration of Control of Money and Credit,* Washington, D.C.: Government Printing Office. (Referred to as Pujo Committee Report.)
U.S. House of Representatives (Committee on the Judiciary, Anti-trust Subcommittee)
   1965   *Interlocks in Corporate Management.* Washington, D.C.: Government Printing Office.
U.S. House of Representatives (Committee on Banking and Currency, Subcommittee on Domestic Finance)
   1968   *Commercial Banks and Their Trust Activities: Emerging Influences on the American Economy.* Washington, D.C.: Government Printing Office.
U.S. House of Representatives (Committee on Banking)
   1970   "Investment and Interlocks between Major Banks and Major Corporations." In Maurice Zeitlin (ed.), *American Society, Inc.* Chicago: Markam.
U.S. Internal Revenue Service
   1970   *Business Income Tax Returns,* 1967, Washington, D.C.: Government Printing Office.
U.S. National Resources Committee
   1939   *The Structure of the American Economy.* Washington, D.C.: Government Printing Office. Reprinted in Paul M.

Sweezy, *The Present as History*, New York: Monthly
Review Press, 1953.

U.S. Senate (Committee on Government Operations, Subcommittee on
Inter-Government Relations, and Budgeting, Management and
Expenditures)
1974   *Disclosure of Corporate Ownership.* Washington, D.C.:
Government Printing Office.

U.S. Senate (Select Committee on Presidential Campaign Activities)
1974   *Draft of Final Report: Part 2, Campaign Financing.*
Washington, D.C.: Government Printing Office.

U.S. Senate (Committee on Banking)
1977   *Community Credit Needs (Hearings).* Washington, D.C.:
Government Printing Office.

U.S. Senate (Committee on Governmental Affairs)
1978   "Interlocking Directorates among Major U.S. Corporations."
(staff study prepared by the Subcommittee on Reports,
Accounting, and Management.) Washington, D.C.:
Government Printing Office.

Useem, Michael
1978   "The Inner Group of the American Capitalist Class." *Social
Problems* 25 (February):225–240.
1979a   "The Social Organization of the American Business Elite and
Participation of Corporation Directors in the Governance
of American Institutions." *American Sociological Review*
44:553–572.
1979b   "Studying the Corporation and the Corporate Elite." *American
Sociologist* 14 (May):97–107.
1980a   "Corporations and the Corporate Elite." *Annual Review of
Sociology* 6:41–77.
1980b   "Which Business Leaders Help Govern?" In G. William
Domhoff (ed.), *Power Structure Research.* Beverly Hills,
CA: Sage.
1980c   "The Upper Class, the Corporate Elite, and the Changing Mode
of Class Reproduction in Elite Higher Education." Paper
presented at the Askwith Symposium on Inequality and
Schooling in America, Harvard Graduate School of
Education, Cambridge, MA.
1981   "Business Segments and Corporate Relations with American
Universities." *Social Problems* 29 (December):129–141.
1982   "Classwide Rationality in the Politics of Managers and Directors
of Large Corporations in the United States and Great
Britain." *Administrative Science Quarterly* 27:199–226.
1983   "Business and Politics in the United States and United
Kingdom." *Theory and Society* 12:281–308.
1984   *The Inner Circle: Large Corporations and the Rise of Business
Political Activity in the U.S. and U.K.* New York: Oxford
University Press.

Vickers, L.
1934   *Fare Structures in the Transit Industry.* Ph.D. dissertation,
Columbia University.

Villarejo, Don
    1961   "Stock Ownership and the Control of Corporations" (pamphlet).
           Somerville, MA: New England Free Press.
Vogel, David
    1978   "Why Businessmen Distrust Their State: The Political
           Consciousness of American Corporate Executives."
           British Journal of Poilitical Science 8:45–78.
    1979   "Business's 'New Class' Struggle." *Nation* (December 15):609.
    1980   "Businessmen United." *Wall Street Journal* (January 14).

Wallin, J. E. W.
    1916   "Who Is Feeble Minded." *Journal of the American Institute of Criminal Law and Criminology* 6:706–16.
Ward, D.
    1971   *Cities and Immigrants: A Geography of Change in Nineteenth Century America.* New York: Oxford University Press.
Warner, S., Jr.
    1976   *Streetcar Suburbs.* New York: Atheneum.
Warner, W. L. and D. B. Unwalla
    1967   "The System of Interlocking Directorates." In W. L. Warner, D. B. Unwalla, and J. H. Trim (eds.), *The Emergent American Society, Vol. 1, Large Scale Organizations.* New Haven: Yale University.
Weidenbaum, Murray L.
    1977   *Business, Government and the Public,* Englewood Cliffs, NJ: Prentice-Hall.
    1978   *The Impacts of Government Regulation.* St. Louis: Center for the Study of Business, Washington University.
Weinstein, James
    1968   *The Corporate Ideal in the Liberal State, 1900–1918,* Boston: Beacon.
Weiss, L.
    1961   *Economics and American Industry.* New York: Wiley.
Whitt, J. A.
    1982   *Urban Elites and Mass Transportation: The Dialectics of Power.* Princeton, NJ: Princeton University Press.
Wilcox, D. F.
    1919   "Solving the Traction Problem from the Public Point of View." Paper presented at the tenth anniversary of the New York State Conference of Mayors and City Officials, Schenectady, New York, June 12.
    1921   *Analysis of the Electrical Railway Problem.* New York: author.
Wissler, C.
    1901   "The Correlation of Mental and Physical Traits." *Psychological Monographs* 3:16.
Woodward, Bob and Carl Bernstein
    1974   *All the President's Men.* New York: Simon and Schuster.
Wu, Sen-Yuan
    1986   *Plant Closings and Local Fiscal Crisis.* Ph.D. dissertation, State University of New York at Stony Brook.

Yago, Glenn
 1980 "Corporate Power and Urban Transportation." In M. Zeitlin
    (ed.), *Classes, Class Conflict, and the State.* Cambridge,
    MA: Winthrop.
 1984 *The Decline of Public Transportation in Germany and the*
    United States, 1970–1980. New York: Cambridge
    University Press.
Yerkes, R. M.
 1918 "Psychology in Relation to the War." *Psychological Review*
    25:85–115.
Yerkes, R. M. (ed.)
 1921 *Psychological Examining in the United States Army* (Memoirs
    of the National Academy of Sciences, Vol. 15).
    Washington, DC: Government Printing Office.
 1923 "Testing the Human Mind." *Atlantic Monthly* (March): 358–
    370.
Young, Richard
 1973 "Liberalism: The American Creed." In Edward Greenberg and
    Richard Young (eds.), *American Politics Reconsidered.*
    Belmont, CA: Wadsworth.

Zeitlin, Maurice A.
 1974 "Corporate Ownership and Control: The Large Corporation and
    the Capitalist Class." *American Journal of Sociology*
    79:1073–1119.
 1976 "On Class Theory of Large Corporations: Reply to Allen."
    American Journal of Sociology 8:894–903.
Zeitlin, Maurice A., W. Lawrence Neumen, and Richard E. Ratcliff
 1976 "Class Segments: Agrarian Property and Political Leadership in
    the Capitalist Class in Chile." *American Sociological*
    Review 41:1000–1029.
Zeitlin, Maurice A., Richard E. Ratcliff, and Lynda Ewen
 1974 "The Inner Group: Interlocking Directorates and the Internal
    Differentiation of the Capitalist Class." Paper presented at
    the annual meeting of the American Sociological
    Association, Montreal.
Zinn, Howard
 1965 *SNCC: The New Abolitionists.* Boston: Beacon.

Contributors

Michael Schwartz (editor)	*State University of New York Stony Brook*
Laura Anker	*State University of New York College at Old Westbury*
James Bearden	*State University of New York College at Geneseo*
Dan Clawson	*University of Massachusetts Amherst*
Mary Ann Clawson	*Wesleyan University*
David Gersh	*Houston Community College*
Tom Koenig	*Northeastern University*
Beth Mintz	*University of Vermont*
Mark S. Mizruchi	*Columbia University*
Donald Palmer	*Stanford University*
Richard Ratcliff	*Syracuse University*
Peter Seybold	*Indiana University Bloomington*
Michael Useem	*Boston University*
J. Allen Whitt	*Louisville University*

INDEX